Is Xi-Jinping's China a New Superpower

Is Xi-Jinping's China a New Superpower

Capt. R K Sirohi

PRASHANT PUBLISHING HOUSE
DELHI-110094

Published by :
Prashant Publishing House
C-34, 28 Foota Road, Gali-3,
West Karwal Nagar, Delhi-110094
Phone : 011-22963970, Mob. : 9810396373
e-mail.: prashantpublishinghouse@gmail.com

Is Xi-Jinping's China a New Superpower

Reserved
First Published 2018

ISBN 978-81-938012-4-6

PRINTED IN INDIA
Published by Mr. R.K. Jha M/s Prashant Publishing House and Published at H.S. Offset House Press, Delhi.

Contents

Preface

President Xi Jinping warned of "severe" challenges while laying out a road map to turn China into a leading global power by 2050, as he kicked off a twice-a-decade party gathering expected to cement his influence into the next decade.

Mr Xi has vigorously pursued what he has called a "great rejuvenation of the Chinese nation" with his China Dream vision. Under him, China has enacted economic reform to combat slowing growth, such as cutting down bloated state-owned industries and reducing pollution, as well as its One Belt One Road trade project. The country has become more assertive on the global stage, from its continued dominance in the South China Sea despite international protestations, to its exercise of soft power by pumping billions of dollars into Asian and African investments.

Chinese President Xi Jinping is on a roll. In October, the Communist Party he dominates used its national congress to accord him even more authority for his second term, embedding his core position and "thought" in its constitution. The party's Politburo is now stacked with Xi loyalists, and two important players on foreign policy, State Councillor "Tiger" Yang Jiechi and party doctrine-shaper Wang Huning, have been elevated to support their leader's ambitious global agenda.

This month Xi powered serenely through a series of high-level diplomatic meetings, including a summit parley with US President Donald Trump. Despite all the attention it attracted, the US chief executive's "state visit plus" was more about pageantry, managing risks and deflecting potential problems. More indicative of Xi's plans was his speech at the Asia-Pacific Economic Cooperation summit in Vietnam, where he called for "profound change", and visits to Vietnam and Laos on which he sought to warm and deepen relations.

Some believe Xi might seek a third term as general secretary (or as party chairman) in 2022, which would allow him to remain at the helm until 2027. So far, no CPC general secretary has held that post for more than two terms, even if the party charter does not impose term limits. Adding fuel to the speculation is the fact that no potential successor to Xi was named in the new Politburo Standing Committee.

Today's Chinese see themselves as the heirs of a millennium-old civilization that was the world leader in culture, science, technology and administration right up to the 16th century. In this ideal conception, China — the "Middle Kingdom," as it is still called in Chinese today — was at the center of the world, surrounded by barbarians, who were willing to pay tribute to the luminosity of Chinese civilization.

This is a reference book. All the matter is just compiled and edited in nature, taken from the various sources which are in public domain.

The book examines how since his appointment to China's three top posts– Xi Jinping has deftly used ideology and nationalism to accumulate power and ensure the Chinese Communist Party (CCP)'s legitimacy and monopoly on power.

—*Editor*

1

China's President Xi Jinping

He has been front and centre of China's push to cement its position as a superpower, while also launching crackdowns on corruption and dissent.

A consummate political chess player who has cultivated an enigmatic strongman image, the leader of the ruling Chinese Communist Party has rapidly consolidated power, having his ideas mentioned by name in the constitution - an honour that had been reserved only to Mao Zedong until now.

The "Xi Jinping Thought" means that any challenge to the president will now be seen as a threat to Communist Party rule.

A seven-man leadership committee unveiled in October 2017 included no obvious heir, raising the prospect that Mr Xi intended to govern beyond the next five years. The Communist Party has now confirmed that aim, with a proposal to remove a clause in the constitution that limits the presidency to two terms.

Princeling, peasant, president

Born in Beijing in 1953, Xi Jinping is the son of revolutionary veteran Xi Zhongxun, one of the Communist Party's founding fathers and a vice-premier.

Because of his illustrious roots, Mr Xi is seen as a "princeling" - a child of elite senior officials who has risen up the ranks. But his family's fortunes took a drastic turn when his father was purged in 1962 prior to the Cultural Revolution and imprisoned. At the age of 15, the younger Xi was sent to the countryside for "re-education" and hard labour in the remote and poor village of Liangjiahe for seven years - an experience that would later figure largely in his official story.

Far from turning against the Communist Party, Mr Xi embraced it. He tried to join it several times, but was rebuffed because of who his father was.

Once he was finally accepted in 1974, he worked hard to rise to the top - first as a local party secretary in Hebei province, before moving on to more senior roles in other places including party chief of Shanghai, China's second city and financial hub.

His increasing profile in the party propelled him to its top decision making body, the Politburo Standing Committee, and in 2012 he was picked as president.

The Tsinghua University chemical engineering graduate is married to the glamorous singer Peng Liyuan, and the two have been heavily featured in state media as China's First Couple. It's a contrast from previous presidential couples, where the first lady has traditionally kept a lower profile.

They have one daughter, Xi Mingze, but not much is known about her apart from the fact that she studied at Harvard University.

Other family members and their overseas business dealings has been a subject of scrutiny in the international press.

China Dream

Mr Xi has vigorously pursued what he has called a "great rejuvenation of the Chinese nation" with his China Dream vision.

Under him, China has enacted economic reform to combat slowing growth, such as cutting down bloated state-owned industries and reducing pollution, as well as its One Belt One Road trade project.

The country has become more assertive on the global stage, from its continued dominance in the South China Sea despite international protestations, to its exercise of soft power by pumping billions of dollars into Asian and African investments.

This has been accompanied by a resurgence in patriotic nationalism whipped up by state media, with a particular focus on Mr Xi as China's strongman leader, leading some to accuse him of developing a personality cult like that of former leader Mao Zedong.

Media captionSongs have been written celebrating Chinese President Xi Jinping, one even has an accompanying dance routine

At home, Mr Xi has waged a ruthless war on corruption which has punished more than a million "tigers and flies"- a reference to both high and low-ranking party officials.

Some observers believe that the campaign is aimed at rooting out opponents, and is part of a series of political manoeuvres by Mr Xi aimed at consolidating his power.

Meanwhile China has seen increasing clampdowns on freedoms, from rising online censorship to arrests of dissidents and human rights lawyers, leading some to describe Mr Xi as "the most authoritarian leader since Chairman Mao".

Despite this, Mr Xi is still thought to enjoy reasonably widespread support among ordinary Chinese citizens - and is expected to keep shaping the country for the next few years.

Chinese leaders have traditionally hinted at one or more possible heirs to the leadership body, the Standing Committee, at the beginning of their final term. But in October 2017, Mr Xi did not do so.

The leaders unveiled were all in their 60s and likely to retire at the end of this term.

And in a clear sign of Mr Xi's influence, the Communist Party voted, in 2017, to write his philosophy, called "Xi Jinping Thought on Socialism with Chinese Characteristics for the New Era", in its constitution.

Only founder Mao and Deng Xiaoping, who introduced economic reforms in the 1980s, have made it into the all-important fundamental law of the land.

RISE TO POWER

Xi joined the Communist Youth League of China in 1971 and he applied in 1973 to join the Communist Party of China 10 times and finally got in on the tenth attempt in 1974. In 1982, he was sent to Zhengding County in Hebei as deputy Party Secretary of Zhengding County. He was promoted in 1983 to Secretary, becoming the top official of the county. Xi subsequently served in four provinces during his regional political career: Hebei (1982–1985), Fujian (1985–2002), Zhejiang (2002–2007), and Shanghai (2007).

Xi held posts in the Fuzhou Municipal Party Committee and became the president of the Party School in Fuzhou in 1990. In 1997, Xi was named an alternate member of the 15th Central Committee of the Communist Party of China. However, out of the 151 alternate members of the Central Committee elected at the 15th Party Congress, Xi received the lowest number of votes in favour, placing him in last place in the rankings of members, ostensibly due to his status as a princeling.

In 1999, he was promoted to the office of Vice Governor of Fujian, then he became governor a year later. In Fujian, Xi made efforts to attract investment from Taiwan and to strengthen the private sector of the provincial economy. In February 2000, he and then-provincial Party Secretary Chen Mingyi were called before the top members of the Party Central Politburo Standing Committee of the Communist Party of China – general secretary Jiang Zemin, Premier Zhu Rongji, Vice-President Hu Jintao and Discipline Inspectionsecretary Wei Jianxing – to explain aspects of the Yuanhua scandal.

In 2002, Xi left Fujian and took up leading political positions in neighbouring Zhejiang, eventually taking over as provincial party chief after several months as acting governor, occupying a top provincial office for the first time in his career. In 2002, Xi was elected a full member of the 16th Central Committee, marking his ascension to the national stage. While in Zhejiang, Xi presided over reported growth rates averaging 14% per year. His career in Zhejiang was marked by a tough and straightforward stance against corrupt officials, which earned him a name on the national media and drew the attention of China's top leaders.

Following the dismissal of Shanghai Party Chief Chen Liangyu in September 2006 due to a social security fund scandal, Xi was transferred to Shanghai in March 2007 to become the party chief of Shanghai. Xi spent only seven months in Shanghai, but his appointment to one of the most important regional posts in China sent a clear signal that Xi was highly regarded by China's top leadership. In Shanghai, Xi avoided controversy, and was known for strictly observing party discipline. For example, Shanghai administrators attempted to earn favour with Xi by arranging a special train to shuttle him between Shanghai and Hangzhou in order for him to complete handing off his work to his successor as Zhejiang party chief Zhao Hongzhu. However, Xi reportedly refused to take the train, citing a loosely enforced party regulation which stipulated that special trains can only be reserved for "national leaders". While in Shanghai, he worked on preserving unity of the local party organization, and made a pledge that there would be no 'purges' during his administration, despite the fact that many local officials were thought to have been implicated in the Chen Liangyu corruption scandal. On most issues Xi largely echoed the line of the central leadership. Xi's career is notable in that during his regional tenures, he was never implicated in any serious scandals, nor did he face serious political opposition.

CHINESE PRESIDENT XI CEMENTS HIS GRIP ON POWER WITH RARE PARTY MOVE

The move puts Xi on par with Chairman Mao Zedong who founded the People's Republic of China in 1949 and paramount leader Deng Xiaoping, who oversaw China's opening up to the world.

Deng Xiaoping Theory was added to the constitution six months after his death in February 1997. China's previous two presidents, Hu Jintao and Jiang Zemin, haven't had their names enshrined in the constitution in this way.

What is Xi's new era? Socialism with Chinese Characteristics has long been used to describe how Marxism has been adapted for China. The term was closely associated with Deng Xiaoping as a way to promote economic development.

However, there's little agreement on what Xi's new spin means. Willy Lam, at the Chinese University of Hong Kong, says domestically it's about tightening Communist Party control over all aspects of Chinese life in the internet age. Globally, it's about making sure China becomes a superpower that gets to make the rules.

"Xi Jinping now has an institutional guarantee of support. He can be emperor for life — staying in power as long as his health allows," said Willy Lam, an adjunct professor at the Chinese University of Hong Kong's Center for China Studies.

Xi looks set to emerge from the 19th National Congress of the Communist Party of China stronger than ever, both domestically and on the international stage.

At home, Xi has taken down senior leaders in his anti-corruption drive, launched an unprecedented crackdown on free speech, and radically overhauled the two-million strong People's Liberation Army, the world's largest fighting force.

Globally, the world will now likely see China continue to step into a global leadership vacuum as the US turns inward under President Donald Trump.

As Xi presided over the closing session in the Great Hall of the People, more than 2,200 delegates raised their hands in unison to approve the party charter amendments, with staffers announcing "meiyou" ("none") to indicate the lack of dissenting or abstaining votes.

Sweeping vision

Xi repeatedly referred to "Socialism with Chinese Characteristics for a New Era," during a three-and-a-half-hour opening speech to the National Party Congress last week. And the resolution passed Tuesday echoed many of the same themes.

The address detailed his sweeping vision for the country, charting its future in a world where China's reach is now extending — and being felt — further than ever before.

Xi declared that China should "take center stage in the world," and that its brand of socialism offers "a new choice for other countries." He added that, "no one should expect China to swallow anything that undermines its interests."

Lam said Xi's "new era" philosophy sought to establish China as a superpower that "plays a rule-setting role in global affairs."

Domestically, Lam said the move to enshrine Xi's name in the party charter would signify greater party control over all aspects of life in China.

Lam said Xi had managed to "totally repudiate" a tradition of collective leadership instituted by Deng: "It's a return to one-man rule. It's a backward step."

When asked what he thought of Xi Jinping Thought, Sun Yongkang, a 24-year-old photographer in Beijing, said: "I really like the key word New Era. President Xi is a trailblazer, he opens up a new model for China's development."

Who's in, who's out

On Wednesday, Xi is expected to be formally granted a second five-year term as the party's general secretary and reveal the new members of the Politburo Standing Committee (PBSC), the top decision-making body in the one-party system.

Who's included and who's not will shed light on the magnitude of Xi's grip on power and his future plans.

Some analysts have speculated that Xi will seek to stay on beyond 2022, when his second term is due to end, breaking a tradition followed by his two predecessors and emulating Russian President Vladimir Putin.

However, it looks like that Wang Qishan, Xi's anti-corruption czar, will be retiring despite some speculation that Xi would bend the rules and allow him to stay on in the PBSC — despite being older than the customary retirement age of 68.

His name wasn't on a list of Central Committee members from which the politburo and its standing committee are named.

Retaining Wang would have set a precedent for any future power play by Xi, 64, to stay in the top job beyond 2022.

CHINESE FOREIGN POLICY WITH XI JINPING CHARACTERISTICS

The past five years have witnessed significant transformations in Chinese foreign policy. For decades, the People's Republic of China (PRC) pursued Deng Xiaoping's strategy of keeping a 'low profile' in international affairs. However, since the ascendance of Xi Jinping to Chinese presidency, the country has adopted what many observers interpret as a more aggressive foreign policy. This *Focus Asia* piece challenges this interpretation and rather highlights that Beijing is dependent and remains sensitive to the perceptions, interests and needs of its international environment. Indeed, China's international partners, including the European Union (EU) and its member states, possess significant potential leverage over the trajectory of the PRC's foreign policy. To realize this potential, Europe should stick to its traditional role as a "regulatory superpower".

BEWARE OF THE NEW XI JINPING, CHINA'S PRESIDENT FOR LIFE

Chinese President Xi Jinping is now officially the most powerful Chinese leader since Mao Zedong who died more than 40 years ago after the National People's Congress voted overwhelmingly in favour of a constitutional amendment which gives Xi the right to remain in office indefinitely. Not that there was any doubt about it but when it finally happened it seemed to be marking another red line in China's evolution as the pre-eminent global power of our times.

It was only last month that China's ruling Communist Party had moved a proposal to remove a constitutional clause limiting presidential service to just two terms in office. This is one of the most significant developments in global politics today given China's growing heft in the global order.

Xi began his second term as head of the party and military last October at the end of a once-every-five-years party congress. His real source of authority emanates from him being the CPC's General Secretary — a post that has no term limit — as well as being the head of the powerful Central Military Commission. His political doctrine, "Xi Jinping Thought on Socialism with Chinese Characteristics for a New Era", is now part of the amended constitution. This takes China back to the good old days of Mao when he was the supreme leader, deciding on the fate of millions based on his whims and fancies. Xi's elevation also marks a significant change in Chinese political thought. Recognising the dangers of one man rule, Deng Xiaoping got the limit of two five-year presidential terms written into China's constitution in 1982 after Mao's death. That seems to have been put aside for now.

But let there be no doubt that this is all about Xi's ambition. In a marathon address to the 19th party congress last October, Xi had unveiled his vision of China's future of achieving 'moderate' prosperity in the next four years, and emerging as an advanced socialist nation by 2050.

Underlining that China would pursue its own path of developing "socialism with Chinese characteristics" and inviting "peoples of all countries to join China's effort to build a common destiny for mankind and enduring peace and stability," he was building a case for the "Beijing Consensus" as an alternative to the so-called Washington Consensus.

Like the rest of the world, India will also be affected by this change in manifold ways. New Delhi has no option but to deal pragmatically with whoever is ruling China, given the enormous stakes in Sino-Indian relations. Yet at a time when Sino-Indian bilateral ties are passing through one of their worst times, a centralising figure in China's governing system will only complicate matters.

China has always managed to have a consistent strategic approach towards India — to contain Indian within the confines of South Asia by assisting Pakistan to balance India. It has refused to recognise New Delhi's global aspirations and not budged an inch on key issues pertaining to Indian interests. But the growing power disparity between India and China as well as lack of any effective leverage vis-à-vis China has also meant that India has not been in any position to challenge China.

The Modi government started off promisingly by resetting the terms of engagement with China. Its principled position on the BRI has been effective in shaping the global discourse and its effective handling of last year's Doklam crisis enhanced its stature. But there is a danger now of slipping back into the old mode of China policy where a mistaken belief that only if India can brush aside the hard issues, a semblance of normalcy will return to Sino-Indian ties.

It is a myth and especially now when Xi who remains unambiguous about his desire to make China a global superpower and has all the time and resources at his command to do so. It is highly unlikely that New Delhi can attain a win-win outcome from Beijing.

Xi's growing authority will mean that he will double down on his efforts to militarise the Indian Ocean and expand Chinese influence in South Asia. His pet project BRI will also see a renewed focus and Indian opposition will rankle at his ambitious outreach. He will also wait to teach New Delhi a lesson for what many in China feel was a diplomatic drubbing for Beijing in Doklam. And this will happen when India goes into election mode and political bickering will attain new heights.

The Indian political class is yet to learn to speak in one voice in national security matters. How easy it is to divide the Indian polity was clear when even at the height of the Doklam crisis, the leaders of India's main Opposition party decided to get a briefing from the Chinese Ambassador than its own government! So as Xi's power rises to its zenith, there are many reasons to worry, but mostly it is India's own ability to get its own house in order which should concern us the most.

WHY XI JINPING IS ONCE AGAIN LETTING CHINA'S MILITARY HAVE A DIRECT LINK TO LOCAL AUTHORITIES

With little fanfare, it said "Comrade" Ma Tao would be a member of the standing committee of the Hubei branch of the Communist Party. It coincided with a flurry of similarly brief announcements in official media across the country, from Liaoning in the north to Anhui in the east.

But while the statements may have seemed small, they were a big signal from the top. They were a subtle but significant sign that Chinese President Xi Jinping had the confidence to let the armed forces once again forge links with local civilian authorities following an anti-graft campaign and a sweeping restructure of the military.

Why China's armed police will now only take orders from Xi and his generals

Party standing committees are the main decision-making bodies of any administration in China and the military has long had a presence on them at all levels. The practice dates back to the 1950s when then-defence minister Peng Dehuai suggested that officers from the People's Libration Army (PLA) join government meetings to improve coordination between military and civilian affairs.

The presence has allowed the PLA to advocate for military interests in those areas without becoming involved in the day-to-day running of the administrative regions.

But that came to an abrupt halt in late 2016 when the central government embarked on a massive restructure of the armed forces, including cutting 300,000 personnel from the payroll.

The changes were part of Xi's big plan to streamline the military and transform it into a modern fighting force, regrouping the previous seven military regions, which used to command local garrisons, into five "battle zones". It also came amid a nationwide crackdown on corruption that claimed some of the PLA's biggest names, including Guo Boxiong and Xu Caihou, former PLA generals and vice-chairmen of the Central Military Commission, the body that oversees the armed forces. Many of those top officers also had a web of corrupt with local government officials, thanks in some part to their presence on the standing committees.

The announcements that PLA officers would once again be taking up seats on the party standing committees is a strong signal that the military reforms have been completed and the PLA is regrouping, analysts say. Ni Lexiong, a Shanghai-based military expert, said the PLA personnel were deployed to ensure the civilian governments supported the operations of the modernising army.

China brings People's Armed Police under control of top military chiefs

"When the army has people in the party standing committees, it has more influence in issues involving local garrisons and retired soldiers." The welfare of retired military personnel has already erupted as a major concern, with hundreds of veterans demonstrating in the capital in the last year or so, demanding unpaid benefits and better treatment. As more military personnel are retrenched, local governments have been charged with finding new jobs for veterans, increasing the importance of good connections between the PLA and local authorities.

Xi Jinping shakes up China's military leadership ... what changes at the top mean for world's biggest armed forces

The officers on the standing committees will also play an important role in the drive to integrate military and civilian industries in weapons production, analysts say. For the programme to succeed, local governments will need to encourage the transfer of technology across military and civilian sectors as well as back military-related industries.

Better civilian-PLA coordination will also be needed now that the 1.5 million members of the People's Armed Police are under the military's sole control. Those powers are now the sole province of the PLA, making communication between the civilian and military authorities ever more important.

A Chinese political analyst said military commanders in local party leadership would help make sure the armed forces responded to local emergencies while answering to the army.

"The officers will solve the disconnect in paramilitary work," the analyst said. "And when the army has a conflict of interest with a local administration, there has to be someone who speaks for the military."

CHINA MILITARY SPENDING QUICKENS AS XI SEEKS 'WORLD CLASS' FORCE

China said defense spending would increase at the quickest pace in three years, as President Xi Jinping pursues a "world-class" military capable of projecting force further from the country's coasts.

The central government's military outlays are expected to rise 8.1 percent to 1.11 trillion yuan ($175 billion) this year, the Chinese Ministry of Finance said Monday in its annual report to the national legislative session in Beijing. Last year's budget called for an increase of 7.1 percent, the slowest pace since at least 1991.

The spending figure is one of the few pieces of official data available as the U.S. and Asian neighbors seek to gauge the development of the 2 million-member People's Liberation Army. While the figure equals about one-quarter of U.S. outlays, the Stockholm International Peace Research Institute estimates that China's actual spending is about 55 percent more than officially stated.

Vice Foreign Minister Zhang Yesui, a spokesman for the National People's Congress, said at a briefing Sunday that China's defense spending was proportionate to the size of its economy and budget. The country's military outlays were equal to about 1.9 percent of gross domestic product in 2016, according to Sipri, compared with about 3.3 percent for the U.S. "China is committed to a path of peaceful development and China pursues a defense policy that is defensive in nature," Zhang said. "China's development will not pose a threat to other countries."

Besides approving the government's budget, the National People's Congress was also expected to appoint Xi to a second term as president and repeal constitutional term limits requiring him to step down in 2023. The amendment may give Xi more time to advance a pledge in October to complete China's restoration as a global power by the mid-century mark, including the most significant military overhaul in six decades.

"China is continuing its sustained effort to increase the funding for the PLA — and a good part of that increase will go into efforts to improve China's nuclear forces and projection capabilities," said Tim Huxley, executive director of the International Institute for Strategic Studies-Asia in Singapore. "We are seeing consistent long-term Chinese investment in the development of military technology, which will increasingly rival or better those of the U.S. and Western countries."

The Trump administration has expressed concern about China's growing military and economic influence, calling the country a "revisionist power" intent on disrupting the current global order. A U.S. defense strategy document published in January said China "seeks Indo-Pacific regional hegemony in the near-term and displacement of the United States to achieve global preeminence in the future."

China Defense, Surveillance Stocks Do Best Since Xi's Power Grab

Xi has been carrying out a sweeping military overhaul to create a U.S.-style joint command structure and establish a force that can "fight and win wars." Since 2015, Xi has cut 300,000 troops, arrested scores of generals for corruption and created a new Rocket Force to manage China's missiles and Strategic Support Force to oversee cyber operations.

As Xi saves money by trimming troops, he's extending China's military reach, including launching the country's first domestically built aircraft carrier in April. Last year, the PLA established its first overseas military base near the U.S.'s Camp Lemonnier naval facility in the tiny West African nation of Djibouti, strategically located near some of China's top oil sources.

Since 2000, China's seven biggest naval shipyards have produced more submarines, destroyers, frigates and corvettes than the combined output of India, Japan and South Korea — all of which have ramped up production — according to IISS's latest annual report on the global military balance.

Premier Li Keqiang said in his opening address to the National People's Congress that China had "basically completed" its push to reduce the PLA's ranks.

"Our people's armed forces have achieved a remodeling of their political ecosystem, of the way they are organized, of the structure of their forces, and of their conduct and image," he said.

THE RISE OF CHINA AND THE FUTURE OF THE WEST

The rise of China will undoubtedly be one of the great dramas of the twenty-first century. China's extraordinary economic growth and active diplomacy are already transforming East Asia, and future decades will see even greater increases in Chinese power and influence. But exactly how this drama will play out is an open question. Will China overthrow the existing order or become a part of it? And what, if anything, can the United States do to maintain its position as China rises?

Some observers believe that the American era is coming to an end, as the Western-oriented world order is replaced by one increasingly dominated by the East.

The historian Niall Ferguson has written that the bloody twentieth century witnessed "the descent of the West" and "a reorientation of the world" toward the East. Realists go on to note that as China gets more powerful and the United States' position erodes, two things are likely to happen: China will try to use its growing influence to reshape the rules and institutions of the international system to better serve its interests, and other states in the system — especially the declining hegemon — will start to see China as a growing security threat.

The result of these developments, they predict, will be tension, distrust, and conflict, the typical features of a power transition. In this view, the drama of China's rise will feature an increasingly powerful China and a declining United States locked in an epic battle over the rules and leadership of the international system.

And as the world's largest country emerges not from within but outside the established post-World War II international order, it is a drama that will end with the grand ascendance of China and the onset of an Asian-centered world order. That course, however, is not inevitable. The rise of China does not have to trigger a wrenching hegemonic transition. The U.S.-Chinese power transition can be very different from those of the past because China faces an international order that is fundamentally different from those that past rising states confronted.

China does not just face the United States; it faces a Western-centered system that is open, integrated, and rule-based, with wide and deep political foundations. The nuclear revolution, meanwhile, has made war among great powers unlikely — eliminating the major tool that rising powers have used to overturn international systems defended by declining hegemonic states. Today's Western order, in short, is hard to overturn and easy to join.

This unusually durable and expansive order is itself the product of farsighted U.S. leadership. After World War II, the United States did not simply establish itself as the leading world power. It led in the creation of universal institutions that not only invited global membership but also brought democracies and market societies closer together. It built an order that facilitated the participation and integration of both established great powers and newly independent states. (It is often forgotten that this postwar order was designed in large part to reintegrate the defeated Axis states and the beleaguered Allied states into a unified international system.) Today, China can gain full access to and thrive within this system. And if it does, China will rise, but the Western order — if managed properly — will live on.

As it faces an ascendant China, the United States should remember that its leadership of the Western order allows it to shape the environment in which China will make critical strategic choices. If it wants to preserve this leadership, Washington must work to strengthen the rules and institutions that underpin that order — making it even easier to join and harder to overturn. U.S. grand strategy should be built around the motto "The road to the East runs through the West." It must sink the roots of this order as deeply as possible, giving China greater incentives for integration than for opposition and increasing the chances that the system will survive even after U.S. relative power has declined.

The United States' "unipolar moment" will inevitably end. If the defining struggle of the twenty-first century is between China and the United States, China will have the advantage. If the defining struggle is between China and a revived Western system, the West will triumph.

2

'The Chinese Dream' and Xi Jinping's Power Politics

China's leader Xi Jinping ends 2017 in an unassailable position of power, having consolidated his grip over the Communist Party and state. Xi's ultimate goal is to transform China into a global superpower. China's President and Communist Party General Secretary Xi Jinping has managed to tighten his hold over the party and state this year. This was in full display during the 19th congress of the Communist Party of China (CPC) held in October, when the 64-year-old president won a second five-year term as leader.

Some believe Xi might seek a third term as general secretary (or as party chairman) in 2022, which would allow him to remain at the helm until 2027. So far, no CPC general secretary has held that post for more than two terms, even if the party charter does not impose term limits. Adding fuel to the speculation is the fact that no potential successor to Xi was named in the new Politburo Standing Committee.

While Xi had already positioned himself as the "core" leader of the CPC, the party congress also enshrined the president's political philosophy – dubbed "Xi Jinping Thought on Socialism with Chinese Characteristics for a New Era" – in the country's constitution. The move was, in fact, not unusual, experts say. "As always, the party congress has adopted changes to the constitution to incorporate the ideological inclinations of the incumbent leader and praise them as a great development of Marxism," China analyst Felix Wemheuer told DW.

The inclusion of Xi's name into the constitution accorded him a higher status than his two immediate predecessors, Hu Jintao and Jiang Zemin. "But Xi's ideas have not been put on the same level as Mao Zedong's ideas," said Wemheuer.

Mao's thoughts are viewed as something that are valid for all times, while Xi's are regarded as relevant only to the current era of the CPC, observers say.

POLITICAL POSITIONS AND CHINESE DREAM

Xi and Communist Party ideologues coined the phrase "Chinese Dream" to describe his overarching plans for China as its leader. Since 2013, the phrase has emerged as the distinctive quasi-official ideology of the party leadership under Xi Jinping, much as the "Scientific Outlook on Development" was for Hu Jintao and the "Three Represents" was for Jiang Zemin. The origin of the term "Chinese Dream" is unclear. While the phrase has been used previously by journalists and scholars, some publications have posited that the term likely drew its inspiration from the concept of the American Dream. *The Economist* noted the abstract and seemingly accessible nature of the concept with no specific overarching policy stipulations may be a deliberate departure from the jargon-heavy ideologies of his predecessors.

While the Chinese Dream was originally interpreted as an extension of the American Dream, which emphasizes individual self-improvement and opportunity, the slogan's use in official settings since 2013 has taken on a noticeably more nationalistic character, with official pronouncements of the "Dream" being consistently linked with the phrase "great revival of the Chinese nation". The policy implications of the "Chinese Dream" remain unclear.

Xi first used the phrase during a high-profile visit to the National Museum of China on 29 November 2012, where Xi and his Standing Committee colleagues were attending a "national revival" exhibition. Since then, the phrase has become the signature political slogan of the Xi era.

"Xi Jinping Thought"

On September 18, 2017, the Chinese state media announced that the Communist Party Central Committee had decided that Xi's political philosophies, generally referred to as "Xi Jinping Thought" by western media, would become part of the Party Constitution.

Xi first made mention of the "Thought on Socialism with Chinese Characteristics for a New Era" in the opening day speech delivered to the 19th Party Congress in October 2017. His Politburo Standing Committee colleagues, in their own reviews of Xi's keynote address at the Congress, prepended the name "Xi Jinping" in front of "Thought".

Xi himself has described the Thought as part of the broad framework created around Socialism with Chinese Characteristics, a Dengist term that places China in the "primary stage of socialism". In official party documentation and pronouncements by Xi's colleagues, the Thought is said to be a continuation of Marxism–Leninism, Mao Zedong Thought, Deng Xiaoping Theory, the "Three Represents", and the Scientific Development Perspective, as part of a series of guiding ideologies that embody "Marxism adopted to Chinese conditions" and contemporary considerations.

On 24 October 2017, at its closing session, the 19th Party Congress approved the incorporation of Xi Jinping Thought into the Constitution of the Communist Party of China.

The concepts and context behind Xi Jinping Thought are elaborated in Xi Jinping's *The Governance of China* book series, published by the Foreign Languages Press for an international audience. Volume one was published in September 2014, followed by volume two in November 2017.

Foreign policy

Xi has reportedly taken a hard line on security issues as well as foreign affairs, projecting a more nationalistic and assertive China on the world stage. Xi's political program calls for a China more united and confident of its own value system and political structure.

Under Xi China has also taken a more critical stance on North Korea, while improving relationships with South Korea. China-Japan relations have soured under Xi's administration; the most thorny issue between the two countries remains the dispute over the Senkaku/Diaoyu islands. In response to Japan's continued robust stance on the issue, China declared an Air Defense Identification Zone in November 2013.

Xi has called China–United States relations in the contemporary world a "new type of great-power relations", a phrase the Obama administration had been reluctant to embrace. Under his administration the Strategic and Economic Dialogue that began under Hu Jintao has continued. On China-U.S. relations, Xi said, "If [China and the United States] are in confrontation, it would surely spell disaster for both countries". Xi met with President Obama privately at the Sunnylands ranch in California in 2013 in what became known as the "shirtsleeves summit". The U.S. has been critical of Chinese actions in the South China Sea. In 2014, Chinese hackers compromised the computer system of the U.S. Office of Personnel Management, resulting in the theft of approximately 22 million personnel records handled by the office.

Xi has cultivated stronger relations with Russia, particularly in the wake of the Ukraine crisis of 2014. Xi seems to have developed a strong personal relationship with President Vladimir Putin, both of whom are viewed as strong leaders with a nationalist orientation who are not afraid to assert themselves against Western interests. Xi attended the opening ceremonies of the 2014 Winter Olympics in Sochi. Under Xi, China signed a $400 billion gas deal with Russia; China has also become Russia's largest trading partner.

Xi has signaled a greater interest in Central Asia as evidenced by China's One Belt One Road initiative. Xi made the announcement while in Astana, Kazakhstan and called it a "golden opportunity".

BRICS leaders Vladimir Putin, Narendra Modi, Dilma Rousseff, Xi and Jacob Zuma at the G-20 summit in Brisbane, Australia, 15 November 2014

Xi has also indirectly spoken out critically on the U.S. "strategic pivot" to Asia. Addressing a regional conference in Shanghai on 21 May 2014, Xi called on Asian countries to unite and forge a way together, rather than get involved with third party powers, seen as a reference to the United States. "Matters in Asia ultimately must be taken care of by Asians. Asia's problems ultimately must be resolved by Asians and Asia's security ultimately must be protected by Asians", he told the conference.

In November 2014, in a major policy address, Xi has called for a decrease in the use of force, preferring dialogue and consultation to solve the current issues plaguing the relationship between China and its South East Asian neighbors.

In April 2015 Xi led a large delegation on a state visit to Pakistan. During his visit he signed energy and infrastructure deals worth $45 billion including the China–Pakistan Economic Corridor. Pakistan's highest civilian award, the Nishan-e-Pakistan, was also conferred upon him.

In April 2015, new satellite imagery revealed that China was rapidly constructing an airfield on Fiery Cross Reef in the Spratly Islands of the South China Sea. In May 2015, U.S. Secretary of Defense Ash Carter warned the government of Xi Jinping to halt its rapid island-building in disputed territory in the South China Sea.

In spite of what seemed to be a tumultuous start of Xi Jinping's leadership vis-à-vis the United-States, on 13 May 2017 Xi said at the *Belt and Road Forum* in Beijing: "We should foster a new type of international relations featuring 'win-win cooperation', and we should forge a partnership of dialogue with no confrontation, and a partnership of friendship rather than alliance. All countries should respect each other's sovereignty, dignity and territorial integrity; respect each other's development path and its social systems, and respect each other's core interests and major concerns... ...What we hope to create is a big family of harmonious coexistence."

Role of the Communist Party

Early on in his term, Xi repeatedly issued pronouncements on the supremacy of the Communist Party, largely echoing Deng Xiaoping's line that effective economic reform can only take place within the one-party political framework. In Xi's view, the Communist Party is the legitimate, constitutionally-sanctioned ruling party of China, and that the party derives this legitimacy through advancing the so-called "mass line"; that is the party represents the interests of the overwhelming majority of ordinary people.

Xi's position has been described as preferring highly centralized political power as a means to direct large-scale economic restructuring. Xi believes that China should be 'following its own path' and that a strong authoritarian government is an integral part of the "China model", operating on a "core socialist value system", which has been interpreted as China's alternative to Western values.

However, Xi and his colleagues acknowledge the challenges to the legitimacy of Communist rule, particularly corruption by party officials. The answer, according to Xi's programme, is two-fold: strengthen the party from within, by streamlining strict party discipline and initiating a large anti-corruption campaign to remove unsavoury elements from within the party, and instituting Mao-style "mass line" campaigns externally to make party officials better understand and serve the needs of ordinary people.

Xi believes that just as the party must be at the apex of political control of the state, the party's central authorities (i.e., the Politburo, PSC, or himself as general secretary) must exercise full and direct political control of all party activities.

Xi's policies have been characterized as "economically liberal but politically conservative" by Cheng Li of the Brookings Institution.

Censorship

The "Document No. 9" is a confidential internal document widely circulated within the Communist Party of China in 2013 by the party's General Office. The document was first published in July 2012. The document warns of seven dangerous Western values: constitutional democracy, universal values of human rights, civil society, pro-market neo-liberalism, media independence, historical nihilism [criticisms of past errors], and questioning Reform and Opening. Coverage of these topics in educational materials is forbidden. The release of this internal document, which has introduced new topics that were previously not "off-limits", was seen as Xi's recognition of the "sacrosanct" nature of Communist Party rule over China.

Since Xi Jinping became the General Secretary of the CPC censorship has been "significantly stepped up". His administration has also overseen more internet restrictions imposed in China, and is described as being "stricter across the board" on speech than previous administrations. Xi's term has resulted in a further suppression of dissent from civil society. Xi's term has seen the arrest and imprisonment of activists such as Xu Zhiyong, as well as numerous others who identified with the New Citizens' Movement.

Prominent legal activist Pu Zhiqiang of the Weiquan movement was also arrested and detained. The situation for users of Weibo has been described as a change from fearing that individual posts would be deleted, or at worst one's account, to fear of arrest. A law enacted in September 2013 authorized a three-year prison term for bloggers who shared more than 500 times any content considered "defamatory". A group of influential bloggers were summoned by the State Internet Information Department to a seminar instructing them to avoid writing about politics, the Communist Party, or making statements contradicting official narratives. Many bloggers stopped writing about controversial topics, and Weibo went into decline, with much of its readership shifting to WeChat users speaking to very limited social circles.

In July 2017, the character Winnie-the-Pooh was blocked on Chinese social media sites because bloggers had been comparing the plump bear to China's leader Xi Jinping. This follows an incident where Chinese authorities censored a 9-year-old for comments about Xi's weight.

CONTINUED ANTI-GRAFT CAMPAIGN

For Xi, having a strong CPC is indispensable for a "reinvigorated China," which features constantly in the president's speeches. The massive anti-corruption campaign undertaken under Xi's leadership is also aimed at achieving this objective. According to official numbers published in the *South China Morning Post*, since 2012, China's anti-graft body, the Central Commission for Discipline Inspection (CCDI), has ousted over 250 senior officials from the CPC and the military. Up to two million lower-level officials have also been investigated.

But critics say that corruption is so ingrained in Chinese political culture that Xi's claims of a widespread reduction in corruption have been superficial. And whether or not the crackdown has led to an actual reduction in graft is difficult to observe, even though Xi's detractors say the campaign helped him purge his political opponents. 2017 marks the fifth year since the anti-graft drive began.

Merging party and state

In 2018, the anti-corruption drive is set to be taken to a new level. A new "National Supervision Commission" will work alongside the CPC's anti-graft body, the Central Commission for Discipline Inspection (CCDI), sharing much of its power and resources, and will merge multiple additional anti-graft units. It will also expand the purview of Xi's anti-graft campaign to include employees at state-backed institutions who are not necessarily party members. Suspects could then be detained for several months without legal assistance.

In his congress address, Xi also said China would keep up with the "irreversible" momentum of the anti-corruption campaign, and announced a central leading group responsible for overseeing China's law-based governance. Observers view these developments as evidence that Xi doesn't intend to separate party from state.

China as a 'global player'

Xi also wants to dedicate his power and energy to turning China into a global superpower and the world's preeminent nation. This vision, which Xi calls the "Chinese dream," includes Beijing's claim to global leadership. Xi underlined this during his address at the World Economic Forum in Davos, where he presented himself as a champion of free trade and global cooperation.

This was in sharp contrast to the "America First" protectionist rhetoric adopted by US President Donald Trump, who appears to want to withdraw the US from all multilateral trading arrangements. In May, Xi organized a pompous ceremony in Beijing - attended by representatives from around 100 countries, including 29 heads of state and government - to give international impetus to his signature "Belt and Road Initiative" – an ambitious and coordinated infrastructure project planned from Beijing, which will connect China on land and sea with Europe, Africa, the Middle East and South, Central and Southeast Asia.

Expanding influence

The year 2017 has also seen Beijing expand its political and economic clout in other parts of the world. The development of artificial islands in the controversial Spratly Islands in the South China Sea and their conversion into military bases was completed on schedule.

China also opened its first overseas naval base in Djibouti, in the Horn of Africa, despite Beijing officially calling it only a "logistics center." Although it is primarily intended to support ongoing peace and anti-piracy operations in China, this move is "an indicator of the global expansion of China and its economic interests," said Bernt Berger, a China expert and founder of

Engagement Policy Center, a Berlin-based think tank."The US is slowly getting used to the fact that China's civilian and military facilities will be set up even more frequently near US facilities in the future."

Cooperation and confrontation

It remains uncertain whether this development will lead to more cooperation between China and the US or more rivalry, and possibly confrontation. During his state visit to Beijing in November, Trump appeared to admire Xi and praised him as a strong national leader. But in mid-December, Trump labelled China - together with Russia – as a "revisionist state" that is determined to "challenge American power, influence, and interests, attempting to erode American security and prosperity."

The Communist Party leadership, meanwhile, is not in favor of a direct confrontation with the US. Instead, China accepts the existing world order for now and intends to emerge as a global superpower in the long run. This desire, said China expert Wemheuer, was reflected in Xi's speech to the party congress, where he underlined Beijing's aim to turn the country into a global superpower and a modern socialist industrial state by 2049, the centenary of the founding of the People's Republic of China.

Likewise, the People's Liberation Army is to be transformed into a modern fighting force capable of winning wars by 2035. Despite geopolitical rivalry, the US and China have been forced to cooperate on the North Korean nuclear issue to prevent a catastrophic escalation.

And both countries have reached their limits with North Korea: Even with all his power, Xi Jinping - like Donald Trump and his predecessors - has not been able to stop Kim Jong Un from pursuing nuclear weapons and advanced missiles.

XI JINPING AND THE 'CHINESE DREAM'

The rest of the world rubs its eyes in astonishment. In just under three decades, China has transformed itself from being a bitter-poor developing country into a global economic power. Beijing now has set its eyes on becoming a world superpower. For now, at least, fears about China's rising power and influence are mixed with admiration for the rapid pace of its growth and development.

The Chinese people, on the other hand, and especially the political class in Beijing, see the strengthening of their country as the correction of a historical anomaly. This view is promoted by Beijing's propaganda departments and President Xi Jinping's "Chinese Dream" is meant to address it.

Since Xi took over the reins of his country in 2012, China's state and party leaders have promised the Chinese people the return to the grandeur of past dynasties. By doing so, Xi has attempted to tap into the historical consciousness of the Chinese.

Today's Chinese see themselves as the heirs of a millennium-old civilization that was the world leader in culture, science, technology and administration right up to the 16th century. In this ideal conception, China — the "Middle Kingdom," as it is still called in Chinese today — was at the center of the world, surrounded by barbarians, who were willing to pay tribute to the luminosity of Chinese civilization.

'Century of humiliation'

The so-called "century of humiliation" stands out all the more against this background. It began with China's defeat in the First Opium War (1839-1842) by Great Britain. In the first of the so-called "unequal treaties," China was forced to cede control of Hong Kong to the British. The century has a formal end that suits official propaganda: The founding of the People's Republic of China in 1949 by the Communist Party.

The Century of Humiliation forms the antithesis to the rise of China. Who knows that China's share of world economic output in 1820 was over 30 percent? Following internal Chinese rebellions, colonial exploitation, state collapse, Japanese occupation and civil war, this share had fallen to just 5 percent in the early 1950s.

The phantom pain of losing imperial greatness is kept alive in the collective memory. History books, television series and newspaper articles repeatedly evoke the humiliation of the Chinese nation by foreign powers, the decline and misery. This culture of remembrance has paved the way for the mass appeal of Xi Jinping's Chinese Dream. In doing so, as a collective vision proclaimed from above, it is the exact opposite of the "American Dream" of the realization of individual happiness.

'Global superpower by 2049'

The plans for the "great rejuvenation of the Chinese nation" extend to 2049, the year marking the 100th anniversary of the founding of the People's Republic of China. By then, China should once again emerge as a global superpower. It seems as if the nobler the goals and the farther into the future their fulfilment, the greater the sacrifices one can demand from the people. When it comes to the "rejuvenation of the Chinese nation," nothing like civil liberties or cumbersome constitutional processes should come in the way, according to Beijing's view. Dissenters, human rights activists, even their lawyers end up in jail. The previously hard-won liberties, even in the media, are again being scaled back.

The vision of the Chinese Dream is so vague and at the same time so comprehensive that different messages can fit under its roof.

Anyone who has the authority to interpret the content of the vision can define almost anything as an element for the realization of the Chinese Dream. When Xi Jinping visited the Three Gorges Dam in April, for instance, the ability to independently develop technology was declared essential to realizing the dream. When Xi met with senior military officials in mid-March, it was the greater integration of the civilian and military spheres. Furthermore, there have been repeated exhortations for unity and the development of strength.

In its ambiguity, the Chinese Dream is also suitable as a tool for fomenting Chinese nationalism, which has been gaining traction for the past two decades. It is important as a source of legitimacy for the rule of the Communist Party, as the party's legitimacy, in ideological terms, has been eroded due to its role as the organizer of a highly effective form of state capitalism, with party workers and government officials as main beneficiaries despite Xi's unprecedented anti-corruption campaign.

China's robust maneuvering in the territorial spat with Japan in the East China Sea, and the building of artificial islands in the South China Sea to enforce its claims to the region, also serve the purpose of deliberately stirring the Chinese people's nationalist fervor.

With the Silk Road to the middle of the world

Against this backdrop, Xi's signature project — the Belt and Road Initiative — also fits under the umbrella of the Chinese Dream. China is deploying immense resources to build infrastructure that will connect it to parts of Asia, Africa and Europe and boost its trading links to these regions.

This ambitious project makes China the only country in the world currently pursuing a global vision. And it is certainly no coincidence that the Belt and Road Initiative, regarded as a modern-day version of the ancient Silk Road, also linguistically ties up with times of former splendor.

With its clever investment policy, China has been increasingly able to translate its economic strength into political influence. The new transport links and economic corridors will definitely play their part in the development of the Chinese Dream, by strengthening Beijing's role as a Eurasian center of gravity and turning it once again into the "Middle Country."

It goes without saying that this center should then radiate out into the world. At the Communist Party's congress last fall, Xi called for "Socialism with Chinese Characteristics for a New Era" and recommended it as a development model for other countries. At the start of the year, *The People's Daily*, an official newspaper of the Communist Party, went as far as to talk of a fusion of the "Chinese Dream" with the "Dream of the Whole World."

CHINA'S POWER STATUS AND ITS IMPLICATIONS

The author believes that in order to study China's power status objectively, we should first understand the true nature of international power and clarify our goal for measuring the differences of national powers. If we fail to do this, then as complexity in these measurements increases, their pragmatic value actually decreases. Therefore, the results of assessment will not benefit us at all in understanding national power status.

Relativity in Assessing China's Power Status

Power status connotes relativity. It refers to ranking the power status of one state with relevance to that of other states in an international sphere. The power status of a state can be understood only through a simultaneous comparative assessment of the power status of other nations. If there is only one nation in the world, then there is no frame of reference with which we can decide if a country's power status is high or low. This means that only when there are two or more countries in the world, that the study of a state's power status and its comprehensive national power has significance.

The term 'power status' contains a connotation of both 'the rank of power status' and 'the differences in power status'. Whereas the difference in power status decides the rank of power status, the rank of power status cannot always truly reflect the real nature and degrees of difference in power status. During the Cold War period, the United States and the Soviet Union ranked first and second, respectively, in their power status. However, the difference in power between them remained at a hierarchical level of superpowers. But in the 1990s, while the United States still kept its top ranking (regardless of which major power stayed in second: Russia, Japan or China), the nature of the ranking gap between the first and the second power states changed substantially, because it became a difference in power status between a superpower and a major power.

The power status of a state is based on, but not decided by, its national power. In other words, the increase of a state's power does not necessarily elevate that state's power status. For example, in the late 19th century during the Qing Dynasty, China had enough industrial capacity to arm its military. Its overall national power was far larger than that of the early Qing Dynasty when there was no modern industry. However, internationally, China's power status during the late Qing Dynasty was far behind that of the early Qing Dynasty. Take the current cases of The Netherlands and South Korea. In 1999, GDP in The Netherlands grew from $393.5 billion to $398.1 billion, with an absolute increase of $4.6 billion. However, according to World Bank statistics, the ranking of The Netherlands fell below that of South Korea, whose GDP in the same period increased from $317.1 billion to $406.1 billion.

The rank of a state's power status is decided by the difference between its own power status and that of other states. However, this absolute difference does not indicate the nature and extent of power differences between states. The absolute value of the disparity in power status between two states indicates which state possesses a mightier power status. Therefore, it reflects the rank of the power status of the two states. However, this absolute difference hardly displays the true nature and class difference of a state's power status. For instance, according to the 2003 World Bank GDP statistics, by currency exchange rates, the GDP difference between Japan and Germany was $1.93 trillion while the GDP difference between Germany and Brazil was $1.97 trillion. The absolute values of the two differences vary little, but this by no means indicates that the difference in economic power between Germany and Japan shares any similarity with the difference between Brazil and Germany. Common sense leads us to conclude that Germany and Japan share the same class status, but that Brazil and Germany do not.

The power status of a state depends on how its national power compares with that of other nations. We can clarify this further by looking at GDP comparisons for Japan, Germany and Brazil. In 2003, Japan's GDP amounted to $4.3 trillion, Germany's to $2.4 trillion and Brazil's to $0.5 trillion. Despite the fact that the difference in GDP between Germany and Japan almost equals that between Brazil and Germany, Japan's GDP was only 1.8 times Germany's GDP while Germany's GDP amounted to 4.8 times that of Brazil. This helps us understand that using common knowledge leads us to conclude that Germany and Japan share the same economic class, whereas Brazil and Germany are quite different.

In short, it is the proportional relationship between the power statuses of two states, not the absolute quantity of difference that decides a state's power status. It can be expressed as: $S = A/B$, (where S indicates power status of State A in proportion to that of State B; A refers to the power of State A, and B to the power of State B.) In the reality of international politics, when two states confront each other on a specific issue, the advantages and disadvantages of their powers depend largely on one state's power in proportion to the other. As an example, assume a small military skirmish along a common border between two nations, Side A has three soldiers and Side B only one. Although Side A has only two more soldiers than Side B in absolute number, its power is 200% greater than that of Side B (i.e. the possibility of winning for Side A is three times as much as that for Side B). To cite another example, Side A has 102 soldiers and Side B 100; even if Side A has two more soldiers than Side B, its power strength gains only a 2% advantage. Therefore, the possibility of winning for either side is almost equal. In this analogy, to assess China's power status and its progression, one should focus on China's power status in proportion to the power status of other states, instead of solely on the absolute differences in the power of two states.

Importance of Assessing China's Power Status

Because power status is relative, recognizing China's power status in relation to that of other states is of immediate significance in our study. In order to further understand China's power status we consider the following three aspects. First, by understanding the relativity of power status, we can better understand the major difference in defining the 'Rejuvenation' or 'Rise' of China. In 2003, the Chinese leaders first introduced the term 'Peaceful Rise'. However, in April 2004 at the Boao Asia Forum, it was replaced by 'Peaceful Development'. This was mainly because 'Rise' has a relative meaning in terms of power status. Despite the often heated debates on 'Peaceful Rise', scholars on all sides acknowledge that the word 'Rise' implies attaining superpower status. For the Chinese, 'rejuvenation' bears a similar connotation to 'rise'. Both mean to restore China's power status to the prosperity enjoyed during the prime of the Han, Tang and early Qing Dynasties. It does not simply refer to a regression of China's comprehensive national power down to the ancient level. By early 21st century standards, China's comprehensive national power in the afore-mentioned ancient periods was only equivalent to a state of low power status in the current international system. As power status changes with time and the international environment, China's national rejuvenation will be realized only if its pace of national power growth is faster than that of other countries. Growth at any slower pace will weaken China's power status gradually and thus diminish the hopes of national rejuvenation and rise.

Second, the zero-sum nature of power status helps us understand that there will be no win–win situation in conflicts among international political entities accompanying the rise of China. Power status and international politics share the same zero-sum characteristic.

The rise of a state's power status indicates an expansion of its political power. This in turn causes the fall of other states' power status and political power. Powerful states remain a minority in the world while weaker states remain a majority. Until September 2002, no more than 10 global or regional major powers had been listed among 191 member countries of the UN.

The middle and small powers are represented in greater numbers in this ranking. As the power status of one small state increases, the relative power it gains is drawn from many other middle or small states of similar power status. Thus, an evenly spread decrease in power in every small power is not obvious, and so is unlikely to cause conflict among these states. For instance, the sum of international political power for 100 small states is fixed and stable, and each small state holds 1% of this power sum. When one small state increases its power status to 1.9% of the total power, the share for each of the remaining 99 countries is decreased to 0.99%, i.e. each country loses only 1% of its original power. On the other hand, an increase in power status for a major state usually conveys serious outcomes in this aspect. Great powers are few in number.

Therefore, as a major power gains an advantage in its power status, the remainder of the few major powers feel a tremendous loss of their original power. If the dominant world power belongs to a single state, then this hegemony holds 100% of the power. When the power status of another state increases to the same level, there are two states sharing this world dominant power. That means, among those with dominant power, the former hegemony will be diminished to half, or only 50%. Since a change in a major power's power status may result in the restructuring of international relations and a rearrangement of world resources, studies on comprehensive national strength and power status are of the utmost importance only for those few major powers. The zero-sum nature in power status gives us the insight that a majority of political conflicts along China's path to her rise will bear this zero-sum nature as well. In other words, there will be few win–win situations in China's ascent to a superpower.

Third, by recognizing China's current power status, we can better perceive the strategic relationship between China and the other major powers in the post-Cold War era. In a world configured with one superpower against several major powers, the United States is destined to defend its status against any possible challenging states in the future. As one of the major powers after the Cold War, China automatically becomes an opponent of the United States.

None the less, the United States will decide whether to interpret China as its number one rival on the basis of how China's power status changes. Although China and the Western European major powers have been categorized as regional powers, the geographical distances between them cause fewer conflicts of interest. Thus they may even forge a strategic alliance against the United States' hegemonic pressures. However, in East Asia, China and Japan have fundamental conflicts that will cause inevitable confrontations between the two. In the early post-Cold War period, Japan was the world's second economic power after the United States, and the number one economic power in East Asia. If its economic power status decreases due to an increase in power status of other states, both globally and regionally, Japan may take several measures to protect its existing international status by strengthening its political and military power. Thus, if China's economic power status replaces that of Japan, Japan may confront China politically. A better understanding of China's power status enables us to know why structural conflicts exist in China's strategic relationships with the United States and Japan but not with the major European powers.

THE EVER-GROWING POWER OF CHINA'S XI JINPING

Over four days in the Chinese capital a major political meeting has been taking place between a couple of hundred members of the Central Committee. It is known as the Plenum.

Such gatherings are usually held once a year and allow the Communist Party to make policy decisions which are later shoved through the National People's Congress for approval.

At this week's Plenum, it was pronounced that Party members should unite around the Central Committee "with Comrade Xi Jinping as the core".

Communism's 'core'

The expression is already falling off the lips of senior government officials like a religious mantra. There they were at a press conference explaining the plenum decisions and describing concepts as being in step with "socialism with Chinese characteristics" in order to boost the standing of the Communist Party "with Xi Jinping as the core".

A more mind-numbingly dull and uninformative press conference you would struggle to find, even in China. Pre-ordained questions, pre-scripted answers.

Yet, even amongst the hours of dross, there was this significant new development. "Bla bla bla... Xi Jinping as the core... bla bla... with Xi Jinping at its core... bla bla... Xi Jinping: core... Xi Jinping: core".

What worries China observers is that General Secretary Xi is growing into an untouchable figure the likes of which has not been seen here for quite some time.

This was not the case, for example, with the previous administration of Hu Jintao. Though he too was president and chairman of the Central Military Commission, his was a leadership within a system of collective responsibility. You could imagine a diversity of views amongst the (then nine-member) Politburo Standing Committee.

Since 1949 the most extreme example of an omnipotent ruler was naturally Mao Zedong.

When his disastrous policy known as the Great Leap Forward left millions of people starving to death, Defence Minister Marshal Peng Dehuai challenged him. For this, one of the heroes of the revolution was purged.

Naturally the China of today is nothing like it was in 1959 but the accumulation of power around a single figure "at the core" who cannot be criticised is making plenty of analysts concerned.

Discipline commission

The sprinkles of information which have been released regarding this Plenum's decisions mostly relate to the fight against corruption: Xi Jinping's fight against corruption. Apparently the Central Commission for Discipline Inspection has investigated 1,018,000 officials. Of these 1,010,000 have been punished. Not a bad strike rate.

Because of this rampant fraud, we have been told the rules governing Party behaviour had to be made much more strict. This was needed in order to stamp out election-rigging, the selling of positions and the practice of bargaining with Party organizations in order to secure a promotion or promotions.

For government officials it is now prohibited to "request an official post, honour or special treatment".

The idea must now be that you will wait to be asked. I have no idea how you are supposed to show your interest in a particular job (because they would not take any serious questions at the aforementioned explanatory press conference).

Maybe you just do what you are told and develop an expertise in cotton dying machine technology if your Party requires you to? On this front there is also a rather ominous-sounding new rule amongst those just approved at the Plenum.

'Xi Dada'

For members the disobeying of any decisions made by a Party organisation is now forbidden. Here is another (rather extreme) hypothetical example:

Person giving order: "Excuse me but we have just decided to use extreme force to clear the remaining protestors out from in and around Tiananmen Square so if you would not mind leading your column of tanks down there to sort them out that would be most appreciated."

Response:"Well gee, to tell the truth I have a few moral qualms about firing on my unarmed civilian countrymen."

Person giving order: "Sorry, disobeying any Party decision is now forbidden."

Anecdotally, President Xi Jinping seems very popular amongst ordinary Chinese people: they call him "Xi Dada", loosely translated as "Uncle Xi".

These same average citizens see officials found to have been corrupt being sent to gaol and are cheering all the way.

There is even a television programme here featuring the confessions of regional bosses admitting their crimes on their way to incarceration.

There is a view, though, that so many officials are up to their necks in ill-gotten gains, Xi Dada could have been using a selective anti-corruption campaign to take out only his factional enemies, thus shoring up his own position.

It is a view that we journalists and academics toss about quite a bit. It is not one you will hear expressed amongst the so-called *lao bai xing*, the average Chinese people. To them, who cares if only certain corrupt officials have been taken down? At least some of them have.

Yet the crackdown has been so widespread it has led to one contentious theory.

If Xi Jiping and his people have punished more than a million officials who all have friends and family where does that leave him in terms of amassing enemies who are biding their time for now?

How dangerous might it be for President Xi to ever give up power? Can he find a mechanism to extend his tenure or at least put a wall around himself? Or maybe he just needs a Medvedev-style supporter to come along as a chosen successor? We will not know the answer to any of this until the end of his second term in another six years.

CHINA'S RISE TO WORLD POWER: WILL HISTORY REPEAT ITSELF?

China has been growing at about 9% per annum and its goods and services are rapidly rising in quality and value. In contrast, the US and Europe have wallowed around 0% growth from 2007-2012. China's innovative techno-scientific establishment routinely assimilates the latest inventions from the West (and Japan) and improves them, thereby decreasing the cost of production. China has replaced the US and European controlled "international financial institutions" (the IMF, World Bank, the Inter-American Development Bank) as the principle lender in Latin America. China continues to lead as the prime investor in African energy and mineral resources. China has replaced the US as the principle market for Saudi Arabian, Sudanese and Iranian petroleum and it will soon replace the US as the principle market for Venezuela petroleum products. Today China is the world's biggest manufacturer and exporter, dominating even the US market, while playing the role of financial life line as it holds over $1.3 trillion in US Treasury notes.

Under growing pressure from its workers, farmers and peasants, China's rulers have been developing the domestic market by increasing wages and social spending to rebalance the economy and avoid the specter of social instability. In contrast, US wages, salaries and vital public services have sharply declined in absolute and relative terms.

Given the current historical trends it is clear that China will replace the US as the leading world economic power, over the next decade, if the US empire does not strike back and if China's profound class inequalities do not lead to a major social upheaval.

Modern China's rise to global power faces serious challenges. In contrast to China's historical ascent on the world stage, modern Chinese global economic power is not accompanied by any imperialist undertakings. China has seriously lagged behind the US and Europe in aggressive war-making capacity. This may have allowed China to direct public resources to maximize economic growth, but it has left China vulnerable to US military superiority in terms of its massive arsenal, its string of forward bases and strategic geo-military positions right off the Chinese coast and in adjoining territories.

In the nineteenth century British imperialism demolished China's global position with its military superiority, seizing China's ports – because of China's reliance on 'mercantile superiority'.

The conquest of India, Burma and most of Asia allowed Britain to establish colonial bases and recruit local mercenary armies. The British and its mercenary allies encircled and isolated China, setting the stage for the disruption of China's markets and the imposition of the brutal terms of trade. The British Empire's armed presence dictated what China imported (with opium accounting for over 50% of British exports in the 1850s) while undermining China's competitive advantages via tariff policies.

Today the US is pursuing similar policies: US naval fleet patrols and controls China's commercial shipping lanes and off-shore oil resources via its overseas bases. The Obama-Clinton White House is in the process of developing a rapid military response involving bases in Australia, Philippines and elsewhere in Asia. The US is intensifying its efforts to undermine Chinese overseas access to strategic resources while backing 'grass roots' separatists and 'insurgents' in West China, Tibet, Sudan, Burma, Iran, Libya, Syria and elsewhere. The US military agreements with India and the installation of a pliable puppet regime in Pakistan have advanced its strategy of isolating China. While China upholds its policy of "harmonious development" and "non-interference in the internal affairs of other countries", it has stepped aside as US and European military imperialism have attacked a host of China's trading partners to essentially reverse China's peaceful commercial expansion.

China's lack of a political and ideological strategy capable of protecting its overseas economic interests has been an invitation for the US and NATO to set-up regimes hostile to China. The most striking example is Libya where US and NATO intervened to overthrow an independent government led by President Gadhafi, with whom China had signed multi-billion dollar trade and investments agreements. The NATO bombardment of Libyan cities, ports and oil installation forced the Chinese to withdraw 35,000 Chinese oil engineers and construction workers in a matter of days. The same thing happened in Sudan where China had invested billions to develop its oil industry. The US, Israel and Europe armed the South Sudanese rebels to disrupt the flow of oil and attack Chinese oil workers. In both cases China passively allowed the US and European military imperialists to attack its trade partners and undermine its investments.

Under Mao Tse Tung, China had an active policy countering imperial aggression: It supported revolutionary movements and independent Third World governments. Today's capitalist China does not have an active policy of supporting governments or movements capable of protecting China's bilateral trade and investment agreements. China's inability to confront the rising tide of US military aggression against its economic interests, is due to deep structural problems. China's foreign policy is shaped by big commercial, financial and manufacturing interests who rely on their 'economic competitive edge' to gain market shares and have no understanding of the military and security underpinnings of global economic power. China's political class is deeply influenced by a new class of billionaires with strong ties to Western equity funds and who have uncritically absorbed Western cultural values. This is illustrated by their preference for sending their own children to elite universities in the US and Europe. They seek "accommodation with the West" at any price.

This lack of any strategic understanding of military empire-building has led them to respond ineffectively and ad hoc to each imperialist action undermining their access to resources and markets. While China's "business first" outlook may have worked when it was a minor player in the world economy and US empire builders saw the "capitalist opening" as a chance to easily takeover China's public enterprises and pillage the economy. However, when China (in contrast to the former USSR) decided to retain capital controls and develop a carefully calibrated, state directed "industrial policy" directing western capital and the transfer of technology to state enterprises, which effectively penetrated the US domestic and overseas markets, Washington began to complain and talked of retaliation.

China's huge trade surpluses with the US provoked a dual response in Washington : It sold massive quantities of US

Treasury bonds to the Chinese and began to develop a global strategy to block China's advance. Since the US lacked economic leverage to reverse its decline, it relied on its only "comparative advantage" – its military superiority based on a world wide system of attack bases, a network of overseas client regimes, military proxies, NGO'ers, intellectuals and armed mercenaries. Washington turned to its vast overt and clandestine security apparatus to undermine China's trading partners. Washington depends on its long-standing ties with corrupt rulers, dissidents, journalists and media moguls to provide the powerful propaganda cover while advancing its military offensive against China's overseas interests.

China has nothing to compare with the US overseas 'security apparatus' because it practices a policy of "non-interference". Given the advanced state of the Western imperial offensive, China has taken only a few diplomatic initiatives, such as financing English language media outlets to present its perspective, using its veto power on the UN Security Council to oppose US efforts to overthrow the independent Assad regime in Syria and opposing the imposition of drastic sanctions against Iran.

It sternly repudiated US Secretary of State Hilary Clinton's vitriolic questioning of the 'legitimacy' of the Chinese state when it voted against the US-UN resolution preparing an attack on Syria.

Chinese military strategists are more aware and alarmed at the growing military threat to China. They have successfully demanded a 19% annual increase in military spending over the next five years (2011-2015). Even with this increase, China's military expenditures will still be less than one-fifth of the US military budget and China has not one overseas military base in stark contrast to the over 750 US installations abroad. Overseas Chinese intelligence operations are minimal and ineffective. Its embassies are run by and for narrow commercial interests who utterly failed to understand NATO's brutal policy of regime change in Libya and inform Beijing of its significance to the Chinese state.

There are two other structural weaknesses undermining China's rise as a world power. This includes the highly 'Westernized' intelligentsia which has uncritically swallowed US economic doctrine about free markets while ignoring its militarized economy.

These Chinese intellectuals parrot the US propaganda about the 'democratic virtues' of billion-dollar Presidential campaigns, while supporting financial deregulation which would have led to a Wall Street takeover of Chinese banks and savings. Many Chinese business consultants and academics have been educated in the US and influenced by their ties to US academics and international financial institutions directly linked to Wall Street and the City of London.

They have prospered as highly-paid consultants receiving prestigious positions in Chinese institutions. They identify the 'liberalization of financial markets' with "advanced economies" capable of deepening ties to global markets instead of as a major source of the current global financial crisis. These "Westernized intellectuals" are like their 19th century comprador counterparts who underestimated and dismissed the long-term consequences of Western imperial penetration. They fail to understand how financial deregulation in the US precipitated the current crisis and how deregulation would lead to a Western takeover of China's financial system- the consequences of which would reallocate China's domestic savings to non-productive activities (real estate speculation), precipitate financial crisis and ultimately undermine China's leading global position.

These Chinese yuppies imitate the worst of Western consumerist life styles and their political outlooks are driven by these life styles and Westernized identities which preclude any sense of solidarity with their own working class.

There is an economic basis for the pro-Western sentiments of China's neo-compradors. They have transferred billions of dollars to foreign bank accounts, purchased luxury homes and apartments in London, Toronto, Los Angeles, Manhattan, Paris, Hong Kong and Singapore. They have one foot in China (the source of their wealth) and the other in the West (where they consume and hide their wealth).

Westernized compradores are deeply embedded in China's economic system having family ties with the political leadership in the party apparatus and the state. Their connections are weakest in the military and in the growing social movements, although some "dissident" students and academic activists in the "democracy movements" are backed by Western imperial NGO's. To the extent that the compradors gain influence, they weaken the strong economic state institutions which have directed China's ascent to global power, just as they did in the 19th century by acting as intermediaries for the British Empire. Proclaiming 19th Century "liberalism" British opium addicted over 50 million Chinese in less than a decade. Proclaiming "democracy and human rights" US gunboats now patrol off China's coast. China's elite-directed rise to global economic power has spawned monumental inequalities between the thousands of new billionaires and multi-millionaires at the top and hundreds of millions of impoverished workers, peasants and migrant workers at the bottom.

China's rapid accumulation of wealth and capital was made possible through the intense exploitation of its workers who were stripped of their previous social safety net and regulated work conditions guaranteed under Communism. Millions of Chinese households are being dispossessed in order to promote real estate developer/speculators who then build high rise offices and the luxury apartments for the domestic and foreign elite. These brutal features of ascendant Chinese capitalism have created a fusion of workplace and living space mass struggle which is growing every year. The developer/speculators' slogan "to get rich is wonderful" has lost its power to deceive the people. In 2011 there were over 200,000 popular encompassing urban coastal factories and rural villages. The next step, which is sure to come, will be the unification of these struggles into new national social movements with a class-based agenda demanding the restoration of health and educational services enjoyed under the Communists as well as a greater share of

China's wealth. Current demands for greater wages can turn to demands for greater work place democracy. To answer these popular demands China's new compradore-Westernized liberals cannot point to their 'model' in the US empire where American workers are in the process of being stripped of the very benefits Chinese workers are struggling to regain.

China, torn by deepening class and political conflict, cannot sustain its drive toward global economic leadership. China's elite cannot confront the rising global imperial military threat from the US with its comprador allies among the internal liberal elite while the country is a deeply divided society with an increasingly hostile working class. The time of unbridled exploitation of China's labor has to end in order to face the US military encirclement of China and economic disruption of its overseas markets. China possesses enormous resources. With over $1.5 trillion dollars in reserves China can finance a comprehensive national health and educational program throughout the country.

China can afford to pursue an intensive 'public housing program' for the 250 million migrant workers currently living in urban squalor. China can impose a system of progressive income taxes on its new billionaires and millionaires and finance small family farmer co-operatives and rural industries to rebalance the economy. Their program of developing alternative energy sources, such as solar panels and wind farms – are a promising start to addressing their serious environmental pollution. Degradation of the environment and related health issues already engage the concern of tens of millions. Ultimately China's best defence against imperial encroachments is a stable regime based on social justice for the hundreds of millions and a foreign policy of supporting overseas anti-imperialist movements and regimes – whose independence are in China's vital interest. What is needed is a pro-active policy based on mutually beneficial joint ventures including military and diplomatic solidarity. Already a small, but influential, group of Chinese intellectuals have raised the issue of the growing US military threat and are "saying no to gunboat diplomacy".

Modern China has plenty of resources and opportunities, unavailable to China in the 19th century when it was subjugated by the British Empire. If the US continues to escalate its aggressive militaristic policy against China, Beijing can set off a serious fiscal crisis by dumping a few of its hundreds of billions of dollars in US Treasury notes. China, a nuclear power should reach out to its similarly armed and threatened neighbor, Russia, to confront and confound the bellicose rantings of US Secretary of State, Hilary Clinton. Russian President-to-be Putin vows to increase military spending from 3% to 6% of the GDP over the next decade to counter Washington's offensive missile bases on Russia's borders and thwart Obama's 'regime change' programs against its allies, like Syria.

China has powerful trading, financial and investment networks covering the globe as well as powerful economic partners.These links have become essential for the continued growth of many of countries throughout the developing world. In taking on China, the US will have to face the opposition of many powerful market-based elites throughout the world. Few countries or elites see any future in tying their fortunes to an economically unstable empire-based on militarism and destructive colonial occupations.

In other words, modern China, as a world power, is incomparably stronger than it was in early 18th century. The US does not have the colonial leverage that the ascendant British Empire possessed in the run-up to the Opium Wars. Moreover, many Chinese intellectuals and the vast majority of its citizens have no intention of letting its current "Westernized comprادors" sell out the country. Nothing would accelerate political polarization in Chinese society and hasten the coming of a second Chinese social revolution more than a timid leadership submitting to a new era of Western imperial pillage.

XI JINPING CHINA'S REJUVENATION MUST BE PEACEFUL, OR IT WON'T HAPPEN AT ALL

Now that China has done away with presidential term limits, Xi Jinping can retain all his current titles and power long into the future. Most commentary defending the move argues that Xi is consolidating power to push through difficult reforms and strengthen China, and that he wants to remain in charge beyond 2022 to preside over China's emergence as a global superpower, achieving the great rejuvenation of the Chinese nation.

That Xi cares about achieving this great rejuvenation is pretty clear. Yet this goal implies not only China's economic transformation into a developed country, but also its change into a superpower with global influence, admired and respected around the world.

If this is truly Xi's ultimate goal, then there is something important that both the outside world and Xi himself need to understand: the great rejuvenation of the Chinese nation will either have to be peaceful or it probably won't happen at all.

Over the next 20 years, as China's power and influence grow, tensions between Beijing and the US, along with other regional powers, will inevitably emerge. This is already happening, whether in the South China Sea or at the Sino-Indian border. Even a limited war might have profound consequences for China's rise, because it could throw its economy into recession or catalyse the formation of an anti-China alliance of Asia-Pacific states, from Japan to Australia to India. This would sabotage both China's economic and strategic goals.

Asia-Pacific countries have already become fearful of China's growing military might, but its economic pull has proved stronger for the time being.

Asian leaders can also comfort themselves with the thought that China hasn't fought a war in almost 40 years, and official Chinese rhetoric at least talks about peaceful settlement of disputes. But if China's military were to show its teeth, it would become clear that a peaceful rise is just a dream and any country in the region could become the next target.

Current economic priorities would give way to the imperatives of defending national security. China's neighbours would rush into the arms of the United States and band together to resist China's expanding influence. Inevitably, they would also start reducing their economic and commercial ties to China, hurting the Chinese economy. US allies worldwide, including the European Union, would follow this trend.

Instead of eliminating US influence and the American military presence in the Asia-Pacific, an aggressive China and any military confrontation would only strengthen them. Instead of respect and admiration for China, this would generate only fear and hatred. Instead of cementing China's position as the centre of an Asia-Pacific that gravitates around it, it would lead to a coalition restraining China's power and influence. The great rejuvenation would remain a mere slogan.

How China's military is girding for battle, and what it means for neighbours

To avoid this, China will need to prioritise its long-term strategic goals and eschew any use of force, even in situations in which Beijing might see a war as justified and as the best way to teach a neighbouring country a lesson.

Because of its indisputable military might, it's highly doubtful that any other country would willingly start a war with China. The only plausible scenario is a political or military act that falls short of war, but which Beijing sees as very aggressive, such as a deadly maritime incident in the East or South China Sea, forward military deployments at the disputed Sino-Indian border, or a Taiwanese declaration of independence.

In any of these instances, Xi and the Communist Party might be inclined to use force, even in a limited manner. But once China does this, its record of four decades of peace will be gone and it will face criticism for what will be seen as an aggressive response. Thus, Xi will need to avoid the pressure for a quick military solution and find a way to negotiate a peaceful settlement.

If Xi is serious about achieving the great rejuvenation of the Chinese nation and building a community with a shared future, he will have to follow the path of peaceful rise, even in moments of crisis. This means prioritising diplomacy and economics over military expansion. The recent 15.6 per cent jump in China's diplomatic budget is a welcome development in this direction. But it also means that China's long-term goals must override short-term imperatives, requiring compromises. Xi's political strength in China should make compromises possible. Hu Jintao and Jiang Zemin, who lacked Xi's control over the party and army, couldn't have delivered such compromises.

China's president for life? Not Xi Jinping, a student of history

The last Chinese leader in a position to negotiate grand bargains and offer concessions was Deng Xiaoping. It was Deng who normalised relations with the US, acquiesced to US arms sales to Taiwan, negotiated the return of Hong Kong and Macau under the "one country, two systems" principle, and agreed to shelve territorial disputes in the East China Sea to focus on cooperation, not conflict. If Xi is as powerful as Deng and driven by a grand vision, he will also have to deliver such agreements.

While it is debatable if this is what they truly believe, it does seem that Xi and the other Chinese leaders would prefer to achieve their goal of rejuvenation through peaceful means. They want to diminish US influence in the Asia-Pacific through non-military means, instead of a full-blown war. Xi's emphasis on the Belt and Road Initiative and the community with a shared future for humanity, both enshrined in either the party or the state constitution, isn't just window dressing. This is his plan to expand China's influence and transform it into a superpower. But the real question is whether Xi's belief in these goals and plans is strong enough to hold a steady course and be willing to compromise to preserve peace.

Xi Jinping as president beyond 2023 may be good for China – though the West won't believe it

If Xi really wants to preside over China's national rejuvenation, he will need to focus on how to expand China's influence through diplomatic and peaceful means, while avoiding any military confrontation. This is even more important now that the US is starting to see China as a geopolitical and economic adversary and tensions are sure to rise. Just as Xi will have to use his greatly expanded power to take tough economic decisions, he will also face the need for difficult diplomatic and geopolitical compromises.

China's goal must be to make friends in the Asia-Pacific, not scare its neighbours away. Whether Xi manages to do this will largely determine if he will be the president of a respected and admired China, returning as a central player on the world stage.

3

Xi Jinping Decision World Superpower's Important Political Change for Decades

The signs that China's President Xi Jinping was looking for more than his two terms as leader were there last October at the Communist party's 19th National Congress. It was there that Mr Xi was elected for a second five-year term of the party's chief, a title that has in recent times been served concurrently with the presidency, as well as the title of chairman of the Central Military Commission, which controls the armed forces. It was then that a new line-up for the all powerful Politburo Standing Committee (PBSC) was unveiled – without an heir apparent to Mr Xi.

In line with other PBSC roles, the post of General Secretary of the Party does do not have official term limits like the presidency. But there is an informal agreement that officials will retire at age 68. Of the five new faces in the seven-member committee, the youngest will be 65 in 2022, when Mr Xi, currently 64, finishes his second term as leader.

CHINA CLEARS PATH FOR XI JINPING TO RULE BEYOND 2023

That has been backed by the latest pronouncement in Xinhua, China's official news agency, on Sunday, that the party leadership "proposed to remove the expression that the president and vice president of the People's Republic of China 'shall serve no more than two consecutive terms' from the country's Constitution". The proposed constitutional changes were released in the name of the Central Committee, a council of hundreds of senior party officials, who will meet from Monday for three days.

The move to get rid of the two-term limit on the presidency is certainly dramatic and would mark the biggest political move the party has made in decades, leaving the door open for Mr Xi to rule well into the next decade, and possibly much beyond that. The changes need to be passed by the party-controlled legislature, the National People's Congress, which holds its annual full session from 5 March. But that would appear little more than a formality, with the Congress having never voted down a proposal from party leaders. Mr Xi will also be elected to second term as president during that March meeting.

While the presidency is seen as the least important of the three roles Mr Xi currently performs, the removal of the term limit would mean the greatest accumulation of personal power by a leader in China since Mao Zedong, who founded the People's Republic.

The state-run *Global Times* suggested in an article on Sunday, quoting an academic source, that the move to abolish presidential term limits would keep the "trinity" of the roles of party leader, military leader and president together and allow China to move forward.

"Especially in the period from 2020 to 2035, which is a crucial stage for China to basically realise socialist modernisation, China... [needs] a stable, strong and consistent leadership. So removal of the section of the clause about the presidency in the Constitution is serving the most important and fundamental national interest and the Party's historic mission," the paper quoted the academic as saying.

At the Communist party's National Congress in October, Mr Xi also had the political thesis bearing his name, "Xi Jinping

Thought on Socialism with Chinese Characteristics for a New Era", written into the party's charter, with Mao the only other leader to have that honour while still alive. In another win for Mr Xi, the latest announcement on Sunday also states that among the amendments to the country's constitution, his "Thought" will also be added.

The Central Committee is said to have approved the constitutional changes last month, but the official announcement at the time made no mention of the dramatic extent of the changes, which show Mr Xi has amassed enough power to rewrite the rules that had constrained his predecessors, Hu Jintao and Jiang Zemin, both of whom stepped down after two terms. It is a power base that resembles Vladimir Putin's centralisation of authority, but would be the envy of even the Russian president.

The absence of term limits would also reverse a trend that began 40 years ago under Deng Xiaoping who aimed at preventing the reappearance of the cult of personality that had surrounded Mao and ensuring more peaceful transitions of power. Jude Blanchette, an expert in Chinese politics from New York's Conference Board research group tweeted: "This is extraordinary ... we're seeing the rapid dismantling of the Deng era project to de-Maoify Chinese politics"

With the power of Chinese leaders tending to begin to wane about halfway through their second term, analysts have cautioned that a clearer picture of whether Mr Xi will stay on for decades will come depending on what China looks like in 2020 or 2021 – but all the signs are there for Mr Xi to hold all the major power for at least a decade and it will be up to him what he does with it. A stark warning came from Joshua Wong, the pro-democracy leader in Hong Kong who was at the forefront of student protests against Chinese rule there.

GLOBAL EFFECTS OF CHINESE INFLUENCE

Overall, President Xi's announcement that China's international engagement will enter a new era brings with it both challenges and opportunities. The PRC aims to rewrite the rules of world affairs and make them more in line with its own interests and intends to soften but not dissolve international institutions. Much the same can be said of international law, as China emphasizes that it complies with international law but tries to redefine core terms and concepts. It prefers vague legal norms that do not comprehensively limit sovereign state control.

However, Beijing is paying particular attention to China's international reputation and is well aware that it needs to closely cooperate with other countries. China's international relations of the new era will not be solely determined by the PRC but to a significant extent by the country's international partners – including the European Union (EU).

A United European Response?

At a time when uncertainties about the U.S.' role in international affairs rise, the task falls to the EU to engage in a dialogue with Beijing in order to shape international affairs in a new era of Chinese foreign and trade policy. I argue that Europe will have to respect the historical legacy of China's preference for sovereign self-determination and non-interference. However, the EU should push for more predictability in its relationship with China and follow a strict rules-based cooperation. The EU should be aware of its leverage and role in responding to China's new foreign policy. Shortly after the Party Congress ended, a Hong Kong-based expert who is intimate with the CPC's foreign policy-making said:

"China's international strategy is evolving. Not even China knows where it will take the country. And the leadership is well aware that it is not only them who will determine how the country can and will reshape the world. To a large extent this depends on China's international partners: It is an interactive process and China knows that it has no other choice than to listen to other nations. [...] Xi takes Europe's interests very serious. There is a great chance for you guys [Europeans] to play a crucial role in determining China's foreign affairs. But you

have to actively pick up this role and develop a pro-active strategy and not react to China like you do right now."

For Europe, it is crucial to speak with one voice and unite vis-à-vis a rising China. In recent years, the PRC has clearly adopted a 'divide-and-rule' policy towards the member states of the European Union. While economically and technologically strong countries like Germany may be able to respond to this Chinese strategy, smaller EU countries may find this more challenging. Thus, Europe should be very cautious of potential internal divisions springing up along the lines of the 16-plus-one format. EU member-states will be better placed if they agree to a more comprehensive, coherent, and inclusive China policy.

THE RESISTIBLE RISE OF XI JINPING

China's 19th Party Congress began Wednesday with a three-and-a-half-hour speech by Xi Jinping, a telling sign of a man who knows he has to be listened to. The general secretary of the Chinese Communist Party — usually referred to in English by his far less important title of "president" — is the heart of a weeklong love fest in Beijing as officials gather to determine the makeup of the leadership for the next five years and more.

But Xi's power in office reaches far beyond the assembled delegates in the Great Hall of the People. Xi has near-absolute command over the ruling party and, through it, a state of 1.3 billion people, a 1.6 million-strong army, and an $11 trillion economy. The United States is still richer and stronger, but the office of the U.S. president — even when the officeholder is not deemed a "moron" by members of his own cabinet — is far more radically limited than the position held by his Chinese counterpart.

Xi's rule has tightened the grip of the party on his country and slashed away space for any opposition. While his predecessors, Hu Jintao and Jiang Zemin, struggled to make their authority felt, even before formally assuming office in 2013 Xi was purging his foes. Under the rules of the party, he's about to reach the halfway mark of his term — but there's a growing consensus that power in 2022 will stay in his hands, with no appointed heir in sight.

But Xi's rise was not inevitable. The speed and range of his purges depended partially on his own political skills but far more critically on opportunities offered him by the rest of the party. Xi arrived at the party's highest echelon at a moment of growing paranoia — triggered by public discontent about rampant corruption, deepened by the revolutionary Arab Spring in 2010, and reinforced by the Ukraine rebellion of 2014. Xi represented the possibility of deliverance for China's autocratic, but consensus-based, political system — and a promise to protect it against any opponent, including Xi's main rival in the Communist elite, Bo Xilai. Bo's fall in 2012 gave Xi the momentum he needed to create a rolling attack on his foes that left him the only man who mattered.

And so Xi managed to thoroughly change the party — imposing absolute security and receiving absolute control — largely, if paradoxically, because he did so in the course of allegedly preserving it. Absent the paranoia-inspired acquiescence of his party colleagues, and the opening provided by Bo's unforeseen fall, Xi would almost certainly still be president of China — but hemmed in by political rivals, restricted in his use of the party's security machinery, and limited in his ambitions.

Before we go on, a caveat. The party's code of *omertà* is tight, and the outside world's knowledge of what happens behind the palace moats of Zhongnanhai, Beijing's Kremlin, minimal. Reliable information has become even harder to come by in the age of Xi, where the fear of talking to media, and especially to foreigners, has become more acute than ever. Tales of the leadership — including entire alternate histories promising supposedly hidden truths — circulate online and among the Chinese dissident diaspora, but most of them are fantasy. This account relies on private conversations with insiders, media accounts, and the opinions of foreign experts to create a rough first sketch of a history that may never be fully revealed. Yet the outlines of the story are clear, as is what they mean for the future direction of the world's largest country.

Xi's ascent to the role of general secretary was fixed in 2007 at the 17th Party Congress, when his position as heir apparent was solidified. The horse-trading around this was part of a semicodified system of succession going back to 1989, when Jiang Zemin became general secretary following the Tiananmen massacre. Hu Jintao became Jiang's heir apparent in 1997 and took on the role in 2002. Stability, as ever for the party, was paramount, but there was also a belief in rule by consensus and committee — at the top. By the late 2000s, however, there was a strong feeling among the Chinese elite that Hu's administration had been a failure. Despite the nominal ease of the succession, Jiang had never abandoned his desire to keep power in his hands, holding on to key military roles until 2005 and working through his political allies to hamstring his successor. Hu, once able to do a passable imitation of a human being, had become increasingly robotic, barely a presence in the public mind despite his constant unsmiling appearances on stage.

By 2007, Hu's weakness had set up Xi's strength; he was expected to be a more assertive, confident, and charismatic leader when he took over in 2012 — but still a party man to the core, one who had risen steadily through the system and was expected to serve it. By 2017 he'd pick a clear heir of his own, establishing a new generation of leadership to continue these traditions. But he would not be ruling alone; instead, he'd be guided, and constrained, by a range of other top figures on the Standing Committee, the seven to nine men who would make up the core leadership, and in the 25-seat Politburo.

Foreign observers often look for familiar patterns of "reformers" and "hard-liners" within authoritarian states. But the most important ties in the party at the time had very little to do with ideology. Instead, they were determined by affiliation: who you had come up with, served under, and were patronizing yourself. And so Xi's new Politburo would be expected to include allies of Hu, Xi, and even the cadaverous Jiang.

The biggest challenge for the new administration would be rampant corruption, from the petty extortion of street vendors through to enormous payoffs for political influence and the wholesale ransacking of state resources. In percentage terms, Chinese corruption's worst point had been the 1990s. But even if corruption had been slightly curbed since then in relative terms, in absolute ones China's economic boom meant that the sums of money involved had become eye-bogglingly large, with scandals running into the billions of dollars.

From the party's point of view, corruption was rotting the public's faith and crippling the nation. From the point of view of most members of the party, however, if everyone else was getting rich, then why couldn't they? Even a cursory glance at China's new social media revealed that officials were seen as skinning the people, not serving them. Worst of all, the military itself was rotten — to the extent that a war, even a small one, could become a disastrous failure. The authorities were jailing 10,000 officials a year on corruption charges, but that was a droplet in a river. Helicopters were disappearing from bases, sold off to private firms; thousands of army license plates were flogged off to truckers so that they could avoid roadside tolls; and military officers — who had officially been told to get out of private business entirely a decade before — were running condom factories and Beijing nightclubs.

One reason why corruption was on everyone's mind, though, was that the spaces available to talk about it had broadened. It can be hard to distinguish how much of the limited online and press openness of the late 2000s was deliberate policy and how much was laziness and indifference within an increasingly corroded system. But for some thinkers in the party, openness was seen as the solution to corruption. Online supervision of lower-level officials by the public, combined with more freedom of the press, would eliminate the rot at the bottom — while remaining carefully limited from going further. Chinese bloggers became adept at pointing out Rolexes on the wrists of city officials supposedly paid less than $1,000 a month. Even those deeply embedded in the system felt the need to talk in this language: "We want democracy and an open press in China," a prominent nationalist provocateur claimed in private conversation. "But we have to go slowly, slowly. China is a complicated country."

The Arab Spring put an end to these ambitions. An already present paranoia about Western cultural infiltration was given new life by the scenes at Tahrir Square. "Color revolution," already a concern after the Central Asian revolts, began to grip the Chinese leadership's imagination. The country's founding legitimacy rests on revolutionary martyrdom — but it's also twice been threatened by passionate (and unemployed) youth taking to the streets, in the Cultural Revolution and in the Tiananmen protests. That gave the scenes from the Arab world an extra edge and made the threat posed by revolt a tangled one: It had to be both discredited as a Western-backed, insincere form of revolution and sincerely crushed.

A few posts by online exiles about a "Jasmine Revolution," a call for protest that never materialized, prompted a massive upping of security in Beijing. Chinese officials were prone to exaggerating the capabilities and role of U.S. intelligence in these events. "The Green Revolution was just caused by CIA spies!" one yelled down the phone when his account of how much the Iranian people loved their government, based on a weeklong trip, was questioned. Yet Edward Snowden's revelations about the extent of U.S. capabilities further escalated the sense of threat from the West — as did the discovery and elimination of an extensive CIA network between 2010 and 2012. A renewed urgency about the reach of the West, and the need to reassert the dominance of the party, began to seize the leadership.

A security state demands a strongman to lead it. Yet by early 2012, it wasn't Xi who worried the country's liberals most but one of his rivals — the consummate politician Bo Xilai.

Like Xi, Bo was a scion of red aristocracy; their fathers, Bo Yibo and Xi Zhongxun, had helped forge the revolution, fell in the chaos of the 1960s, re-emerged under Deng Xiaoping, and then worked hard to promote their sons' careers. Both had divorced their first wives and made advantageous marriages: Xi to the celebrity army singer Peng Liyuan and Bo to Gu Kailai, the daughter of a revolutionary general and a prominent lawyer.

Bo's campaigning for higher office had initially been seen as gauche, but his publicity skills proved better suited to the 2000s, as the internet and the rise of a less controlled media opened up new means of campaigning that eluded most of Bo's peers. Bo's TV-friendly good looks and smooth talk were as winning to foreign politicians as they were to Chinese crowds.

As party chief of Chongqing, one of the country's largest cities, Bo was in the national papers almost daily — a rarity for a provincial leader. He arrived in 2008 with a blaze of furious activity, running a highly publicized anti-gangster campaign that purported to have ended organized crime in the city. Bo followed that cleanup with an extensive cultural campaign, ordering "frivolous" shows off the air in prime time to be replaced with party propaganda (and crashing ratings) and organizing mass singalongs to "red songs" — a mix of revolutionary classics and modern patriotic numbers. It inspired imitations throughout the country — and won lengthy praise from Xi himself on a Chongqing visit in 2010. In 2011, it became an official part of the party's 90th anniversary celebrations.

Alongside the cultural campaign, a simultaneous expansion of public services, new parks, and urban housing made Bo genuinely popular in the city. Journalists, academics, and other officials rushed to praise the "Chongqing model," incentivized both by a belief that Bo was the coming man and by the all-expense-paid (plus a few red envelopes) trips that the city administration offered. Even Henry Kissinger, a national hero in China for his role in Richard Nixon's 1972 visit, blessed Bo at a red songs event before a crowd of 100,000 people.

All of this worried both China's embattled liberals and Bo's rivals within the party. Dissidents and intellectuals saw the red songs as an unhealthy reminder of Cultural Revolution fervor. His peers saw him as dangerously charismatic and ambitious and a potential threat to the established consensus-based order, where politicking was supposed to be a matter of backroom deals, not open campaigning. There were hints that Bo might even be able to overturn Xi's succession. At 63 in 2012 — four years older than Xi — he wasn't able to wait for a chance at the top job. "Bo would almost certainly have been elevated into the standing committee and then he would have been untouchable.... That was a very frightening prospect for his rivals, who thought of him as a Hitler-like figure," a senior Chongqing official told the *Financial Times* in 2012.

At that year's 18th Party Congress, fixed as usual for the autumn, the stage seemed set for Bo to join the ranks of China's most powerful men in the Politburo and to provide a permanent counterweight to Xi. And then it all came crashing down — and opened up a chance for Xi to rule unchallenged.

On Feb. 2, 2012, Wang Lijun, Bo's brash police chief, was suddenly demoted to a minor position. On Feb. 6, he turned up at the American consulate in Chengdu, 200 miles away from Chongqing, begging to be given political asylum.

Bo's wife, Gu Kailai, had, Wang claimed, murdered a British businessman and fixer, Neil Heywood. The Americans were firm, though; there was no way they could give Wang refuge — especially with Chinese police surrounding the consulate. A day later, he was on a first-class flight back to Beijing, accompanied by the vice minister of state security.

Whatever really happened, Wang's very public flight gave Bo's rivals, especially Xi, a golden chance to take him down. By March 15, he was out as party chief; by April 10, he was officially under investigation. He languished in detention for more than a year before charges were officially brought the next July, culminating in public show trials for him and his wife alike.

Tens of thousands of people had hitched a ride on Bo's bandwagon, and now the scrabble to get off left many of them trampled underfoot. Ambitious underlings sent clippings of their bosses' praise of Bo to the authorities. Regular pundits disappeared from the opinion pages for a while, like expert sycophant and "top journalism educator" Li Xiguang, who had made the mistake of praising Bo too loudly. (Like many others, Li would re-emerge a couple of years later with his tongue ready for Xi's broad posterior.)

Gu Kailai became "Bogu Kailai" in reports, a linguistic aberration something along the lines of saying "Mrs. Bill-Hillary Clinton." There were wide speculations that this was a deliberate attempt to remind everyone of Bo's culpability. But the real answer lay in the desperation to prove that you were on the right side — especially among journalists who had heaped fulsome praise on the Chongqing model. "It was a misprint in a piece of Xinhua [the state news agency] copy," an experienced Xinhua reporter claimed. "And then everybody imitated it because they thought it must mean something — and then nobody could stop."

Bo's purge had been technically initiated under Hu's auspices. But that made it the perfect cover for Xi to move against other potential opponents — and to carry out his own version of Bo's policies at the same time, putatively in service of the party's integrity rather than his own personal ambition. Even as the "Chongqing model" was officially discredited (and Xi's own praise for it erased from media archives), Xi was imitating his former enemy's techniques. He entered office with a promise of national cleanup, sparing neither the great ("tigers") nor the petty ("flies"). Unlike previous campaigns, retired officials, civilian and military alike, were in the crosshairs despite being theoretically out of the game. Like Bo's gang crackdown, the anti-corruption campaign was broadly popular among a public increasingly fed up with the vagaries of bribery — although it was hard to distinguish genuine enthusiasm from the mandatory praise of the leader's schemes. And, at least at first, it was also popular among a party establishment desperate for a renewed sense of order and public legitimacy.

Perhaps the most significant scalp claimed by Xi in his early years was that of Zhou Yongkang, a powerful deal-maker under Hu who had retired from his post on the Standing

Committee in 2012. After Bo's fall, rumors about his ties to Bo circulated widely, possibly prompted by Xi himself. "Bo and Zhou were nowhere near as close as claimed," the daughter of one of Zhou's fallen allies said. "But Xi wanted to link the two of them together so that he could go after Zhou." In the year before Zhou's own arrest was announced, his appointees were systematically accused of corruption and removed from office.

Ling Jihua, a close ally of Hu's, was another early victim, rendered particularly vulnerable when his son died in a Ferrari crash the same month that Bo fell — another stroke of luck for Xi. Senior army officials, once thought untouchable due to the military's fierce resistance to any inquiry into its own ranks, were also hit — one literally arrested in his hospital bed.

Xi's weapon in this campaign was the Central Commission for Discipline Inspection (CCDI), the party's internal watchdog. He put his close ally Wang Qishan in charge of it, a friend since childhood and former colleague. Before the arrival of Wang, the CCDI had been much more limited in who it could target, wary of offending the powerful and circumscribed, in particular, by the feared Ministry of State Security. But it had been closely tied to Zhou, and several of its former ministers and vice ministers were among the first to be reaped. It was the CCDI that now gave officials bad dreams.

The CCDI's procedural tool was *shuanggui*, the rapid seizure and isolation of suspects in order to prevent them from contacting their own networks of power. It literally means "double designation," referring to the official notice to appear at a "designated time and designated place." In practice, it was quasi-legal kidnapping, carried out under the authority of "party discipline." A CCDI team would turn the wing of a local hotel into an improvised detention center, where they would force confessions — and information on other targets — out of their subjects using every means possible, including torture. By 2013, the purges had become so widespread that the major state-owned oil enterprises established a routine of calling senior staff in the early morning to check that nobody had disappeared into detention overnight.

In ordinary times, those targeted would have been able to fight back, drawing on the wealth of personal friendships, mutual blackmail material, and institutional loyalties that every Chinese leader accumulates on the way up. But back-footed by Bo's fall, and their networks disrupted by the numerous retirements, changes in title, and prosecutions that had followed, they were never able to mount any kind of resistance. Chinese political plotting requires getting people from across a vast country together in the same room — surveillance makes communications too risky to use. But the very act of getting high-ranking officials together, outside of approved occasions, could now be taken as evidence of a conspiracy. Previous purges, although frequent, had been followed by a cooling-down period, an ebb and flow that gave the chance for recovery and resistance. But the shock and awe of Xi's campaign never let up.

Xi's crackdown did curb much of the mid-level corruption and especially the wild banqueting and brothel culture that had become the norm among officials and businessmen. But referring to it solely as an anti-corruption campaign misses the point. There was no doubt that many — virtually all — of those who had fallen had been corrupt. But so had *everyone*. Chinese government salaries had fallen far behind inflation, so even with the packages of benefits that came with the post it was impossible to keep up one's neighbors without taking something on the side. And an official who insisted on being clean would be seen as either dangerously naive or up to something, a Frank Serpico among dirty cops. Xi's own family had accumulated billions of dollars.

Perhaps the fallen had been a little dirtier than most. But those picked for sacrifice in the campaign, however, tended to come from areas where Xi's rivals had strong power bases: the southern provinces, especially Sichuan; the energy sector; and the army. Not that the inequities of Xi's approach made any difference to the public, which was pleased to see high officials receive any comeuppance at all. "Oh, they all sing the same tune," a guard at the Tangshan Prison said wearily, describing the fallen party officials he now oversees. "'Everyone was doing it. Everyone was taking money. I was just unlucky, poor me.'"

The other plank of Xi's new program was the reassertion of total party dominance over all sectors of public life, especially over policing its own people. When Xi arrived, there had been the usual wide-eyed speculations that he could be a new Mikhail Gorbachev. His Western enthusiasts pointed to his time in Iowa as a sign that he must be eager to embrace the wonders of freedom. But it turned out that a lifetime spent as the heir to a Leninist party was more influential on Xi's thought than two weeks among the cornfields. The paranoia of Western infiltration and rebellious youth prompted by the Arab Spring gave Xi unrestrained access to the full possibilities of China's security state, turned against both his foes inside the party and the party's potential rivals in civil society.

Again imitating Bo's Chongqing techniques, he began a mass roundup of potential critics and a freeze of civil society. 2012 immediately saw an assault on Weibo, the country's most popular microblogging platform, which had become a way for journalists to call out (suitably minor) corrupt officials and for thinkers to post calls for reform.

The "big Vs" of Weibo (the equivalent of Twitter's blue-checked "verified accounts") were silenced, either banned from the service or scared off after several of them were forced into televised confessions of wrongdoing. Human rights lawyers, once given a limited space to operate, were shut down or arrested. A new NGO law was introduced, modeled on Russia's, that limited the ability of organizations to receive foreign funding and scared many into closing. Foreign textbooks were forced out of Chinese universities. The newspapers became an endless drumbeat of praise for Xi mixed with territorial jingoism.

Each of the campaigns fed into the other. Since the primacy of the party was at stake, resisting Xi's purges could be framed as treason. Meanwhile, the fall of the great was rupturing local networks and kicking the brutally Darwinian political economy of Chinese officialdom into high gear. Ideological vehemence was necessary, not just to show allegiance to the new leader but to prove that you were doing something, anything, to justify your post. And the easiest thing to do was to pick on acceptable targets, like feminists, fans of yaoi, churches, and ethnic minorities — and remind them just who was in charge.

Both these campaigns are still going on. Fresh scalps of public officials were culled just before the Party Congress. The political situation remains frozen, the language of media and academia stilted and sycophantic. Unauthorized contact with foreigners is understood to be dangerous for anyone in a position of power. Sources who would once go on record now speak anonymously; those who always preferred cover now won't speak at all. The government is doubling down on big data, offering the possibilities of a surveillance state that can trace every purchase, movement, and online posting — or claim to, at least.

In the run-up to the Party Congress, Xi has been given a prominence far exceeding any Chinese leader since Mao Zedong. Even when he was general secretary, it was very easy to forget that Hu Jintao existed; late at night, Hu himself might have had doubts. But Xi is everywhere — slogans, posters, daily television. The contrast in visual imagery between the blank-faced Hu, never allowing an iota of emotion to slip, and the easily confident, in-command Xi is startling. New slogans now circulate with Xi's name attached in a way that Hu's own effort, the "harmonious society," never managed. "Xi Jinping's Chinese dream." "Xi Jinping's Belt and Road Initiative." Some of this was mandated, but much of it is voluntary, eager signaling by everyone from academics to businesses that they are on board. Xi's name can be crammed into anything, no matter how irrelevant or insignificant. What will Xi do with this power? There are still a few optimists who believe that economic reform is the next step, now that he has the power to override resistance. But all indications so far have been of the primacy of the party-state in the economy, just as in every other aspect of life — a fact reiterated by Xi in his opening speech at the Party Congress. As Americans have found since 9/11, it's harder to wind down a security state than it is to crank it up.

As for how popular Xi genuinely is, it's hard to judge; he certainly seems to have a strong base with the middle-aged homeowners who make up the central pillar of party support. Inside the party, things seem far less certain.

One of the underappreciated achievements of Xi's earlier predecessor, Deng Xiaoping, was to break the country out of the cycles of political revenge that had begun in 1949. Part of that bargain was the collective leadership system, upheld even by those temporarily at the top in the knowledge that the winds could change. Xi has snapped some, if not all, of the links that kept things from getting out of hand.

So now, even as they smile and grovel to survive, many inside the party are nurturing private hatreds — which means that Xi can ill-afford to let go of the power he's taken into his hands, even if he gives up his official titles in 2022. In Chongqing and Dalian, nobody will criticize Xi directly — but they'll still speak fondly of Bo, a coded indication of their feelings about the man who built his rule off their former favorite's fall.

CHINA: RISE, FALL AND RE-EMERGENCE AS A GLOBAL POWER

China 's re-emergence as a world economic power raises important questions about what we can learn from its previous rise and fall and about the external and internal threats confronting this emerging economic superpower for the immediate future.

First we will outline the main contours of historical China 's rise to global economic superiority over West before the 19th century, following closely John Hobson's account in The Eastern Origins of Western Civilization. Since the majority of western economic historians (liberal, conservative and Marxist) have presented historical China as a stagnant, backward, parochial society, an "oriental despotism", some detailed correctives will be necessary. It is especially important to emphasize how China , the world technological power between 1100 and 1800, made the West's emergence possible. It was only by borrowing and assimilating Chinese innovations that the West was able to make the transition to modern capitalist and imperialist economies.

In part two we will analyze and discuss the factors and circumstances which led to China 's decline in the 19th century and its subsequent domination, exploitation and pillage by Western imperial countries, first England and then the rest of Europe, Japan and the United States .

In part three, we will briefly outline the factors leading to China's emancipation from colonial and neo-colonial rule and analyze its recent rise to becoming the second largest global economic power.

Finally we will look at the past and present threats to China 's rise to global economic power, highlighting the similarities between British colonialism of the 18 and 19th centuries and the current US imperial strategies and focusing on the weaknesses and strengths of past and present Chinese responses.

China: The Rise and Consolidation of Global Power 1100 - 1800

In a systematic comparative format, John Hobson provides a wealth of empirical indicators demonstrating China 's global economic superiority over the West and in particular England . These are some striking facts:

As early as 1078, China was the world's major producer of steel (125,000 tons); whereas Britain in 1788 produced 76,000 tons.

China was the world's leader in technical innovations in textile manufacturing, seven centuries before Britain 's 18th century "textile revolution".

China was the leading trading nation, with long distance trade reaching most of Southern Asia, Africa, the Middle East and Europe . China's 'agricultural revolution' and productivity surpassed the West down to the 18th century.

Its innovations in the production of paper, book printing, firearms and tools led to a manufacturing superpower whose goods were transported throughout the world by the most advanced navigational system.

China possessed the world's largest commercial ships. In 1588 the largest English ships displaced 400 tons, China 's 3,000 tons. Even as late as the end of the 18th century China 's merchants employed 130,000 private transport ships, several times that of Britain . China retained this pre-eminent position in the world economy up until the early 19th century.

British and Europeans manufacturers followed China 's lead, assimilating and borrowing its more advanced technology and were eager to penetrate China 's advanced and lucrative market.

Banking, a stable paper money economy, manufacturing and high yields in agriculture resulted in China 's per capita income matching that of Great Britain as late as 1750.

China 's dominant global position was challenged by the rise of British imperialism, which had adopted the advanced technological, navigational and market innovations of China and other Asian countries in order to bypass earlier stages in becoming a world power.

Western Imperialism and the Decline of China

The British and Western imperial conquest of the East, was based on the militaristic nature of the imperial state, its non-reciprocal economic relations with overseas trading countries and the Western imperial ideology which motivated and justified overseas conquest.

Unlike China , Britain 's industrial revolution and overseas expansion was driven by a military policy. According to Hobson, during the period from 1688-1815 Great Britain was engaged in wars 52% of the time. Whereas the Chinese relied on their open markets and their superior production and sophisticated commercial and banking skills, the British relied on tariff protection, military conquest, the systematic destruction of competitive overseas enterprises as well as the appropriation and plunder of local resources. China 's global predominance was based on 'reciprocal benefits' with its trading partners, while Britain relied on mercenary armies of occupation, savage repression and a 'divide and conquer' policy to foment local rivalries. In the face of native resistance, the British (as well as other Western imperial powers) did not hesitate to exterminate entire communities.

Unable to take over the Chinese market through greater economic competitiveness, Britain relied on brute military power. It mobilized, armed and led mercenaries, drawn from its colonies in India and elsewhere to force its exports on China and impose unequal treaties to lower tariffs. As a result China was flooded with British opium produced on its plantations in India – despite Chinese laws forbidding or regulating the importation and sale of the narcotic. China 's rulers, long accustomed to its trade and manufacturing superiority, were unprepared for the 'new imperial rules' for global power. The West's willingness to use military power to win colonies, pillage resources and recruit huge mercenary armies commanded by European officers spelt the end for China as a world power.

China had based its economic predominance on 'non-interference in the internal affairs of its trading partners'. In contrast, British imperialists intervened violently in Asia , reorganizing local economies to suit the needs of the empire (eliminating economic competitors including more efficient Indian cotton manufacturers) and seized control of local political, economic and administrative apparatus to establish the colonial state.

Britain 's empire was built with resources seized from the colonies and through the massive militarization of its economy. It was thus able to secure military supremacy over China . China 's foreign policy was hampered by its ruling elite's excessive reliance on trade relations. Chinese officials and merchant elites sought to appease the British and convinced the emperor to grant devastating extra-territorial concessions opening markets to the detriment of Chinese manufacturers while surrendering local sovereignty. As always, the British precipitated internal rivalries and revolts further destabilizing the country. Western and British penetration and colonization of China 's market created an entire new class: The wealthy Chinese 'compradores' imported British goods and facilitated the takeover of local markets and resources. Imperialist pillage forced greater exploitation and taxation of the great mass of Chinese peasants and workers. China 's rulers were obliged to pay the war debts and finance trade deficits imposed by the Western imperial powers by squeezing its peasantry. This drove the peasants to starvation and revolt.

By the early 20th century (less than a century after the Opium Wars), China had descended from world economic power to a broken semi-colonial country with a huge destitute population. The principle ports were controlled by Western imperial officials and the countryside was subject to the rule by corrupt and brutal warlords. British opium enslaved millions.

British Academics: Eloquent Apologists for Imperial Conquest

The entire Western academic profession – first and foremost British imperial historians – attributed British imperial dominance of Asia to English 'technological superiority' and China's misery and colonial status to 'oriental backwardness', omitting any mention of the millennium of Chinese commercial and technical progress and superiority up to the dawn of the 19th century.

By the end of the 1920's, with the Japanese imperial invasion, China ceased to exist as a unified country. Under the aegis of imperial rule, hundreds of millions of Chinese had starved or were dispossessed or slaughtered, as the Western powers and Japan plundered its economy. The entire Chinese 'collaborator' comprador elite were discredited before the Chinese people.

What did remain in the collective memory of the great mass of the Chinese people – and what was totally absent in the accounts of prestigious US and British academics – was the sense of China once having been a prosperous, dynamic and leading world power. Western commentators dismissed this collective memory of China 's ascendancy as the foolish pretensions of nostalgic lords and royalty – empty Han arrogance.

CHINA: THE SUPERPOWER OF MR. XI

In the almost one-hundred-year existence of the Chinese Communist Party (CCP), its current general secretary, Xi Jinping, is only the second leader clearly chosen by his peers. The first was Mao Zedong. Both men beat out the competition, and thus secured a legitimacy their predecessors lacked. Why was Xi chosen?

The Beijing rumor mill had long indicated that the outgoing elders were looking for a "princeling" successor, that is the son of a senior first- generation revolutionary. Princelings, it was apparently felt, had a bigger stake in the revolution than most people, and thus would be the most determined to preserve the rule of the CCP.

Xi's father, Xi Zhongxun, was a respected vice-premier and member of the CCPCentral Committee known for his moderate views, but he fell afoul of Mao in 1962 and was purged, then was rehabilitated and returned to high office after the Chairman's death. Xi Jinping thus has the additional legitimation of being "born red," as Evan Osnos put it recently in *The New Yorker*.

Doubtless this heritage partly accounts for Xi's evident self-confidence, but another factor could be the toughening he underwent as a young teenager, fending for himself in the face of hostile Red Guards and thereafter working in the countryside for six years. According to an official biography, "he arrived at the village as a slightly lost teenager and left as a 22-year-old man determined to do something for the people." Unlike his predecessors Jiang Zemin, who had the benefit of studying in the Soviet bloc and then rising through the relative stability of the industrial bureaucracy, and Hu Jintao, who started in the industrial bureaucracy and then made his way up the ranks of the Communist Youth League, Xi had no such protective carapace in his early years. That background could explain why

Xi has been taking far greater risks after becoming general secretary than either Jiang or Hu did. What is widely accepted among China hands is that Xi is the most powerful leader of China since Deng Xiaoping, with a developing personality cult.

Xi is not *primus inter pares* like Jiang and Hu; he is simply *primus*. In his recent book, *Chinese Politics in the Era of Xi Jinping*, Willy Wo-Lap Lam, a veteran observer of Chinese elites, explains that since taking over as general secretary in November 2012 and president of China in March 2013, Xi has centralized power under his leadership to an extraordinary degree, creating and chairing the new Central National Security Commission, which has jurisdiction over the army, the police, and all foreign-related and national security agencies, along with chairing the Central Military Commission, which comes with his job as CCP general secretary. In a move that surely undercuts the regime's second-ranking member, Premier Li Keqiang, supposedly the economic czar, Xi has created and taken the chair of a new Central Leading Group on Comprehensively Deepening Reforms. Xi has also taken on the leadership of central leading groups on foreign affairs, Internet security, and information technology.

In fact, Xi is arguably even more powerful than Deng was, though Lam does not suggest this. In promoting his reform program, Deng had to bob and weave under pressure from equally senior colleagues who disliked reform. The only possible threat to Xi could have been his fellow princeling Bo Xilai, but he had been conveniently purged by Hu Jintao in a lurid case that involved his wife's murder of a foreigner. Xi's current colleagues in the Politburo and its Standing Committee (PSC), passed over for the top job, seem less of a threat than the charismatic Bo might have been.

The Sisyphean task that Xi has set himself is to stamp out corruption in the CCP. Both Jiang Zemin and Hu Jintao had warned about the dangers arising from this pervasive problem. According to Hu, failure to eradicate corruption could "deal a body blow to the Party and even lead to the collapse of the Party and country." Xi has echoed Jiang and Hu, saying that "upholding integrity and combating corruption are vital for the survival of the Party and the state." On another occasion he emulated Mao by quoting from an ancient philosopher: "Many worms will disintegrate wood, and a big enough crack will lead to the collapse of a wall." But in contrast with the efforts of Jiang and Hu to stem corruption, Xi has launched a very high-profile campaign. In his words: "We should fight corruption with strong determination,...persevere in our anticorruption effort till we achieve final success rather than start off full of sound and fury and then taper off in a whimper." He may come to regret promising not to end with a whimper.

Xi had been preaching the need to fight corruption long before he became Party leader. At an antigraft conference in 2004, he warned officials: "Rein in your spouses, children, relatives, friends and staff, and vow not to use power for personal gain." Xi knew of what he spoke. His sister and her family were accumulating investments worth hundreds of millions of dollars while he was rising up the ranks of the leadership, though Western investigative reporters found no evidence that Xi's immediate family was involved in any way. Nor was this an isolated case among the top leadership. Shortly before Wen Jiabao retired as premier in March 2013, it was reported, by another Western news source, that his family, including his mother, wife, children, and siblings, were rich to the tune of $2.7 billion. Such foreign investigative reports require months of painstaking research, but within the top ranks of the CCP, knowledge of the riches of other leaders' families must be easier to come by.

To deal with corruption, Xi has put Wang Qishan, a trusted, longtime colleague, drawn from the seven-member Politburo Standing Committee, in charge of the Party's Central Discipline Inspection Committee (CDIC). The committee's remit is to pursue both "tigers" and "flies," to root out corruption at all levels. In 2014, Wang's investigators' work resulted in over 71,000 officials being punished for violating the eight-point anticorruption rules. Many doubtless were guilty only of living high off the hog on the public purse, not confining their banquets to "four dishes and a soup," the traditional CCP measure of restraint. But dozens of senior officials have been dismissed; in one province, the ranks of the Party have been decimated from top to bottom. Perhaps the CDIC's biggest achievement last year was to repatriate five hundred fugitive officials from abroad and recover almost $500 million of their ill-gotten gains. Wang hopes to persuade even countries like the US, with which China has no extradition treaty, to assist him in this endeavor.

The prime tiger to be bagged so far is Zhou Yongkang, a member of the ruling Politburo Standing Committee until he had to retire for age reasons in 2012. He had been in charge of the Central Political and Legal Affairs Commission, supervising the security apparatus and law enforcement, including the police, paramilitary forces, and domestic intelligence: not the profile of one easily purged even in retirement. So before arresting him, the CDIC cut the ground from under his feet by rounding up his subordinates in the provincial and state organizations he had run. Last month, Zhou was sentenced to life in prison, the most senior official to be purged for corruption in the history of the People's Republic.

Up till this point, there seemed to have been a comradely agreement that former members of the Politburo Standing Committee were to be allowed to retire in peace, so senior Chinese officials may hope that Zhou has really been arrested for factional reasons rather than corruption, having been a supporter of the purged Bo Xilai, Xi Jinping's onetime rival princeling. In that case, past and future ex-PSC members could breathe more easily. But if Zhou turns out not to be the last tiger but the first, then existing tensions in the top ranks of the Party will rise. Mao's colleagues were too afraid of him to unite against him even when they were falling like ninepins in the Cultural Revolution: besides, to have brought down Mao—the Lenin and Stalin of the revolution—would have deprived the CCP of its legitimacy. Xi does not have that stature, so to continue his tiger hunt will require nerve.

Like Mao before him, Xi relies on the People's Liberation Army (PLA) as his last line of defense. A year ago, eighteen leading active-service generals, including the officers commanding central PLA departments and the seven regional commanders, swore their loyalty to Xi as chairman of the CCP's Military Affairs Commission. But this demonstration that the PLA had his back was a sign of weakness as well as strength. Mao had no need for so public a demonstration of military loyalty. And since the anticorruption campaign has already targeted some senior generals, including a former vice-chairman of the Military Affairs Commission and Politburo member—as high as a soldier can get—these eighteen pledges may have been designed as keep-out-of-jail cards. It remains to be seen how loyal the generals stay if the campaign targets more top brass.

Swatting flies also involves considerable risks. In many ways, it is a more important task than bagging tigers. Chinese citizens may cheer as another tiger is laid low, but it is the flies, the lower-level cadres, whose predatory activities affect their everyday lives. If corruption among the well over 80 million Party members is as widespread as Chinese leaders imply and the Chinese people believe, then tens of millions could be involved.

Suppose that only 10 percent of grassroots Party cadres are corrupt, almost certainly a gross underestimate: that's 8 million people. Then add in family members, who the Wen Jiabao case suggests may well also be corrupt. With a spouse, the figure becomes 16 million; add in a child, 24 million; add in a sibling, 32 million; and with the sibling's spouse, one has 40 million people who should be prosecuted. And that's with only a 10 percent corruption rate. Party morale would crumble along with its organizational strength, as it did during the Cultural Revolution. Already, compulsory visits by officials to incarcerated colleagues must be intimidating.

Indeed, Xi is attempting a cultural revolution of his own. Whereas Mao wanted to make Chinese leaders revolutionary, Xi wants to make them righteous, because moral purity is essential for Marxist parties to stay pure, and moral integrity is a fundamental trait for officials to remain clean, honest and upright. In the 1980s, party officials jumped on Deng Xiaoping's "to get rich is glorious" bandwagon and many used their positions for corruption.

Under Mao, those officials had been told to "serve the people," but Mao had betrayed them by making them the victims of Red Guard violence during the Cultural Revolution. Corruption, beginning in the Deng era but far worse now, was a payback for what they had endured. Now Xi wants to withdraw that perk of Party membership. Will Party members fall into line or seek to subvert the campaign? What will be the impact on potential Party members?

This problem is exacerbated by Xi's lack of any persuasive ideology to enthuse Party members. He has conjured up the "Chinese dream," the "rejuvenation of the Chinese nation," and according to an official document from the CCP's Central Committee, "we are...rapidly arousing mass fervor, proclaiming that socialism with Chinese characteristics and the Chinese dream are the main theme of our age." But the Chinese dream is too distant to arouse "mass fervor" among citizens whose personal dream is to be able to afford an urban apartment or their son getting a good job after college. As for "socialism with Chinese characteristics," Deng Xiaoping's justification for putting Marxism on the shelf, any educated Chinese knows that the nearest facsimile to that can be found only in Singapore. Taiwan could be labeled democracy with Chinese characteristics. Capitalism with Chinese characteristics? Hong Kong. And China? 1.3 billion people with Chinese characteristics. There is no ideological there there.

Neither the "Chinese dream" nor "socialism with Chinese characteristics" has the intellectual plausibility of Marxism-Leninism, and certainly does not arouse the mass fervor of Mao Zedong Thought at its height. Marxism- Leninism, like Confucianism, was a philosophy that embraced state and society, that guided officials and prescribed rules for families. It was a doctrine that glued cadres and people together. But however much Chinese leaders proclaim that Marxism-Leninism is still their lodestar, and Xi Jinping proposes the study of Marxism in institutions of higher learning, in practice the works of Paul Samuelson and his successors are far more relevant to officials who seek to engineer the Chinese dream than those of Marx and Engels. Chinese who seek something to fill the spiritual void have turned in their tens of millions to a different Western doctrine, Christianity. The spread of a Western religion is a prime example of the problems that face Xi in his avowed aim to keep out Western doctrines, though the Party seems confident of containing it with a policy of knocking off crosses and knocking down churches.

Without a substantive positive ideology to grip the Chinese people, Xi has been forced to go negative, listing alien doctrines to be extirpated. According to a central Party document, there are six "false ideological trends, positions, and activities" emanating from the West that are advocated by dissident Chinese: constitutional democracy; universal values; civil society; economic neoliberalism; Western-style journalism, challenging China's principle that the media and the publishing system should be subject to Party discipline; and promoting historical nihilism, trying to undermine the history of the CCP by emphasizing the mistakes of the Maoist period.

There is nothing particularly surprising about this listing except for its confirmation of the extent to which "opening up" has resulted in the spread of Western values among Chinese citizens. But the sixth concern, "historical nihilism," is a particular worry of Xi's, connected with his understandable obsession with preventing the CCP going the way of the Soviet Communist Party. He believes the rot started in the Soviet Union when Party leader Nikita Khrushchev denounced Stalin's record in 1956, thereby dividing Soviet history into a bad era (Stalin's) and a good one (post-Stalin).

For Xi, it was historical nihilism to write off the Maoist period, with its Great Leap famine and its Cultural Revolution—"the devastation that Mao left in his wake," as Andrew Walder puts it in his major new book, *China Under Mao: A Revolution Derailed*—as all bad, for he fears that would ultimately mean denigrating Mao, and, as his portrait on Tiananmen demonstrates, the Chairman is still the legitimator of the regime. According to Xi, an important reason why the Soviet Union disintegrated and the Soviet Communist Party collapsed was that their ideals and convictions wavered.... Finally, all it took was one quiet word from Gorbachev to declare the dissolution of the Soviet Communist Party, and a great party was gone.... In the end nobody was a real man, nobody came out to resist.

Xi clearly intends that the members of the CCP should have their ideals and convictions strengthened and he will be the "real man" who will lead the resistance to infiltrating Western doctrines.

What Xi did not acknowledge was that when Gorbachev came to power in 1985, his aim was to revive the Party and the country after two decades of corruption and stagnation under Brezhnev. He believed in communism, state ownership, and central planning, probably more deeply than Xi. Like Deng Xiaoping, Gorbachev launched reform (perestroika) and opening up (glasnost). But unlike in China, the Soviet bureaucracy had been in power for many decades and had not been terrorized and undermined by a cultural revolution. Resistance to perestroika was strong, even within the Politburo. Glasnost became the more important route for changing the Soviet system, and authors and journalists exploited their new freedom. Hitherto banned books were published. Informal groups were set up in favor of perestroika. Public opinion became important. The regime came under open attack. And gradually Gorbachev became more radical in his effort to shock his countrymen into change. Ultimately, the Soviet Communist Party was dissolved and the Soviet Union fell apart.

Xi Jinping is as concerned as Gorbachev was to transform the Communist Party that he leads and to prevent the collapse of the People's Republic. The Soviet example proves to him that glasnost is not the way to go. With an estimated five hundred demonstrations a day across China, 60 percent of them provoked by "land grabs" by local officials, opening the door further must seem imprudent. Rather, closing down has been the order of the day. The atmosphere in intellectual circles has become chillier than under Hu Jintao. Even anticorruption whistle-blowers are punished; Xi wants a centrally controlled campaign, not an unpredictable free-for-all.

So Xi has chosen his form of perestroika. In addition to the anticorruption campaign, it comprises thoroughgoing economic reform. But almost forty years after the end of the Cultural Revolution, Chinese bureaucrats have recovered their self-confidence. Insofar as economic reform now will hurt their vested interests, including their power over the economy, they drag their feet. Local governments with no hope of increased central subsidies also are recalcitrant.

How foot dragging can work was illustrated in an outburst by China's premier against ministers in April this year when he upbraided them for allowing cabinet decisions to become mired among their subordinates. A further factor, unmentioned by the premier, is probably a reluctance to take initiatives because of the anticorruption campaign.

If one compares this campaign to Gorbachev's perestroika, the dangers to the system become apparent. Gorbachev had to use weapons of the weak: volunteer intellectuals from the ranks of journalists, editors, publishers, and academia. Xi, on the other hand, is using a powerful, long-established central party organization that can wreak havoc in any provincial or ministerial organization it selects. In Mao's Cultural Revolution, victims were often chosen at random. Xi's "cultural revolution" is anything but random, and since a high proportion of Party cadres are allegedly corrupt, they must all dread the arrival of a CDIC team in their area. In principle, there is nothing to stop the investigators from criticizing, dismissing, or indicting sufficient tigers and flies to paralyze the whole CCP.

Clearly Xi cannot want that. He has few options. He can gradually reduce the tempo of the anticorruption campaign, allow it to taper off, instruct Wang Qishan to send out fewer investigation teams, and to pursue only the most egregious sinners. Simultaneously he could tell the elite that they can keep what they have, but from now on any new instance of corruption will be punished severely. The tiger shoot would be over and the flies would go unharmed. Xi would have to accept the humiliation of ending the campaign with a "whimper."

This would hardly be a satisfactory outcome. Citizens would know that the rich and powerful had got away with it again. They would characterize the campaign as simply factional fighting at the top, as they will already have noticed that Xi's campaign has so far not targeted any princelings. And they would continue to demonstrate against the flies. The "China dream" would be dismissed as a joke.

Alternatively, Xi can pursue the campaign vigorously, if not to the bitter end—which would never be reached—then at least for a few more years. The dangers are clear: a coup against him by fearful tigers; demoralization among the flies, the Party rank and file; the generals refusing to maintain their support as they, too, continue to be besieged by the CDIC.

Or Xi could try to divert attention, either by stoking the fires of nationalism with further provocative moves in the East and South China Seas or by folding anticorruption into a new campaign that would benefit both the people and the country. This would be an attack on the third great disaster that the CCP has visited upon the Chinese people, the degradation of the environment, a tragedy whose impact will be longer lasting than the famine or the Cultural Revolution. Since the land grabbed from peasants by officials is often sold to a polluting industry, corruption would still be targeted. And if Xi took the chair of a new National Environmental Protection Committee, finally a serious effort would be made to purify China's earth, air, and water.

4

Xi Envisions China as a Superpower Built on One-party Rule

Having cemented himself as China's leader for years to come, President Xi Jinping on Tuesday outlined his vision for a rejuvenated nation leading the world order as a superpower rivaling the U.S.

And such global ambitions, he believes, can be realized only through the strong leadership of the Communist Party. China will play an active role in changing and shaping the world order, said Xi at the close of the National People's Congress, signaling his intentions to have Beijing's wishes reflected in a global landscape currently led by Washington.

Xi highlighted efforts to build a first-class military, reasserting the goal of becoming a global power by midcentury. On the economic front, Xi pledged to open up the market for "high-quality growth" to bolster overall national power.

With the U.S. in mind, Xi responded to alarm over China's rise by saying that "only those who are accustomed to threatening others see everyone as a threat." He also took aim at independence movements in Taiwan and Hong Kong, declaring that "not a single inch of our land" could be ceded from China. Xi placed particular emphasis on the Chinese Communist Party's social controls, describing the party as an eternal pillar of the Chinese people. "The party is the highest force for political leadership and the fundamental guarantee of the rejuvenation of the Chinese nation," said Xi.

Hopes for democracy raised during predecessor Hu Jintao's presidency have now vanished as the party reasserts its monopoly on power.

Constitutional changes certified by the rubber-stamp congress appear to have emboldened Xi. Lawmakers enshrined social controls by writing into the constitution that the party "leads everything." The two-term limit for presidents also was discarded, allowing him to stay in office beyond the end of his second term in 2023.

At the twice-a-decade National Congress of the party last fall, Xi promised that China would complete the basic modernization of socialism by 2035 and become a modern socialist great power by 2050. By appointing close allies to key posts, the president has solidified his power base and seems determined to extend his rule to see through these goals.

Xi's speech lasted more than 30 minutes, the longest since the presidency became China's top leadership position in 1993. In contrast, predecessors Hu and Jiang Zemin spoke for around 10 minutes on similar occasions.

Speaking at a press conference, Premier Li Keqiang promised to lower tariffs on popular consumer goods and drugs and ban forced technology transfers for foreign manufacturers investing in China. The statement was largely taken as an attempt to ease trade frictions with the U.S.

China plans to eliminate import tariffs for cancer drugs and lower them on imported autos. The government already cut tariffs on everyday consumer goods in December.

The U.S. is considering broad punitive tariffs under Section 301 of the Trade Act to counter China's forced technology transfers. Li stated that there would be no winners in a trade war and that both sides would suffer. He urged the U.S. to "act rationally" and not be led by emotions. Li even touched on China's foreign reserves as the world's largest holder of U.S.

Treasurys. "China diversifies the investment of its foreign exchange reserves on the basis of market principles, and China will remain a responsible long-term investor," he said.

China's annual budget deficit this year will fall to 2.6% of gross domestic product from 3% in 2017. Li said he wants to lower that figure even further to prepare for uncertainties that could create new domestic problems.

The Chinese economy is increasingly dependent on demand from overseas. Li said the government will step up public spending if growth steeply declines from a trade war.

RATIONALE FOR THE REFORMS AND DENG XIAOPING THEORY

While it has been argued by Westerners that the reforms introduced by the CPC under Deng were a rejection of the party's Marxist heritage and ideology, the CPC does not view it as such. The rationale behind the reforms was that the productive forces of China lagged behind the advanced culture and ideology developed by the party-state. In 1986, to end this deficiency, the party came to the conclusion that the main contradiction in Chinese society was that between the backward productive forces and the advanced culture and ideology of China. By doing this, they deemphasized class struggle, and contradicted both Mao and Karl Marx, who both considered that class struggle was the main focus of the communist movement. According to this logic, thwarting the CPC's goal of advancing productive forces was synonymous with class struggle. The classical goal of class struggle was declared by Deng to have been achieved in 1976. While Mao had also emphasized the need to develop productive forces, under Deng it became paramount.

Mao Zedong (left) meets with Richard Nixon, the President of the United States, on 29 February 1972. Some have likened the CPC's position under Deng to that of the Communist Party of the Soviet Union under Joseph Stalin when he introduced the planned economy. Adrian Chan, the author of *Chinese*

Marxism, opposes this view: "To Stalin, the development of productive forces was the prerequisite for the Soviet Union to become communist." He further argues that such a view does not make sense in light of the different situations; Stalin emphasized production because of the Soviet Union's backwardness in all areas, while in China, the reforms were seen as one way to further develop the productive forces. These interpretations, while not in agreement, shed light on the fact that Chinese socialism did change during the Deng era. In 1987, the *Beijing Review* stated that the achievements of socialism were "evaluated according to the level of the productive forces".

Party theoretician and former Politburo member Hu Qiaomu in his thesis "Observe economic laws, speed up the Four Modernizations", published in 1978, argued that economic laws were objective, on par with natural laws. He insisted that economic laws were no more negotiable "than the law of gravity". Hu's conclusion was that the Party was responsible for the socialist economy's acting on these economic laws. He believed that only an economy based on the individual would satisfy these laws, since "such an economy would be in accord with the productive forces". The CPC followed his line, and at the 12th National Congress, the party constitution was amended, stating that the private economy was a "needed complement to the socialist economy". This sentiment was echoed by Xue Muqiao; "practice shows that socialism is not necessarily based on a unified public ownership by the whole society".

The official communiqué of the 3rd plenum of the 11th Central Committee included the words: "integrate the universal principles of Marxism–Leninism–Mao Zedong Thought with the concrete practice of socialist modernization and develop it under the new historical conditions". With the words "new historical conditions", the CPC had in fact made it possible to view the old, Maoist ideology as obsolete (or at least certain tenants). To know if a policy was obsolete or not, the party had to "seek truth from facts" and follow the slogan "practice is the sole criterion of the truth". At the 6th plenum of the 11th

Central Committee, the "Resolution on Certain Questions in the History of Our Party Since the Founding of the People's Republic of China" was adopted. The resolution separated Mao the person from Mao Zedong Thought, claiming that Mao had contravened Mao Zedong Thought during his rule. While the document criticized Mao, it clearly stated that he was a "proletarian revolutionary" (i.e. not all of his views were wrong), and that without Mao there would have been no new China. Su Shaozi, a party theoretician and the head of the Institute of Marxism–Leninism–Mao Zedong Thought, argued that the CPC needed to reassess the New Economic Policy introduced by Vladimir Lenin and ended by Stalin, as well as Stalin's industrialization policies and the prominent role he gave to class struggle. Su claimed that the "exploiting classes in China had been eliminated". Dong Fureng, a Deputy Director at the Institute of Economics, agreed with the reformist discourse, first by criticizing Marx and Friedrich Engels' view that a socialist society had to abolish private property, and secondly, accusing both Marx and Engels for being vague on what kind of ownership of the means of production was necessary in socialist society. While both Su and Dong agreed that it was the collectivization of agriculture and the establishment of People's Communes which had ended rural exploitation, neither of them sought a return to collectivized agriculture.

The creation of a "Socialist market economy"

The term "socialism with Chinese characteristics" was added to the General Program of the party's constitution at the 12th National Congress, without a definition of the term. At the 13th National Congress, held in 1987, Zhao Ziyang, the CPC General Secretary, claimed that socialism with Chinese characteristics was the "integration of the fundamental tenets of Marxism with the modernization drive in China" and was "scientific socialism rooted in the realities of present-day China". By this time the CPC believed that China was in the primary stage of socialism, and therefore needed market relations to develop into a socialist society. Two years earlier, Su had tried to internationalize the term "primary stage of socialism" by claiming that socialism contained three different production phases. China was currently in the first phase, while the Soviet Union and the remaining Eastern Bloc countries were in the second phase. Because China was in the primary stage of socialism, Zhao argued that in "[China] for a long time to come, we shall develop various sectors of the economy, always ensuring the dominant position of the public sector". Further, some individuals should be allowed to become rich "before the objective of common prosperity [pure communism] is achieved". Lastly, during the primary stage of socialism, planning would no longer be the primary means of organization of the economy. Upon hearing this remark, Chen Yun, a cautious reformer and the second-most powerful politician in China, walked out of the meeting.

Why do people support us? Because over the last ten years our economy has been developing ... If the economy stagnated for five years or developed at only a slow rate – for example, at 4 or 5 percent, or even 2 or 3 percent—what effects would be produced? This would be not only an economic problem but also a political one. — *Deng Xiaoping during a conversation with Yang Shangkun and Premier Li in 1990.*

Both Chen Yun and Deng supported the formation of a private market. At the 8th National Congress, Chen first proposed an economy where the socialist sector would be dominant, with the private economy in a secondary role. He believed that by following the "Ten Major Relationships", an article by Mao on how to proceed with socialist construction, the CPC could remain on the socialist road while also supporting private property. Chen Yun conceived of the bird-cage theory, where the bird represents the free market and the cage represents a central plan. Chen proposed that a balance should be found between "setting the bird free" and choking the bird with a central plan that was too restrictive.

Between the time of the 13th National Congress and the Tiananmen Square incident and the ensuing crackdown, the line between right and left within the CPC became clearer. The rift became visible in the run-up to the 7th plenum of the 13th

National Congress (in 1990), when problems arose concerning China's 8th Five-Year Plan. The draft for the 8th Five-Year Plan, supervised by Premier Li Peng and Deputy Premier Yao Yilin, openly endorsed Chen Yun's economic view that planning should be primary, coupled with slow, balanced growth. Li went further and directly contradicted Deng, stating, "Reform and opening up should not be taken as the guiding principle; instead, sustained, steady, and coordinated development should be taken as the guiding principle." Deng retaliated by rejecting the Draft for the 8th Five-Year Plan, claiming that the 1990s was the "best time" for continuing with reform and opening up. Li and Yao even went so far as to try to annul two key resolutions passed by the 13th National Congress: the theory of socialist political civilization, and the resolution that central planning and markets were equals. Deng rejected the idea of reopening discussions on these subjects, and restated that reforms were essential for the CPC's future. Not accepting Deng's stance, party theorist Deng Liqun, along with others, began promoting "Chen Yun Thought". After a discussion with General Wang Zhen, a supporter of Chen Yun, Deng stated he would propose the abolishment of the Central Advisory Commission(CAC). Chen Yun retaliated by naming Bo Yibo to succeed him as CAC chairman. Indeed, when the 7th plenum of the 13th Central Committee did in fact convene, nothing notable took place, with both sides trying not to widen the ideological gap even further. The resolution of the 7th plenum did contain a great deal of ideological language ("firmly follow the road of socialism with Chinese characteristics"), but no clear formulation of new policy was uttered.

Chen Yun's thoughts and policies dominated CPC discourse from 1989 until Deng's Southern Tour in 1992. Deng began campaigning for his reformist policies in 1991, managing to get reformist articles printed in the *People's Daily* and *Liberation Army* during this period. The articles criticized those communists who believed that central planning and market economics were polar opposites, instead repeating the Dengist mantra that planning and markets were only two different ways in which to regulate economic activity. By that time, the party had begun preparing for the 14th National Congress. Deng threatened to withdraw his support for Jiang Zemin's reelection as CPC General Secretary if Jiang did not accept reformist policies. However, at the 8th plenum of the 13th Central Committee, in 1991, the conservatives still held the upper hand within the party leadership.

To reassert his economic agenda, in the spring of 1992, Deng made his famous southern tour of China, visiting Guangzhou, Shenzhen, and Zhuhai, and spending the New Year in Shanghai. He used his travels to reassert his economic policy ideas after his retirement from office.On the tour, Deng made many speeches and generated large local support for his reformist platform. He stressed the importance of economic reform in China, and criticized those who were against further reform and opening up. The tour proved that amongst the party's grassroots organizations, support for reform and opening up was firm. Because of this, more and more leading members of the central party leadership converted to Deng's position, amongst them Jiang Zemin.

In his speech "Deeply Understand and Implement Comrade Deng Xiaoping's Important Spirit, Make Economic Construction, Reform and Opening Go Faster and Better" to the Central Party School, Jiang said it did not matter if a certain mechanism was capitalist or socialist, the key question was whether it worked.Jiang's speech is notable since it introduced the term socialist market economy, which replaced Chen Yun's "planned socialist market economy". In a later Politburo meeting, members voted unanimously, in old communist fashion, to continue with reform and opening up. Knowing that he had lost, Chen Yun gave in, and claimed that because of new conditions, the old techniques of the planned economy were outdated.

At the 14th National Congress, the thought of Deng Xiaoping was officially dubbed Deng Xiaoping Theory, and elevated to the same level as Mao Zedong Thought. The concepts of "socialism with Chinese characteristics" and "the primary stage of socialism" were credited to him. At the congress, Jiang reiterated Deng's view that it was unnecessary to ask if something was socialist or capitalist, since the important factor was whether it worked. Several capitalist techniques were introduced, while science and technology were to be the primary productive force.

CONSTRAINTS ON CHINESE POWER PROJECTION CAPABILITIES

Chinese power projection capabilities beyond its sea borders, despite this modernization program, remain limited due to a lack of amphibious ships, heavy cargo carrying aircraft and other logistical shortcomings. The PLA-N remains technologically underdeveloped and it suffers from "a lack of integration in its command, control, and communication systems; targeting; air defense; and antisubmarine warfare capabilities. PLA-N ships are vulnerable to attack by aircraft, torpedoes, and antiship missiles. The navies of the ASEAN nations could, if able to cooperate together, exclude the PLA-N from the South China Sea."

While the SA-N-7 "Gadfly" and SA-N-12 "Grizzly" SAM systems, acquired from Russia, doubles the range of the PLA-N air defence capabilities, China's inferior fire-control system will limit their effectiveness. These will only provide protection for the fleet from air raids and to provide air defence cover when landing on individual islands. They have no capability to screen larger areas of operations, especially if operating against land based airpower in the littoral waters of an adversary.

The PLA-N submarine fleet, while currently being upgraded with the purchase of the Russian *Kilo class* submarines, is severely limited in its effectiveness as there are serious questions as to the seaworthiness of most of the fleet. The catastrophic accident onboard the Ming class submarine No. 361 earlier this year puts doubt as to the reliability of the remaining *Ming* and *Romeo* class submarines. Even the *Kilo* submarines are proving to be problematic for China as there were reports in 2002 of major battery failures on the two older EKM877 type.

China might have a large quantity of military equipment but its lacks quality, especially in aircraft and submarines. The Chinese have not yet developed the capabilities for a "blue water" navy and it will take them a considerable amount of time to do so. The much speculated Chinese aircraft carrier is unlikely to be developed over the short-term as China possesses neither the technology nor the resources to build or buy one. While China has long aspired to an aircraft carrier capability, there are currently no plans or even tentative proposals to introduce such a capability. China would require at least two or three carriers to maintain a single carrier on operations at any one time, the others being in refit, transit, or replenishment. The cost of procuring a carrier task force of this size is significant, and China is unlikely to have sufficient defence funding in the foreseeable future. In addition, the technology necessary to develop a carrier battle group is not readily available to China. Even a modest vertical/short take-off and landing (VSTOL) carrier would be expensive and problematic to deploy within the next 20 years, especially given the difficulty in obtaining VSTOL technology aircraft.

Given the current state of the Chinese equipment and training, the Chinese have no capability to pursue an expansionist maritime policy. The Chinese are attempting to address the training problem by increasing the amount of combined military exercises. Since the late 1980s the Chinese have increasingly included army, air force, naval, and rapid reaction forces in their military exercises. While initial exercises were designed to respond to an invasion of the Chinese mainland, these have been expanded to include training in the rapid deployment of troops by air and sea, including airborne and seaborne landing operations.

Beijing's military training exercises are increasingly focusing on the United States as an adversary and on preparing for combined and joint operations under more realistic conditions. The PLA continues to focus on training to counter a more militarily advanced adversary and to incorporate the *Three Attacks and Three Defences* initiative-air defence training that concentrates on attacking stealth aircraft, cruise missiles, and helicopters, while defending against precision strikes, electronic warfare, and enemy reconnaissance. Moreover, the adoption of military training reforms in 2002 are designed to improve training of the army in general and the officer corps in particular, eventually resulting in a more professional military force. In 2002, PLA training emphasized maritime and amphibious operations, and the integration of conventional ground units with marines, airborne, and special operations forces (SOF). However, for the most part, while PLA ground, air and naval forces might have been in the field at the same time, there was no integration of the PLA-N marine and PLA-AF airborne units with the ground forces.

The Hong Kong Chinese language newspaper, *Kuang Chiao Ching*, described a potential assault task force that the PLA-N could assemble for an assault on the Spratlys. This would include one *Luhu* class destroyer, six Luda class destroyers, two frigates, 30 missile patrol boats, 10 landing ships, 10 minelayers, and 18 submarines. In addition, the task force would comprise 30 to 50 support ships and two to three battalions of marines. The task force would be supported by strike and fighter aircraft from the PLA-AF and the PLA-NAF. The strike aircraft would include the H-6 bomber, armed with C-601 anti-ship cruise missiles, and the new H-7, all-weather bomber, armed with C-801 anti-ship missiles. The 24 PLA-AF Su-27s along with the J-7 and J-8 fighters would also be included to provide air cover for both bombers and the fleet. Even today the likelihood of such a force being assembled or effective is highly doubtful. While a similar task force today could be extended to include the newer guided-missile frigates and Su-30s, the PLA-N lacks any long-range amphibious capability and almost no effective logistical or support infrastructure to supply their forces over long distances for a protracted period of time. They have three oil and fuel from port to port) and some 56 amphibious landing ships.

Moreover, the limited number of Sukhois in the Chinese inventory will not guarantee them control of the sky over the

South China Sea. Even with the latest agreement to purchase additional aircraft this does not give the Chinese enough aircraft to continuously control the skies over the Spratlys. The Sukhois have an effective combat radius of 1,400 kilometres and as the nearest Chinese airbase, on Woody Island in the Paracels, is approximately 1,000 kilometres from the main group of the Spratlys the fighters will have very little time to patrol any potential combat area.

In addition, the Sukhois are part of the PLA-AF not the PLA-NAF. As such, they are not equipped for naval operations, nor are the pilots trained for operations over water or to provide tactical support for naval units, which would severely restrict their effectiveness over the Spratlys. The Chinese bomber force is also limited in regards to its combat radius as the H-6 has an effective range of just over 1,600 kilometres, so while they can reach the Spratlys they would have only a limited amount of time to search for such mobile targets as warships.

While the PLA-AF have modified some of its H-6 aircraft into aerial refuellers the small size of these aircraft only provide a limited extension of the Chinese fighters' combat radius, especially in time of war when the tankers would be targets of enemy fighters. Moreover, aerial refuelling is a complex task requiring the tanker and fighters to rendezvous at specific coordinates, altitude, speed, and direction and the Chinese do not regularly practice in-air refuelling.

Finally, to date the Su-27 and Su-30s are stationed considerably inland in the Beijing, Nanjing, Guangzhou, Jinan, Shenyang, and Chengdu military regions while the airbases closest to the Spratlys, on Hainan and Woody Island, are PLA-N airfields rather than PLA-AF bases. Questions need to be raised about the ability of the Chinese to operate the new weapons and weapon systems that they are have purchased due to the fact that they are buying a wide variety of off-the-shelf high technology systems from several different suppliers. The technological leap that these systems represent for the Chinese maintenance crews as well as the mix of suppliers will severely limit the ability of the Chinese to properly maintain all the systems. The PLA-AF ground crews have had serious problems in maintaining the new Sukhois for flight training operations and many have reportedly crashed.

CHINA: FROM IMPERIAL DEPENDENCY TO WORLD CLASS COMPETITOR

China's sustained growth in its manufacturing sector was a result of highly concentrated public investments, high profits, technological innovations and a protected domestic market. While foreign capital profited, it was always within the framework of the Chinese state's priorities and regulations. The regime's dynamic 'export strategy' led to huge trade surpluses, which eventually made China one of the world's largest creditors especially for US debt.

In order to maintain its dynamic industries, China has required huge influxes of raw materials, resulting in large-scale overseas investments and trade agreements with agro-mineral export countries in Africa and Latin America.

By 2010 China displaced the US and Europe as the main trading partner in many countries in Asia, Africa and Latin America.

Modern China's rise to world economic power, like its predecessor between 1100-1800, is based on its gigantic productive capacity: Trade and investment was governed by a policy of strict non-interference in the internal relations of its trading partners. Unlike the US , China did initiate brutal wars for oil; instead it signed lucrative contracts. And China does not fight wars in the interest of overseas Chinese, as the US has done in the Middle East for Israel.

The seeming imbalance between Chinese economic and military power is in stark contrast to the US where a bloated, parasitic military empire continues to erode its own global economic presence. US military spending is twelve times that of China. Increasingly the US military plays the key role shaping policy in Washington as it seeks to undercut China's rise to global power.

RISE IN THE COMMUNIST PARTY

After numerous unsuccessful attempts, in 1974 Xi Jinping was accepted into the Communist Party. The following year he began to study chemical engineering at Beijing's Tsinghua University, earning a degree in 1979. From that point forward, he steadily rose through the ranks of the Communist Party.

Between 1979 and 1982, Xi served in the Central Military Command as vice premier, gaining valuable military experience. It was around this time that he married his first wife, Ke Lingling, the daughter of the Chinese ambassador to Great Britain. The marriage ended in divorce within a few years.

From 1983 to 2007, Xi Jinping served in leadership positions in four provinces, beginning with Hebei.

During his tenure in Hebei, Xi Jinping traveled to the United States and spent time in Iowa with an American family, learning the finer points of agriculture and tourism.

After his return, he served as vice mayor of Xiamen in Fujian, where in 1987 he married folk singer Peng Liyuan, who also holds the rank of army general in the People's Liberation Army. The couple has a daughter, Xi Mingze, who studied at Harvard University under a pseudonym.

National Prominence

Xi would make a steady ascent in the ensuing decades, with postings as governor of the Fujian and Zhejiang provinces and as party secretary.

In 2007, his career got a further boost when a pension-fund scandal rocked the leadership of Shanghai and he was named as its party secretary.

He spent his tenure promoting stability and restoring the city's financial image, and that same year was chosen for the Politburo Standing Committee. In early 2008, Xi's visibility became even greater when he was elected vice president of the People's Republic of China and placed in charge of preparations for the 2008 summer Olympics in Beijing.

Elected Leader of the People's Republic of China

In early 2012, Xi Jinping traveled to the United States to meet with President Barack Obama and members of his cabinet. He also made a nostalgic trip back to Iowa and then visited Los Angeles. During his visit, he spoke of increasing trust and reducing suspicions between the two countries while respecting each other's interests in the Pacific-Asian region.

Later that year, on November 15, Xi Jinping was elected general secretary of the Communist Party and chairman of the Central Military Commission. In his first speech as general secretary, Xi broke from tradition and sounded more like a Western politician, speaking about the aspirations of the average person and calling for better education, stable jobs, higher income, a more reliable safety net of retirement and health care, better living conditions and a better environment. He also vowed to take on corruption within the government at the highest levels. He referred to his vision for the nation as the "Chinese Dream."

On March 14, 2013, Xi completed his ascent when he was elected president of the People's Republic of China, a ceremonial position as head of state. In his first speech as president he vowed to fight for a great renaissance of the Chinese nation and a more prominent international standing.

Achievements and Controversies

Fulfilling one of his early promises, Xi almost immediately embarked on a campaign to deal with government corruption. He arrested some of the country's most powerful figures, including former security chief Zhou Yongkang, and by the end of 2014 the CCP had disciplined more than 100,000 officials.

Xi also set about stimulating a slowing economy. In 2014, China introduced the "One Belt, One Road" initiative to bolster trade routes and launched the ambitious Asian Infrastructure Investment Bank. Domestically, his party expanded the power of private banks and allowed international investors to trade shares directly on the Shanghai stock market.

Xi has also changed some of the laws enacted by predecessors, formally ending China's one-child policy in 2015. His elimination of the "reeducation through labor" system, which punished individuals charged with petty crimes, was viewed favorably.

However, the Chinese leader has drawn scrutiny for his methods. Critics have noted that his crackdown on government corruption mainly targeted political opponents, and the CCP has come under fire by human rights groups for jailing journalists, lawyers and other private citizens. Under Xi's reach, censors have sought to eliminate Western influence in school curriculums and limited the public's internet access.

Xi has also overseen economic regulations that have reverberated beyond his country's borders. The government stepped in to prop up a sagging housing market in 2014, and suddenly devalued the yuan in the summer of 2015. Despite promising during a trip to the United States in September that China would never manipulate currency to increase exports, Xi has been accused of that very approach.

Global Standing

As part of his goal to establish China as a 21st century global superpower, Xi has pushed for military reform to upgrade naval and air forces. Already chairman of the Central Military Commission, in 2016 he added the title of commander in chief of its joint battle command center.

In recent years, Xi has asserted China's naval capacities through the construction of artificial islands within disputed territories of the South China Sea. Despite his claims to the contrary, satellite photographs indicated that the islands were being used to house military developments. In July 2016, an international tribunal in The Hague ruled that China had illegally claimed those territories, although China refused to accept the authority of that ruling.

While often at odds with the U.S. over trade issues, Xi has publicly acknowledged the need for China to cooperate with its Western counterpart on the issue of climate change. In

September 2016, Xi and U.S. President Barack Obama announced they were formally adopting the international climate-change agreement reached in Paris the previous December to reduce emissions from the world's two largest economies.

In November 2017, Xi met with U.S. President Donald Trump for a two-day summit in Beijing. Despite earlier accusing China of being a currency manipulator, Trump offered praise this time around for the country taking advantage of financial opportunities. For his part, Xi spoke about a "win-win" cooperation between the two economic superpowers, announcing memorandums of understanding to increase trade by $253 billion.

However, the two leaders then contrasted one another during their subsequent appearances at the Asia-Pacific Economic Cooperation summit in Vietnam. In his speech, Trump criticized the development of globalization for harming American workers and companies, declaring, "we are not going to let the United States be taken advantage of anymore." Taking the stage immediately afterward, Xi painted a glowing picture of the collective benefits of globalization, saying, "let more countries ride the fast train of Chinese development."

Tensions between the two sides mounted after Trump ordered stiff tariffs on aluminum and steel imports in March 2018, as part of U.S. efforts to level the "out of control" trade deficit with its Asian counterpart. China responded by slapping tariffs on a range of American goods, including fruits, nuts and pork products, prompting Trump to threaten to escalate the matter further.

Xi sounded a conciliatory note during his speech at the Boao Economic Forum in April, in which he pledged to "significantly broaden market access" for foreign companies by easing restrictions in the financial and auto sectors and lowering import tariffs for vehicles. Additionally, he promised greater protection for intellectual property. "China does not seek a trade surplus," the president said. "We have a genuine desire to increase imports and achieve greater balance of international payments under the current account." Amid the escalating tensions of a potential trade war, the yuan fell to a six-month low against the dollar in late June, sparking speculation that China would let that course continue and make their goods cheaper on the world market. Meanwhile, the matters of military deployments in the disputed South China Sea and American support of Taiwan's claims of independence also remained delicate subjects in discussions with Washington.

Xi indicated as much in a meeting with U.S. Defense Secretary James Mattis in June. "Our stance is steadfast and clear-cut when it comes to China's sovereignty and territorial integrity," the president said. "We cannot lose one inch of territory passed down by our ancestors. Meanwhile, we want nothing from others."

Expansion of Power

In October 2017, during a meeting of the 19th National Congress of the Communist Party, delegates voted to add the words "Xi Jinping Thought for the New Era of Socialism with Chinese Special Characteristics" to the party constitution. The addition was meant to serve as a guiding principle for the party moving forward, with Xi's vision paving the way for global leadership in the years to come.

Furthermore, the constitutional change boosted Xi's status to match those of exalted former Communist Party heads Mao Tse-tung and Deng Xiaoping. It was believed that, as one of the country's strongest leaders in decades, Xi possessed the ability to hold on to power as long as he desired.

In late February 2018, the Communist Party's Central Committee proposed scrapping term limits for China's president and vice president, potentially setting the table for Xi to govern indefinitely. The National People's Congress formally voted to make the constitutional change the following month, shortly before Xi was confirmed for a second five-year term.

In a speech to close the 16-day legislative session, Xi spoke of forging unification with Taiwan, promoting "high-quality" development that values innovation and expanding his signature

Belt and Road foreign policy initiative. "The new era belongs to everyone, and everyone is a witness, pioneer and builder of the new era," he said. "As long as we are united and struggle together, there will be no power to stop the Chinese people from realizing their dreams."

THE STATE OF THE WORLD: A FRAMEWORK

The evolution of geopolitics is cyclical. Powers rise, fall and shift. Changes occur in every generation in an unending ballet. However, the period between 1989 and 1991 was unique in that a long cycle of human history spanning hundreds of years ended, and with it a shorter cycle also came to a close. The world is still reverberating from the events of that period.

On Dec. 25, 1991, an epoch ended. On that day the Soviet Union collapsed, and for the first time in almost 500 years no European power was a global power, meaning no European state integrated economic, military and political power on a global scale.

What began in 1492 with Europe smashing its way into the world and creating a global imperial system had ended. For five centuries, one European power or another had dominated the world, whether Portugal, Spain, France, England or the Soviet Union. Even the lesser European powers at the time had some degree of global influence.

After 1991 the only global power left was the United States, which produced about 25 percent of the world's gross domestic product (GDP) each year and dominated the oceans. Never before had the United States been the dominant global power. Prior to World War II, American power had been growing from its place at the margins of the international system, but it was emerging on a multipolar stage. After World War II, it found itself in a bipolar world, facing off with the Soviet Union in a struggle in which American victory was hardly a foregone conclusion.

The United States has been the unchallenged global power for 20 years, but its ascendancy has left it off-balance for most of this time, and imbalance has been the fundamental characteristic of the global system in the past generation. Unprepared institutionally or psychologically for its position, the United States has swung from an excessive optimism in the 1990s that held that significant conflict was at an end to the wars against militant Islam after 9/11, wars that the United States could not avoid but also could not integrate into a multilayered global strategy.

When the only global power becomes obsessed with a single region, the entire world is unbalanced. Imbalance remains the defining characteristic of the global system today.

While the collapse of the Soviet Union ended the European epoch, it also was the end of the era that began in 1945, and it was accompanied by a cluster of events that tend to accompany generational shifts.

The 1989-1991 period marked the end of the Japanese economic miracle, the first time the world had marveled at an Asian power's sustained growth rate as the same power's financial system crumbled.

The end of the Japanese miracle and the economic problem of integrating East and West Germany both changed the way the global economy worked. The 1991 Maastricht Treaty set the stage for Europe's attempt at integration and was the framework for Europe in the post-Cold War world.

Tiananmen Square set the course for China in the next 20 years and was the Chinese answer to a collapsing Soviet empire. It created a structure that allowed for economic development but assured the dominance of the Communist Party. Saddam Hussein's invasion of Kuwait was designed to change the balance of power in the Persian Gulf after the Iraq-Iran war and tested the United States' willingness to go to war after the Cold War.

In 1989-1991 the world changed the way it worked, whether measured in centuries or generations. It was an extraordinary period whose significance is only now emerging. It locked into place a long-term changing of the guard, where North America replaced Europe as the center of the international system. But generations come and go, and we are now in the middle of the first generational shift since the collapse of the European powers, a shift that began in 2008 but is only now working itself out in detail.

What happened in 2008 was one of the financial panics that the global capitalist system periodically suffers. As is frequently the case, these panics first generate political crises within nations, followed by changes in the relations among nations. Of these changes, three in particular are of importance, two of which are directly linked to the 2008 crisis. The first is the European financial crisis and its transformation into a political crisis.

The second is the Chinese export crisis and its consequences. The third, indirectly linked to 2008, is the shift in the balance of power in the Middle East in favor of Iran.

THE EUROPEAN CRISIS

The European crisis represents the single most significant event that followed from the financial collapse of 2008. The vision of the European Union was that an institution that would bind France and Germany together would make the wars that had raged in Europe since 1871 impossible.

The vision also assumed that economic integration would both join France and Germany together and create the foundations of a prosperous Europe. Within the context of Maastricht as it evolved, the European vision assumed that the European Union would become a way to democratize and integrate the former Communist countries of Eastern Europe into a single framework.

However, embedded in the idea of the European Union was the idea that Europe could at some point transcend nationalism and emerge as a United States of Europe, a single political federation with a constitution and a unified foreign and domestic policy. It would move from a free trade zone to a unified economic system to a single currency and then to further political integration built around the European Parliament, allowing

Europe to emerge as a single country. Long before this happened, of course, people began to speak of Europe as if it were a single entity. Regardless of the modesty of formal proposals, there was a powerful vision of an integrated European polity.

There were two foundations for it. One was the apparent economic and social benefits of a united Europe. The other was that this was the only way that Europe could make its influence felt in the international system. Individually, the European states were not global players, but collectively they had the ability to become just that. In the post-Cold War world, where the United States was the sole and unfettered global power, this was an attractive opportunity.

The European vision was smashed in the aftermath of 2008, when the fundamental instability of the European experiment revealed itself. That vision was built around Germany, the world's second-largest exporter, but Europe's periphery remained too weak to weather the crisis. It was not so much this particular crisis; Europe was not built to withstand any financial crisis. Sooner or later one would come and the unity of Europe would be severely strained as each nation, driven by different economic and social realities, maneuvered in its own interest rather than in the interest of Europe.

There is no question that the Europe of 2012 operates in a very different way than it did in 2007. There is an expectation in some parts that Europe will, in due course, return to its old post-Cold War state, but that is unlikely. The underlying contradictions of the European enterprise are now revealed, and while some European entity will likely survive, it probably will not resemble the Europe envisioned by Maastricht, let alone the grander visions of a United States of Europe. Thus, the only potential counterweight to the United States will not emerge in this generation.

CHINA AND THE ASIAN MODEL

China was similarly struck by the 2008 crisis. Apart from the inevitably cyclical nature of all economies, the Asian model, as seen in Japan and then in 1997 in East and Southeast Asia, provides for prolonged growth followed by profound financial dislocation. Indeed, growth rates do not indicate economic health. Just as it was for Europe, the 2008 financial crisis was the trigger for China.

China's core problem is that more than a billion people live in households earning less than $6 a day, and the majority of those earn less than $3 a day. Social tensions aside, the economic consequence is that China's large industrial plant outstrips Chinese consumer demand.

As a result, China must export. However, the recessions after 2008 cut heavily into China's exports, severely affecting GDP growth and threatening the stability of the political system. China confronted the problem with a massive surge in bank lending, driving new investment and supporting GDP growth but also fueling rampant inflation.

Inflation created upward pressure on labor costs until China began to lose its main competitive advantage over other countries.

For a generation, Chinese growth has been the engine of the global economic system, just as Japan was in the previous generation. China is not collapsing any more than Japan did. However, it is changing its behaviour, and with it the behaviour of the international system.

Looking Ahead

If we look at the international system as having three major economic engines, two of them — Europe and China — are changing their behaviour to be less assertive and less influential in the international system. The events of 2008 did not create these changes; they merely triggered processes that revealed the underlying weaknesses of these two entities.

Somewhat outside the main processes of the international system, the Middle East is undergoing a fundamental shift in its balance of power.

The driver in this is not the crisis of 2008 but the consequences of the U.S. wars in the region and their termination. With the U.S. withdrawal from Iraq, Iran has emerged as the major conventional power in the Persian Gulf and the major influence over Iraq. In addition, with the continued survival of the al Assad regime in Syria through the support of Iran, there is the potential for Iranian influence to stretch from western Afghanistan to the Mediterranean Sea. Even if the al Assad regime fell, Iran would still be well-positioned to assert its claims for primacy in the Persian Gulf.

Just as the processes unleashed in 1989-1991 defined the next 20 years, so, too, will the processes that are being generated now dominate the next generation. Still powerful but acutely off-balance in its domestic and foreign policies, the United States is confronting a changing world without yet having a clear understanding of how to deal with this world or, for that matter, how the shifts in the global system will affect it. For the United States strategically, the fragmentation of Europe, the transformation of global production in the wake of the Chinese economy's climax, and the dramatically increased power of Iran appear as abstract events not directly affecting the United States.

Each of these events will create dangers and opportunities for the United States that it is unprepared to manage. The fragmentation of Europe raises the question of the future of Germany and its relationship with Russia. The movement of production to low-wage countries will create booms in countries hitherto regarded as beyond help and potential zones of instability created by rapid and uneven growth. And, of course, the idea that the Iranian issue can be managed through sanctions is a form of denial rather than a strategy.

Three major areas of the world are in flux: Europe, China and the Persian Gulf. Every country in the world will have to devise a strategy to deal with the new reality, just as 1989-1991 required new strategies. The most important country, the United States, had no strategy after 1991 and has no strategy today. This is the single most important reality of the world. Like the Spaniards, who, in the generation after Columbus' voyage, lacked a clear sense of the reality they had created, Americans have no clear sense of the world they find themselves in. This fact continues to define how the world works.

'RISING CHINA' POSE A THREAT TO INTERNATIONAL SECURITY

The collapse of the Soviet Union in 1991 marked the conclusion of a bipolar political order that had defined the world since 1945. In its place emerged a global framework, largely characterised by the hegemonic ascendance of the United States of America (U.S.). The primacy of the U.S. in this unipolar system has led theorists such as Waltz to claim, 'never since Rome has one country so nearly dominated its world' (2002: 350). Assertions such as this, however, have been problematised by the rapid rise of China as a global power. Increasingly, contemporary China is being re-conceptualised as a realistic economic, political and military counterbalance to U.S. hegemony. For much of the world, this perception has led to growing anxiety that the rise of China poses a significant threat to international security. This essay, however, will dispute this claim, arguing that China's potential as a threat to international security is consistently exaggerated and a relatively benign rise is entirely possible. This will be done by first establishing the ways in which the current rise of China is viewed as a threat to international security by many states and individuals. The inevitability of China 'rising' to achieve hegemon status will next be critiqued, as well as current perceptions regarding emerging Chinese foreign policy. Next, the importance of China's economic integration with the rest of the world will be highlighted. Lastly, the likelihood of a more powerful China leading to regional insecurity, particularly surrounding relations with Taiwan, will be examined.

For numerous states, the sustained military, political and economic ascension of China is increasingly viewed as a likely threat to international security. The rapid pace in which China has managed its societal transformation is arguably without historical comparison. China's subsequent increase in military spending, as well as its commitment to modernising its military capabilities, is cited by many, including the U.S., as clear evidence of its growing potential to threaten international security. This concern was evident in the 2006 Quadrennial Defence Review, which cited China, of all major and emerging powers, as having the 'greatest potential to compete militarily' with the U.S. and highlighted China's ability to field military technology 'that could over time offset traditional U.S. military advantages' (2006: 29).

As well as China's general military capacity, the U.S. has grown increasingly concerned over Chinese nuclear ambitions. This was highlighted in the 2010 Nuclear Posture Review Report (NPRR) which cited China's 'qualitative and quantitative modernisation' of its nuclear arsenal, as well as its relative lack of transparency, as significant factors in growing regional and international anxiety (U.S. Department of Defence 2010: V). China's strengthening military, coupled with a perceived increase in regional antagonism, has generated additional concern for international security. Regarding Chinese regional aspirations, it is the claim of many that China ultimately wished to assert a "Monroe Doctrine", throughout East Asia, excluding non-regional powers (Bowring 2010: 2). Given the continued U.S. involvement in much of East Asia, if this assessment proves accurate, the ramifications for international security would indeed be severe.

As well as China's military advancements, its economic growth has continued at an unrivalled pace. The meteoric ascent of China's economy over the last twenty-five years has transformed regional and international power dynamics (Blij 2005: 129). This very phenomena, however, has been cited as a likely cause of future international insecurity. Realists such as Mearsheimer argue that if the rapid economic growth of China continues over the coming decades, an intense security competition between the U.S. and China is likely to result, with a significant potential for war (2006:160). In order to more accurately assess China's capability to disrupt international security, a more reasoned analysis of China's current and potential strength as a state must be undertaken.

Threats to international security generated by China's challenge to U.S. hegemony must be viewed more soberly, particularly given the uncertainty of China's 'rise'. While China's economic growth and surge in GDP has been dramatic, its long-term continuation has been challenged by some. One study suggests that by 2015, the odds of China experiencing a significant slowdown in GDP growth rates were over 70% (The Economist 2011: 2).

This makes assertions on the inevitability of war, generated by an economic rivalry between the U.S. and China, increasingly problematic. Additionally, while China has indeed experienced an unprecedented surge in national GDP, wealth disparity continues to impede the state's development. The decision of Chinese leadership to identify inequality as one of the greatest political challenges currently facing its society (Klein 2008: 07:33), clearly demonstrates the continued uncertainty surrounding China's rise. Similarly, growing anxiety surrounding China's military spending must also be properly contextualised, particularly given the continued dominance of the U.S. military. In 2009 the U.S. military spent over USD $738 billion, whereas estimates of China's annual military budget range from USD $69.5 billion to USD $150 billion (Thomson 2010: 87). Additionally, China's potential nuclear threat, while growing, is still comparatively small and vulnerable when viewed alongside that of the U.S. China's nuclear stockpile is currently between a tenth and a hundredth the size of the U.S. arsenal (Glaser 2011: 91).

These figures suggest that, despite China's military modernisation attempts, any military exchange between the two states would be hugely asymmetrical. The continued pre-eminence of the U.S. military will be a significant factor in the potential of a growing China to disrupt international security. China, fully aware that an increase in bellicosity can be challenged by the U.S., with overwhelming force, will attempt a peaceful transition to great power status. This is further apparent through an examination of China's current foreign policy.

An analysis of China's foreign policy suggests that its growth in power and influence will present a minimal threat to international security. Among those who claim that a rising China constitutes a significant risk to international stability, comparisons are often drawn between current U.S./China friction and the Cold-War relationship between the U.S. and the U.S.S.R. This, however is misleading. The Cold-War was essentially a conflict of incompatible ideologies. While the capitalist U.S. model advocated individual freedoms, the free market, and political and civil rights; communism sought to promote class equality and an emancipation of the working class (Brady and Said 1993: 591).

Crucially, both models were expansionist in nature, ensuring tensions between the two superpowers would escalate in the post-WWII years. This ensuing conflict would play a dominant role in world politics, with both superpowers transforming global security into a zero-sum game (Bisley 2007: 233). The relationship between contemporary China and the U.S. is vastly different, with a far greater likelihood of non-zero-sum solutions arising to emerging problems. Jisi argues that China currently has little interest in transforming itself into a hegemon, viewing its core interests as security, sovereignty, and development, as well as the elevation of its people's living standards (2011: 5).

This challenges the assertions of offensive realists, who claim that achieving hegemon status within the global system is a state's ultimate goal (Mearscheimer 2001, cited in Snyder 2002:152). Concern over the rise of China often stems from fears that an increase in parity between China and the U.S. will trigger an accelerated security dilemma between the two states. Hertz contends that the security dilemma is an unavoidable condition that results from the anarchical nature of the international system, whereby the defensive security measures of a state can cause a perception of hostile intent by other states (1950, cited in Burke 2007: 148). This can lead to a military build-up in response, resulting in an overall loss of security and increase in anxiety for all states. Given China's primarily domestic focus, as opposed to the expansionist grand strategy of the Soviet Union, predictions of international insecurity resulting from an emerging security dilemma seems exaggerated. This is made further apparent with an examination of the economic interconnectedness that exists between China and the rest of the world.

The continued economic benefits of a rising China for the rest of the world, will largely mitigate any potential threat it poses to international security. A key determinant in the likelihood of international hostilities resulting from a growth in China's status, is China's current position in the world economy. Unlike the rise of the Soviet Union, which was characterised by confrontation and autarky, China has opted for global integration through its own form of capitalism (Jacques 2005: 1). China's entry into global economic institutions, such as the World Trade Organisation (WTO), represents an encouraging development in international security. Liberal theory suggests that the creation of institutions and regimes, such as the WTO, are crucial in blunting the more destructive features of international anarchy and ensuring the prevention of the security dilemma (Booth and Wheeler 2008: 139), which as previously established, is a crucial component in the increase of international insecurity. The economic inter-dependence that exists between China and the rest of the world has hugely increased the potential costs of war, while decreasing its probable gains. This is apparent by observing growing trade between China and other states. Between 2000 and 2005, Chinese imports from the U.S. climbed from USD$16 billion to USD$42 billion, while Chinese exports to the U.S. rose from USD$100 billion to USD$243 billion (Hufbaur, Wong and Sheth 2006: 4). As well as the U.S., China has economically integrated itself with large areas of the globe. States that have recently forged closer bonds with China include Australia, which currently experiences unprecedented and growing economic ties with the rising power (Taylor 2005: 193), and the European Union (EU), which has considered lifting its twenty year arms embargo of China in the hopes of guaranteeing more lucrative trade deals (Cendrowicz 2010: 2). Despite global economic integration contributing to a more benign rise of China, some fear that China's demand for resources may trigger conflict with other great powers. Bijan suggests that this is unlikely, as China, through efficiency, alternative energies, and conservation, hopes to develop non-zero sum measures to transcend resource scarcity (2005: 22). Even if this is possible, however, many contend that the true threat to international security lies in China's dealings with other regional powers.

Despite alarmist claims to the contrary, the growth of China is unlikely to jeopardise the security of other regional states. When describing the rise of continental powers, Napoleon famously said, 'the policies of such states are inherent in their geography' (cited in Kaplan 2010: 23). This is certainly true regarding the rise of contemporary China. Whatever China's true regional ambitions are, an observation of the East Asian alliance system indicates the improbability of a Chinese "Monroe Doctrine" in the near future. With direct economic and political contestation from both India and Japan, both key allies to the U.S. (Power 2006: 32), any attempt to supplant the U.S. as a regional hegemon, seems increasingly unlikely. Nye states that a more probable scenario for East Asia is one in which the U.S., Japan, Australia, India, and others, from a position of strength, engage China and incentivise it to engage more responsibly with the regional community. By again contrasting the rise of China with that of the Soviet Union, likely regional developments are better able to be ascertained. While the Soviet Union was believed to be a 'highly revisionist state bent on radically overturning the status quo' (Glaser 2011: 85), virtually no evidence suggests China shares these qualities. This highlights the reasonable probability of avoiding war within East Asia, as China continues to rise.

Finally, the maintenance of the regional status quo seems increasingly likely, given the direct advantage to China of a significant U.S. naval presence in East Asia. Strategic analyst Khalid R. Al-Rodhan argues that the U.S. naval dominance of East Asia serves China strategically by providing security against terrorism and smuggling, maintaining the balance of power by preventing Japanese militarisation, and contributing to general stability (2007: 52). The fact that the U.S. East Asian naval presence allows China to better focus on domestic matters, strongly suggests that peace can be maintained regionally, as China continues to strengthen. Despite these positive developments, virtual unanimity can be found among those concerned with China's rise, when focus is placed on the volatility that exists between China and Taiwan.

Despite the severe risk to international security presented by China and Taiwan's fractious relationship, the chances of a peaceful resolution are greater than the alternative of war. Tensions between China and Taiwan, resulting from Taiwan's uncertain international status, have been regularly identified as having the potential to cause massive international instability, and until this point have been dealt with by a combination of legal manipulation, complex diplomacy and a detachment from political realities (DeLisle 2000: 35). Despite the situation's current failure to escalate into internecine conflict, fears are growing that the rapid rise of China may manifest into revisionism of Taiwan's status, triggering hostilities. Given its potential to entangle the U.S. and China in large scale war, the Taiwan Strait is viewed by many as one of the most dangerous areas on Earth. (Mandelbaum 1998/99: 31). Some contend, however, that while potentially grave, the Taiwan situation shows signs of stability. Johnston identifies potential processes between China and Taiwan such as noncooperation and conflictual actions, as well as an escalation of 'malign reciprocation' (2003: 50), as indicators of an emerging security dilemma. The failure of this situation to so far occur should be grounds for guarded optimism. Currently the vast majority of Taiwanese citizens favour either unification with the Chinese mainland, or maintenance of the present status-quo (Chang and Wang 2005: 42). This, combined with an improvement in cross-straight relations and institutional cooperation since the 2008 electoral victory of the Kuomintang Party in Taiwan (Bitzinger and Desker 2008: pg106), should provide additional hope among proponents of peace. Lastly, given that Taiwan's naval power is still technologically superior to China's, it is predicted that even without direct U.S. assistance, were diplomacy to collapse, China would be unable to invade Taiwan for at least ten years, *if not considerably longer* (O'Hanlon 2000: 53, my emphasis). These factors, when viewed in concert, suggest a high probability for future peaceful negotiations of the Taiwan situation, despite the strengthening of China.

This essay has sought to challenge the claim that a rising China poses a significant threat to international security. The relatively sudden propulsion of China to great power status, through the exponential growth of both its military and economy, has generated considerable anxiety among numerous states. Some contend that as China grows, its contestation with the U.S. for hegemon status may escalate into large-scale warfare. These concerns, however, seem less credible when a realistic comparison of China and the U.S. is undertaken. While the accelerated growth of China's GDP is indeed enviable, current problems concerning its wealth disparity has the potential to cripple further developments. Additionally, while China and the U.S. are approaching overall economic parity, a huge military asymmetry remains. This will almost certainly inhibit more severe forms of bellicosity from China as it continues to strengthen. Those who fear an emerging Cold War between the U.S. and China consistently fail to comprehend how vastly different the structure of the Chinese state is to that of the former Soviet Union.

While the U.S.S.R was largely defined by its confrontational foreign policy and economic isolationism, contemporary China presents an inversion of this grand strategy. By prioritising domestic issues over expansionist foreign policy, as well as a direct economic engagement with the global community, China has forged strong and lasting financial links with other powerful states, which should prevent an escalation of any emerging hostilities. Despite continued concerns over China's regional ambitions, the strength of the U.S.'s alliance system within East Asia, seems likely to pressure China's acceptance of the regional status-quo for some time to come. Lastly, given the potential for a rapid and irreversible acceleration into a large-scale conflict, the situation involving Taiwan's status does constitute a credible threat to international security. However, given the apparent lack of will from either China, Taiwan, or the U.S. to disrupt the political equilibrium, coupled with indicators that suggest China is not seeking overall regional revisionism, the risk to international security seems manageable. While uncertainties regarding the future of China are legion, the peaceful integration into the international order of a strengthening and influential China is entirely possible. Through interaction and increased inter-dependence, the peaceful rise of China can be assured.

5

Is China Becoming the World's Most Likeable Superpower?

Public diplomacy is perception. Remarkably—and, unthinkably, as recently as one year ago—today China seems to be the world's most likeable superpower.

Compare Donald Trump's recent visit to Europe with that of Premier Li Keqiang, China's second-in-command. Li, who landed in Berlin on Wednesday, hoped to use his three-day trip, with stops in Germany and Belgium, to "voice support for an open economy, free trade and investment [and] global regional peace and stability," according to China's state news wire Xinhua. Trump, on the other hand, failed to support NATO, decried Germany as "very bad" for its trade policies, and even seemingly pushed aside Montenegro's prime minister to barrel his way to the front of a group photo. On Thursday, Li reaffirmed China's support for the Paris Agreement, stating that there is an "international responsibility" to fight climate change. Later on Thursday, Trump announced the United States would exit the landmark climate-change treaty. In that speech, Trump reaffirmed his commitment to his "America First," policy, while Li, in his meetings and speeches in Europe, successfully painted China as a liberal, responsible, globalist power.

Yet in this case, perception is not reality. China is an illiberal, authoritarian nation, run by the Communist Party for the last 68 years. The United States, for all its faults, is a far more natural partner for most of the world's countries. It's a stable, multiparty democracy with a healthy, developed system of alliances, decades of experience in global intervention, and a proud tradition of defending both human rights (in words, if not always in action) and free trade. China is none of these things. But because of Trump's shambolic presidency, a series of disastrous foreign-policy decisions, and Beijing's concerted push to peel away U.S. allies, it currently seems to be winning the global battle for hearts and minds.

China, over the last decade or so, has been prioritizing bilateral and multilateral relations, rather than alliances. Until the Trump presidency came along, that seemed like an obtuse strategy (though better than its decades-long isolationist foreign policy). Why would countries favor a subordinate relationship with Beijing when Washington granted them group security, international recognition, and favorable trade policies? In other words, how could countries like South Korea or Australia—or even, if current trends continue, Germany or France—possibly imagine that their relationships with Beijing, and not Washington, better served their interests?

Since last November, however, America and China's respective strategies and realities have shifted. Some of Trump's statements, like his inauguration address("from this moment on, it's going to be America first") and actions have alienated American allies. And his four months of bungling foreign policy—from his rude and disastrous late-January call with Australia's prime minister to his contentious Europe trip, to his abdication of global responsibility in exiting from the Paris Accords—have worried them.

The result, intentional or otherwise, is that allies and friendly nations have begun to at least think about the alternatives. Consider German Chancellor Angela Merkel's response to Trump's Europe trip. The continent should "take our fate into our own hands," she said on Sunday, adding, "the times in which we could completely depend on others are on the way out." After emphasizing that China "has become a a more important and strategic partner" in a meeting with Li on Thursday, she said "we are living in times of global uncertainty and see our responsibility to expand our partnership in all the different areas and to push for a world order based on law." Merkel's remarks not only indirectly rebuked Trump, but expressed a hope that China would shoulder some of the international responsibility America now seems to be yielding. Consider also the new president of South Korea's surprisingly lukewarm messages towards Trump, and the debatein Australia about moving away from the United States. "Self-reliance and helping ourselves should be the keynote of our foreign policy," Australia's former Prime Minister Paul Keating said in April.

Beijing is providing frameworks for all these nations to plug into a Chinese world order. The most prominent is "One Belt, One Road," Chinese President Xi Jinping's signature trade initiative, which seeks to recreate the old Silk Road trading routes, with China once again at the center of the world's economy. A May forum in Beijing on the initiative gathered Russian President Vladimir Putin, among other leaders, and officials from over three dozen countries, including the United States. China is also increasing its influence over existing frameworks like the United Nations, where it is now the second-largest contributor to the body's peacekeeping budget, and even via the privately held World Economic Forum annual conference in Davos, Switzerland, this January, where Xi portrayed himselfas the patron saint of globalization.

In some prominent cases, the choice by allied or friendly nations to distance themselves from the United States does not necessarily mean they are moving closer to China. Some, including Japan, India, and Germany, are also seeking to diversify their foreign policies. For example, in an endurance test of high-level diplomacy, Merkel managed to host Indian Prime Minister Narendra Modi between Trump and Li's visits. And yet, this trend still benefits China, where many leading strategic thinkers fear that America's alliances seek to contain China, similar to the U.S. Cold-War strategy towards the Soviet Union.

Beijing is not only accepting warmer greetings from nations that feel spurned by the United States; it is actively trying to coerce America's allies to distance themselves from China to assert its power. The prime example is South Korea: After Seoul decided earlier this year to deploy the THAAD anti-missile system, which Beijing fears could shoot down Chinese missiles, but which primarily serve to curtail North Korean aggression, Beijing retaliated economically. It reducedtourism between the two nations, and some South Korean businesses have faced boycotts in China.

In Asia, "we're seeing a region that's equally afraid of being subject to Chinese retaliation as a region fleeing from Donald Trump," Ely Ratner, a former deputy national security advisor to Joe Biden who's now at the Council on Foreign Relations, told me. "I wouldn't underestimate the former."

Beijing wants South Korea to remove THAAD. But it doesn't want Seoul as an ally. Why? Because the world's second-largest economy, and a nation that may dominate the 21st century, has no allies. Chinese diplomats and scholars don't even regard North Korea and Pakistan, two neighboring nations with which it has maintained historically warm relations, as allies. Part of this has to do with timing. "By the time China became a more prominent diplomatic player in the late 1990s and early 2000s, the countries who most desired it were a pretty unsavory bunch: Venezuela, Iran, Burma, Zimbabwe, Sudan," Ratner said. That's not to say China today is diplomatically isolated—far from it. Today, China has mostly shaken its reputation as a coddler of pariah states: Throughout the global financial crisis, Beijing seemed to realize it had more to gain by further integrating itself with the international order, leading to its expanding global influence.

Yes, several eventualities could reverse this trend. Trump's presidency, like the lives of prehistoric men, could be nasty, brutish, but also short. A more engaged America could soothe the damage Trump wrought to American alliances. Xi could decide China needs to manage its domestic issues first, and retreat diplomatically. Or perhaps he could overextend, and alienate friendly countries with unreasonable demands. Beijing could face an economic crisis, or, scarier to the Communist Party, a political one, potentially relieving it of control of China, or forcing it to share power—all possibilities that would distract from the extension of China's power.

In a June 2012 conversation, a high-ranking Chinese diplomat told me Beijing doesn't believe in alliances. Rather, it sees relationships, including with the United States, in bilateral terms. The diplomat said two countries are like neighbors. As Beijing's plants keeps growing—China now has legitimate political and economic interests and entanglements in almost every country in the world—Washington should recognize that new reality and gracefully yield, the diplomat told me.

Five years on, Trump is yielding—neither gracefully, nor altogether intentionally.

THE TRADE IMPLICATIONS OF CHINA'S EMERGENCE

China's economic development has hardly been mono-dimensional. It is not simply a creation of Western capitalists seeking to outsource labour to the lowest bidder; nor is China any longer simply a manufacturing centre of cheap plastic and simple electronic products. Chinese industry has moved rapidly up the production chain and is now producing a very large share of the world's office equipment, DVD players, digital cameras, personal computers as well as clothing and shoes and other simpler manufactured goods.

China's swift development has rerouted global supply chains forged over the last thirty years. It now runs large trade deficits with Eastern Asia while enjoying inexorably expanding trade surpluses with North America and Europe. It has become a trading nation par excellence and currently generates 70% of its national income through foreign trade. China's overall share of world trade has increased from 5% in 2000 to 10% today. (Rossi)

China is also exerting trade pressures on a range of developing and transition countries with which it is directly competing. Mexico and Turkey, for example, are losing market share in textiles to the Chinese without the kind of offsetting compensation that has proven so beneficial to much of Asia.

Central and Eastern Europe now find themselves engaged in a global battle to win new investments. Hungary won important investments for basic assembly manufacturing in the mid-1990s; yet some of those plants have subsequently relocated to China. The Hungarians now recognize that in the face of serious Chinese competition, their best option is to move into ever more sophisticated production if they are to flourish in the emerging global division of labour (Visit to Budapest 2004, NATO PA Secretariat Report).

The net effect of China's rapid growth on the global economy has been highly positive, despite the inevitable dislocation suffered in certain sectors. Its booming economy is generating wealth worldwide. Those benefits accrue through countless channels. Yet, mercantilists and protectionists falsely argue that rising Chinese imports are invariably a bad thing and are simply sparking plant closures and job losses.

Trade economists counter that this is a misleading and partial economic interpretation of what transpires when a large country undergoes economic take-off and emerges as a major global commercial player. First of all, trading with that low cost producer invariably lowers prices for consumers as well as producers, who, as a result, are able to purchase lower cost capital goods. Price falls, in turn, check inflationary pressures in the importing economy, raise consumer welfare, and lower exporters' production costs. The resulting productivity gains help certain domestic industries win market share both domestically and internationally while rewarding workers employed in those sectors. It must also be noted that non-Chinese companies are currently generating over half of China's export earnings and 60% of import revenue. In 2000 alone, U.S corporate earnings generated in China reached $7.2 billion. (Hale and Hale) Western firms are also selling value added inputs to Chinese producers and are thus benefiting from China's place in the international division of labour. These are the winners in the game.

The losers are both the producers of import competing industries that cannot match the price/quality of imported Chinese goods and workers in those industries. Yet, those domestic import competing firms that manage to compete are likely to emerge even stronger. Most empirical work on the broad effects of expanding trade suggests that the gains of the winners in open trading systems significantly outweigh the losses of those suffering from new competition. In this process, moreover, trading countries are likely to grow more specialized in their production, leading to further productivity gains and wealth generation.

Empirical evidence tends to confirm that precisely such processes are at work in those developed and developing countries with growing trade links to China. The Economist recently estimated that if China continues to develop, and if parts of the developing world respond to its competitive challenge by adopting liberal commercial policies, the developed world could enjoy an additional 1% of growth a year, while the developing world would undergo a substantially larger rate of growth despite the dislocation which some economies would obviously undergo. (The Economist, October 2, 2004) The capacity of a single non-oil exporting developing country to have such a broad global economic impact represents an undeniable revolution in international financial and trading systems. As suggested above, it is an economic shift laden with political, diplomatic and strategic significance. Yet, in order to capture the potential gains, Western governments must ensure their economies are ever more agile and flexible. They should increase their respective capacities to shift both capital and labour into those sectors in which they are most competitive and out of those in which they are least productive.

The McKinsey Global Institute recently examined the fate of western workers who lost jobs because of firms moving production facilities to China or India. According to this study,

70% of such American workers find new work within six months, while in Germany only 40% do. This suggests that labour market rigidities can gravely complicate efforts to adapt to changing international market conditions. China is also having a strong effect on global demand. While many casual observers see its most substantial economic impact largely in terms of its enormous exports, China is also a large and growing capital and consumer goods market. It is estimated that if current growth and income distribution were sustained until 2020, China would offer the world 100 million consumers with an average income equivalent to the current income average of Western Europe. (The Economist, October 2, 2004.) Already it has almost single-handedly revived the previously flagging economies of East Asia through high demand for a range of manufacturing inputs, high technology components and consumer goods. Australia - like a range of other commodity exporters - is enjoying a veritable economic boom thanks to burgeoning Chinese demand.

China's imports are growing at a very rapid rate - 40% in 2003 alone. Since 2001, it has accounted for one third of the increase in global import volume. China is the world's third largest importer, and in 2004 accounted for 17% of Japan's exports, 16% of the European Union's, 8.5% of the United States', 38.5% of the rest of Asia's, and 20% for the rest of the World. (Rossi) It is now Japan's leading trade partner and the second largest trade partner of the European Union behind only the United States. EU-China Trade doubled between 1999 and 2003. (Eurostat, 14/6/2004, Kihara and Takeuchi) China is also providing an important market for developing countries; 45% of China's $400 billion in annual imports comes from developing countries, and these rose by $55 billion in 2003. It is, in fact, running a significant trade deficit with the developing world. (Kharas) Some optimistic forecasts suggest that if China continues down the reform path it could be the world's largest exporter and importer within ten years. The US trade with China deficit has reached the enormous sum of $162 billion. (Teather) Yet, imports from China do not explain the explosive growth of the US current account deficit, now at 7% of GDP and rising, partly because China has, in fact, simply replaced other suppliers to the US market. In 1988, for example, only 2% of US shoe imports came from China, while 60% came from Taiwan and South Korea.

Today China has 70% of the US shoe import market, having all but displaced South Korea and Taiwan from the US market, although the Koreans and Taiwanese effectively own many of the Chinese plants selling to the United States.

Many of Taiwan's electronics companies have also relocated to the Chinese mainland and are playing a pivotal role in China's electronics exports to the United States. By the end of 2003, China's deficit with Taiwan stood at $31.5 billion; $13.1 billion with South Korea; $7.6 billion with ASEAN; $5 billion with Japan; and $1.3 billion with Australia. (Hale and Hale) A similar trend can be traced in other goods markets including personal computers. While Asian countries are losing market share in the United States to China, they are being compensated by a massive increase in exports to China in higher end and more valuable products.

The Chinese economy is far more open than the Korean or Japanese economies were at similar points in their economic take-off, and the state seems to have rejected the more dirigiste model of development employed by the Japanese. China's general tariff rates have fallen precipitously from 40% in the early 1990s to 10.4% in 2004. (Beattie) It entered the WTO under highly stringent conditions that have helped to open its market even further. In 2004, exports and imports together accounted for nearly 75% of China's total GDP. This is an extraordinarily high share for such a large country, and more than double that of the United States. Part of the reason is that China's domestic non-tradable economy remains very underdeveloped.

China has also implemented exceedingly open investment rules, although foreign investors still complain about serious administrative burdens and creeping non-tariff barriers in areas like financial services and investment rules. Still, foreign investment in China accounts for some 35% of its GDP. (The Economist, October 2, 2004) It is now the world's fifth largest recipient of foreign direct investment (FDI) and is moving quickly up the list. FDI in the first ten months of 2004 reached $54 billion. These funds are fundamentally transforming China's manufacturing and transport infrastructure.

CHINA 2020: LOOKING TOWARD CHINA'S ECONOMIC FUTURE

The second presenter focused on the future of Chinese economic growth and its implications for internal domestic stability. First, he offered three basic scenarios for China—one in which China will become the world's second largest economy by the year 2020, another in which China experiences a slowdown over the next two decades, which in turns causes a loss of legitimacy for the CCP and possibly leads to disorder, and finally a scenario of economic stagnation.

The presenter noted that the high-growth scenario that is often touted in the popular press is probably not realistic; if it were likely, China's gross domestic product (GDP) would have to reach $11.2 trillion in the year 2020 (compared with the U.S. at $15.4 trillion and Japan at $9.4 trillion).

Four major factors are barriers to high economic growth in China. First, there is the problem of low productivity growth. The presenter asserted that China's productivity growth is much less than is commonly believed and that it is difficult to convert China's high savings rate into useful capital that can then fuel additional productivity. Secondly, there is the problem of "animosity, bureaucracy and corruption".

Animosity refers to growing internal ethnic cleavages in China—such as the Uyghur separatist movement in China's western region. The impediment that bureaucracy presents is related to the "local-central" divide that persists between local governments and Beijing. Local governments often pursue policies that circumvent national directives. Corruption makes the problem worse. China is increasingly recognized as one of the most corrupt countries in the world.

A third factor is reliance on exports to fuel economic growth. Much of the enthusiasm about China's economic growth is rooted in the fact that exports have played such a prominent role. From 1987 to 1995, the real rate of Chinese export growth was 18.1% a year, which was significantly higher than the overall growth of the economy. Yet continued export growth at this rate is not realistic.

If China's exports to the United States, for example, were to continue at their present growth rate, they would constitute almost 80% of U.S. imports and the U.S. would likely have a trade deficit of 48% of GDP, an unlikely scenario. A similar dilemma involves foreign direct investment (FDI). Since 1980, foreign investment in China has grown at a rate of 35% a year; in 1995, moreover, foreign direct investment totaled about $35 billion. However, current evidence suggests that this trend is reversing.

Investors are realizing that China is not as profitable as they once believed. Moreover, continued FDI at past rates is not realistic: "With 35% annual growth, China's receipts of foreign capital will exceed all of Japan's foreign investment in two years and in ten years China would have to receive all of the international capital invested in the whole world."

Other constraints to economic growth in China include energy demand and environmental degradation. Regarding energy, China is already the world's largest energy consumer in the world, consuming 850 million metric tons of oil equivalent. China's energy demand is expected to jump significantly over the next 25 years. To satisfy its growing energy needs, China will most likely increase its dependence on imported energy.

In fact, China will likely become the world's largest energy importer by 2010, with most imports coming from the Persian Gulf and Siberian Russia. Growing energy demand and consumption portends massive environmental consequences. Roughly 300,000 Chinese citizens in urban areas annually suffer premature deaths due to outdoor or indoor pollution.

If environmental standards continued to be ignored by Beijing, the "cumulative effect of deteriorating air and water quality will sharply reduce both the country's productive capacity and the living standards of the Chinese people."

Overall, the presenter proposed three scenarios for the future of Chinese economic growth: the "medium growth" scenario, the "low growth" scenario, and the "economic stagnation" scenario. The presenter argued that the "low growth" scenario was the most likely. Under this scenario, China's real growth would average about 4% a year and by 2020 China's GDP would likely total about $2.6 trillion. This GDP would make China the fifth largest economy, placing it squarely between Korea ($3.2 trillion) and France ($2.4 trillion).

The presenter noted that if the "low growth" scenario actually takes place, it could be devastating for the Chinese Communist Party which, as a substitute for its loss of ideological legitimacy, has maintained a bargain with the Chinese people "to deliver the goods." If the CCP is not able to improve the material welfare of the Chinese people, it will likely face opposition to its rule—most likely from provincial governments—and this could in turn lead to political instability.

The People's Liberation Army: Social and Political Implications of Restructuring

Most of the analysts who follow the People's Liberation Army (PLA) focus on China's military purchases from Russia and the PLA's threat to Taiwan while ignoring the volatility of the internal security problem in China. Members of the PLA are facing the same economic difficulties that other segments of the Chinese population are facing. The demographics of an aging population leave a smaller manpower pool available for military service, a problem exacerbated by the one-child policy. If the government cannot provide the expected social and health safety net for the elderly, leaving the burden on families, the incentive for a young person to serve in the military is lower.

Military pay is barely sufficient to sustain the soldier, let alone a family, and military service takes the child away from the family. Because pay is so low in the security organs of China, whether it be the PLA, People's Armed Police (PAP), or the Public Security Bureau, the incentive to engage in corruption is quite high. In short the leadership cannot isolate the members of its security organs from some of the same problems caused by economic re-structuring that members of the population at large are facing.

If any of the difficulties mentioned earlier grow to the point where the intervention of any of China's security branches is required, the loyalty of those branches in a crisis may be suspect.

Low pay and outside opportunities have created both recruiting and retention problems for the PAP and the PLA. If a family member leaves the farm, he or she tends to migrate to the urban labor market and thereby avoids military or paramilitary service.

The disincentives to join the military and the incentives to avoid conscription are higher now than they ever have been in China for four reasons.

- With the high losses incurred against the attack on Vietnam, it became clear that it was dangerous to send a child into military service.
- Sending a son or daughter into military service is a poor economic choice.
- Due to the actions of the PLA in 1989, entering the military is a distasteful political option.
- As the Party slowly loses its mantle of legitimacy, doing anything for the Party or state organs of power increasingly becomes a meaningless political choice.

The degree of loyalty to the party within the PAP may be more highly suspect than that of the PLA. Following basic training, PAP troops are generally not isolated from the general population as are the troops of the PLA. Because they are not confined to the barracks, they have opportunities to mingle with the populace. They generally enjoy close relationships with the local families and children where they work. Generally speaking, because of this familiarity, the PAP was reluctant or failed to use force against the population in Beijing in 1989.

That is why the PLA was tapped to restore order. To avoid using the PLA in the future, the Central Military Commission has increased the numbers of the PAP by converting whole divisions of the PLA to the PAP.

Thus the Party's leadership hopes that if it again becomes necessary to suppress large segments of the total population, they can depend on the new PAP units.

In addition to suspect loyalty, there is another internal security problem looming in the background. The PLA has demobilized thousands of soldiers who have received basic military training. Moreover, workers in the countryside and in the cities have either served in the military or have received militia training. China now has a large group of people who know how to use violence and manage force in an organized way.

Many people in this large pool are disgruntled due to the economic and social problems mentioned earlier. The problem is further compounded by the previously mentioned state of affairs in the SOEs. The potential for labor unrest in the SOEs is high. The one million-plus officers and soldiers in the reserve forces of the PLA are primarily located in the state or collectively owned enterprises of one form or another. The presenter ended this session with the following questions:

"In the past, the CCP has always been able to call on the PLA to suppress unrest when it was ordered to do so. And in the near term, it can probably count on the PLA again.

But if the PLA faces parts of the PAP and its own reserve divisions, will it act resolutely? Or will things devolve into a general breakdown of the government? This is the dilemma that China's leaders face, and they are riding a tiger they are having difficulty controlling as they liberalize the economy."

Conclusion

Throughout the seminar, two themes remained constant: Because China faces so many internal problems and many nations in the region have experience in managing similar problems, there is ample opportunity for other countries to share their expertise with China. Such cooperation may create an atmosphere that could be extended to more sensitive realms of security as nuclear non-proliferation and border disputes. Secondly, all participants agreed that China is still far away from a Soviet style collapse; however, should China be unable to solve one or more of the many challenges it faces, the result will be some decrease in the internal stability of China. Restructuring the economy has created a degree of fragmentation in China.

Fragmentation can be a destabilizing factor for any regime. The leadership will react but how? Will it become more strict or perhaps even more intolerant of opposition? Will it divert attention away from internal problems by whipping up an already nascent nationalism? The very scale of China (large population, geographic size and location, etc.) implies that any degree of instability in China will likely affect the region as a whole. Hence there is even more incentive for China's neighbors to work with China on cooperative solutions to the challenges that China faces.

CHINA TARGETS MORE GROWTH—AND EVEN MORE XI JINPING

China's government laid out plans to keep economic growth steady this year, as nearly 3,000 lawmakers gathered in the capital with the heftier mandate of entrenching President Xi Jinping's dominance over the nation. Opening the annual session of China's legislature on Monday, Premier Li Keqiang spoke of Beijing's resolve to control debt growth, revamp the country's bloated state sector and open its markets wider for foreign capital, but didn't signal any major shift in tactics.

Calling the tasks of economic and social development "formidable," Mr. Li set a target for economic growth for 2018 at "about 6.5%," a slight recalibration from last year's objective of "around 6.5% or higher if possible."

China's actual growth rate came in at 6.9% in 2017, buoyed by global demand and aggressive government efforts to keep the economy stable. Economists have projected China's economic expansion to moderate to 6.5% this year, as the government continues to rein in risky lending practices and trade tensions with the U.S. rise.

Mr. Li didn't announce any significant new initiatives and the stay-the-course tone of his report signaled that the focus of this year's congress lies elsewhere. On Sunday, lawmakers are due to approve constitutional changes that scrap presidential term limits, allowing President Xi to stay in power indefinitely, and entrench the Communist Party's leading role in governing China.

The National People's Congress will also fill senior government posts—with Xi allies likely to benefit—and review plans to overhaul the government bureaucracy that would give the party greater authority over decision-making, a key step in Mr. Xi's plans to install himself at the center of Chinese political power.

In a policy blueprint Mr. Xi unveiled at a Communist Party congress last October, he demanded greater loyalty and commitment from his 89 million party members as a way of cutting through graft and bureaucratic inertia that has hampered his policy agenda.

In his speech, Premier Li suggested challenges from rising global protectionism but didn't mention the threats of new trade sanctions from the U.S. Senior Chinese officials have mounted a big diplomatic offensive in the past month to seek to fend off such actions. Even so, President Donald Trump has announced plans for new steel and aluminum tariffs and White House officials are preparing broad trade and investment penalties against China.

"Protectionism is mounting and geopolitical risks are on the ascent," Mr. Li said. He pledged to step up efforts to invite in foreign capital and promised tax deferrals for profits reinvested in China. Western officials and industrial executives have largely treated such promises by Beijing with skepticism, pointing to a lack of implementation of them in practice.

Beijing's messages about its resolve to shift to higher-quality growth appeared mixed. Citing the good turn in the economy last year, Mr. Li's report projected a fiscal deficit of 2.6% of economic output, lower than last year's target of 3%. It highlighted the need to rein in rampant borrowing by local governments and eliminated a goal for fixed-assets investment.

At the same time, however, the report reiterated that the government needed to be "proactive," a signal it may step up state investment, and didn't single out debt reduction as an objective. Instead, the report calls for "reasonable" credit expansion in 2018 and said China's overall debt levels will remain "basically steady."

Since late last year, the leadership has softened the goal to deleverage into a mission to control the rise of debt and defuse potential risks. The shift indicates a growing realization of how hard it is to reduce debt without significantly dragging down growth.

The government also reported Monday that China's defense budget will grow by 8.1% this year to 1.11 trillion yuan ($175 billion), up from 7% in 2017 and reversing three years of slowing growth in planned military spending.

Under Mr. Xi, China has been pursuing sweeping military overhauls aimed at creating a modern fighting force capable of defending its expanding global interests. A congress spokesman said Sunday that Beijing's military spending remained low relative to other major countries, when compared as a share of economic output, national fiscal spending, and on a per capita basis.

Meanwhile, Mr. Li said China will continue to reduce excessive industrial overcapacity, slightly lowering targets for cuts in steel-production capacity to 30 million tons. China exceeded its goal for steel cuts last year by eliminating more than 50 million tons in capacity, official data show. Mr. Li said targeted coal-capacity cuts this year were unchanged at 150 million tons. In his speech, the premier also talked up Mr. Xi's Made in China 2025 plan aimed at upgrading the nation's manufacturing capabilities. Many U.S. and other Western officials have expressed concerns over the policy, saying it encourages the government to further subsidize state firms and drive Chinese companies to force technology transfers from their foreign partners.

In his talks with U.S. officials in Washington the past week, Liu He, the top economic adviser to Mr. Xi, played down the importance of this plan in fostering Chinese growth, according to individuals with knowledge of the events.

The push-and-pull over economic policy exposes divisions within the government, according to China watchers. In the past five years, Mr. Xi has consolidated decision-making, including that involving the economy. His trusted adviser, Mr. Liu, is expected to be named as a vice premier in charge of a wide swath of the economy during the legislative session.

In his remarks Monday, Mr. Li also sought to make a stronger point about making China a country of innovators than he had in the past several years.

"China is home to the biggest pool of human resources and talent in the world," he said. "We will provide services that tick every box for inventors, innovators and entrepreneurs."

XI CALLS FOR DEEPENED MILITARY-CIVILIAN INTEGRATION

President Xi Jinping Monday stressed practical efforts to further deepen military-civilian integration to provide impetus and support for realizing the Chinese dream and the goal to build a strong military.

Xi, also general secretary of the Communist Party of China (CPC) Central Committee and chairman of the Central Military Commission, made the remarks when attending a plenary meeting of the delegation of People's Liberation Army (PLA) and armed police at the ongoing session of the 13th National People's Congress, the national legislature.

"Implementing the strategy of military-civilian integration is a prerequisite for building integrated national strategies and strategic capabilities and for realizing the Party's goal of building a strong military in the new era," Xi said.

He called for efforts to promote military development featuring higher quality, efficiency, and scientific and technological levels.

Highlighting coordinated sci-tech innovation in key areas between the military and civilian sectors, Xi asked related parties to promote integrated reasoning and implementation on key sci-tech projects and race to occupy the strategic high ground in terms of sci-tech innovation.

China has achieved a revolutionary restructuring of the military organization and services amid deepened reform on national defense and the armed forces since the 18th CPC National Congress in late 2012, Xi said.

Xi said efforts should be made to speed up the establishment of a modern military policy system. He ordered the military to firmly support the Party and the country's institutional reform and ensure reform tasks concerning both the military and civilian sectors well implemented.

He said efforts to build the system of rule of law in Chinese military should be strengthened. Xi asked every member of the armed forces to uphold the Constitution, and be its loyal supporter, active follower, and firm defender. He said Party committees and governments at all levels should do more to support the cause of defense and military advancement, while the armed forces should render their service to economic and social development.

CHINA 2020: LOOKING TOWARD CHINA'S ECONOMIC FUTURE

The second presenter focused on the future of Chinese economic growth and its implications for internal domestic stability. First, he offered three basic scenarios for China—one in which China will become the world's second largest economy by the year 2020, another in which China experiences a slowdown over the next two decades, which in turns causes a loss of legitimacy for the CCP and possibly leads to disorder, and finally a scenario of economic stagnation.

The presenter noted that the high-growth scenario that is often touted in the popular press is probably not realistic; if it were likely, China's gross domestic product (GDP) would have to reach $11.2 trillion in the year 2020 (compared with the U.S. at $15.4 trillion and Japan at $9.4 trillion).

Four major factors are barriers to high economic growth in China. First, there is the problem of low productivity growth. The presenter asserted that China's productivity growth is much less than is commonly believed and that it is difficult to convert China's high savings rate into useful capital that can then fuel additional productivity. Secondly, there is the problem of "animosity, bureaucracy and corruption".

Animosity refers to growing internal ethnic cleavages in China—such as the Uyghur separatist movement in China's western region. The impediment that bureaucracy presents is related to the "local-central" divide that persists between local governments and Beijing. Local governments often pursue policies that circumvent national directives. Corruption makes the problem worse. China is increasingly recognized as one of the most corrupt countries in the world.

A third factor is reliance on exports to fuel economic growth. Much of the enthusiasm about China's economic growth is rooted in the fact that exports have played such a prominent role. From 1987 to 1995, the real rate of Chinese export growth was 18.1% a year, which was significantly higher than the overall growth of the economy. Yet continued export growth at this rate is not realistic.

If China's exports to the United States, for example, were to continue at their present growth rate, they would constitute almost 80% of U.S. imports and the U.S. would likely have a trade deficit of 48% of GDP, an unlikely scenario. A similar dilemma involves foreign direct investment (FDI). Since 1980, foreign investment in China has grown at a rate of 35% a year; in 1995, moreover, foreign direct investment totaled about $35 billion. However, current evidence suggests that this trend is reversing. Investors are realizing that China is not as profitable as they once believed. Moreover, continued FDI at past rates is not realistic: "With 35% annual growth, China's receipts of foreign capital will exceed all of Japan's foreign investment in two years and in ten years China would have to receive all of the international capital invested in the whole world."

Other constraints to economic growth in China include energy demand and environmental degradation. Regarding energy, China is already the world's largest energy consumer in the world, consuming 850 million metric tons of oil equivalent. China's energy demand is expected to jump significantly over the next 25 years. To satisfy its growing energy needs, China will most likely increase its dependence on imported energy.

In fact, China will likely become the world's largest energy importer by 2010, with most imports coming from the Persian Gulf and Siberian Russia. Growing energy demand and consumption portends massive environmental consequences. Roughly 300,000 Chinese citizens in urban areas annually suffer premature deaths due to outdoor or indoor pollution.

If environmental standards continued to be ignored by Beijing, the "cumulative effect of deteriorating air and water quality will sharply reduce both the country's productive capacity and the living standards of the Chinese people."

Overall, the presenter proposed three scenarios for the future of Chinese economic growth: the "medium growth" scenario, the "low growth" scenario, and the "economic stagnation" scenario. The presenter argued that the "low growth" scenario was the most likely. Under this scenario, China's real growth would average about 4% a year and by 2020 China's GDP would likely total about $2.6 trillion. This GDP would make China the fifth largest economy, placing it squarely between Korea ($3.2 trillion) and France ($2.4 trillion).

The presenter noted that if the "low growth" scenario actually takes place, it could be devastating for the Chinese Communist Party which, as a substitute for its loss of ideological legitimacy, has maintained a bargain with the Chinese people "to deliver the goods." If the CCP is not able to improve the material welfare of the Chinese people, it will likely face opposition to its rule—most likely from provincial governments—and this could in turn lead to political instability.

The People's Liberation Army: Social and Political Implications of Restructuring

Most of the analysts who follow the People's Liberation Army (PLA) focus on China's military purchases from Russia and the PLA's threat to Taiwan while ignoring the volatility of the internal security problem in China. Members of the PLA are facing the same economic difficulties that other segments of the Chinese population are facing. The demographics of an aging population leave a smaller manpower pool available for military service, a problem exacerbated by the one-child policy. If the government cannot provide the expected social and health safety net for the elderly, leaving the burden on families, the incentive for a young person to serve in the military is lower.

Military pay is barely sufficient to sustain the soldier, let alone a family, and military service takes the child away from the family. Because pay is so low in the security organs of China, whether it be the PLA, People's Armed Police (PAP), or the Public Security Bureau, the incentive to engage in corruption is quite high. In short the leadership cannot isolate the members of its security organs from some of the same problems caused by economic re-structuring that members of the population at large are facing.

If any of the difficulties mentioned earlier grow to the point where the intervention of any of China's security branches is required, the loyalty of those branches in a crisis may be suspect.

Low pay and outside opportunities have created both recruiting and retention problems for the PAP and the PLA. If a family member leaves the farm, he or she tends to migrate to the urban labor market and thereby avoids military or paramilitary service.

The disincentives to join the military and the incentives to avoid conscription are higher now than they ever have been in China for four reasons.

- With the high losses incurred against the attack on Vietnam, it became clear that it was dangerous to send a child into military service.
- Sending a son or daughter into military service is a poor economic choice.
- Due to the actions of the PLA in 1989, entering the military is a distasteful political option.
- As the Party slowly loses its mantle of legitimacy, doing anything for the Party or state organs of power increasingly becomes a meaningless political choice.

The degree of loyalty to the party within the PAP may be more highly suspect than that of the PLA. Following basic training, PAP troops are generally not isolated from the general population as are the troops of the PLA. Because they are not confined to the barracks, they have opportunities to mingle with the populace. They generally enjoy close relationships with the local families and children where they work. Generally speaking, because of this familiarity, the PAP was reluctant or failed to use force against the population in Beijing in 1989. That is why the PLA was tapped to restore order. To avoid using the PLA in the future, the Central Military Commission has increased the numbers of the PAP by converting whole divisions of the PLA to the PAP.

Thus the Party's leadership hopes that if it again becomes necessary to suppress large segments of the total population, they can depend on the new PAP units.

In addition to suspect loyalty, there is another internal security problem looming in the background. The PLA has demobilized thousands of soldiers who have received basic military training. Moreover, workers in the countryside and in the cities have either served in the military or have received militia training. China now has a large group of people who know how to use violence and manage force in an organized way.

Many people in this large pool are disgruntled due to the economic and social problems mentioned earlier. The problem is further compounded by the previously mentioned state of affairs in the SOEs. The potential for labor unrest in the SOEs is high. The one million-plus officers and soldiers in the reserve forces of the PLA are primarily located in the state or collectively owned enterprises of one form or another. The presenter ended this session with the following questions:

"In the past, the CCP has always been able to call on the PLA to suppress unrest when it was ordered to do so. And in the near term, it can probably count on the PLA again.

But if the PLA faces parts of the PAP and its own reserve divisions, will it act resolutely? Or will things devolve into a general breakdown of the government? This is the dilemma that China's leaders face, and they are riding a tiger they are having difficulty controlling as they liberalize the economy."

Conclusion

Throughout the seminar, two themes remained constant: Because China faces so many internal problems and many nations in the region have experience in managing similar problems, there is ample opportunity for other countries to share their expertise with China. Such cooperation may create an atmosphere that could be extended to more sensitive realms of security as nuclear non-proliferation and border disputes. Secondly, all participants agreed that China is still far away from a Soviet style collapse; however, should China be unable to solve one or more of the many challenges it faces, the result will be some decrease in the internal stability of China. Restructuring the economy has created a degree of fragmentation in China.

Fragmentation can be a destabilizing factor for any regime. The leadership will react but how? Will it become more strict or perhaps even more intolerant of opposition? Will it divert attention away from internal problems by whipping up an already nascent nationalism? The very scale of China (large population, geographic size and location, etc.) implies that any degree of instability in China will likely affect the region as a whole. Hence there is even more incentive for China's neighbors to work with China on cooperative solutions to the challenges that China faces.

CHINA'S IDENTITY: POWER POLITICS AND NEO-MERCANTILISM

It has to be said that, for the most part, the Chinese elite has managed to keep a low profile and assess China's capabilities and resources rather aptly throughout. Pragmatism reigns supreme, and there is ample cause for this. Despite the fact that China has made enormous progress in the 30 years since the launch of the economic reforms, developing into the world's leading trading power, it still does not score very highly in terms of GDP per capita. In addition, it is also increasingly faced with the fallout generated by the widening gap in levels of prosperity between different regions, urban and rural areas, the rich and poor. Finally, the ecological degradation of the land is spreading ever more rapidly. In view of these factors, Chinese leaders are steering a course where what is needed for the development at home defines the contours of foreign policy.

China's ambitions have to be limited. The current leadership can only maintain its position if it manages to resolve the many problems China faces within a reasonable timeframe. The economic engine must be kept running at all cost, an impossible feat without stable relations with its Asian neighbours and the global community. Beijing has a difficult time navigating between the two dimensions of China's identity. It is constantly involved in a tug-of-war between its "weak power identity" (developing country) and "strong power identity" (great power). It is why China's foreign policy appears so inconsistent at times. While Beijing's foreign policy rhetoric at present points in the direction of a China as responsible global power, there are countervailing pressures. As economic growth continues the need for energy and other strategic resources increases accordingly. Sustainable economic development in a peaceful way may be the final goal, but it cannot be realized without secured access to strategic resources and safe trading routes. Should these become endangered, the nation's wholesale development will be compromised, and consequently the outright survival of the regime would be in jeopardy. This is a tight corner to be in, a kind of self-reliance dilemma if you wish. In such condition it is only natural to put one's own pressing interests first whenever possible and to look for as many ways and places available to secure them. Like it or not, sovereignty and national core interests have to figure centre stage.

China is a "pandragon". It has a double identity, i.e. a "weak power identity" and a "strong power identity". At times, it considers itself a mere developing country that was wronged by the imperialists and is therefore entitled to a great degree of leniency and support. At other times, it sees itself as a great power that is well on its way to restoring the glory of the ancient empires and wants to be treated on an equal footing. That is why Beijing is so sensitive to be taken seriously and be treated as a peer. At the same time however, the Chinese still count on consideration from the other side, some special treatment. China although growing fast is still at a premature stage of development and has to overcome tremendous internal difficulties if it is to survive. Consequently, it cannot as yet take up the full scale of its international responsibilities. To cut a long story short: sustainable domestic economic development is the most pressing challenge; the evolution of China into a responsible global power is the long-term ambition.

On closer examination China's developmental model and asso-ciated economic strategy is neo-mercantilist. It anxiously works to maintain equilibrium between national sovereignty and international integration, particularly between integration in the global market and economic independence. Control by the state apparatus crucially acts as a counterweight to market forces. The state needs to ensure that the market operates, both at home and abroad, in a way that is entirely conducive to the expansion of Chinese influence and power across the globe. At the same time, the government must make sure that this whole process generates enough prosperity, which can then, after the necessary redistributive measures, guarantee social stability and cohesion. Direct domestic investments remain crucial for further economic development and in exchange, the domestic industry must play its part, whilst the government retains a finger in every pie. Ultimately, this entire process needs to be accelerated by a go-out policy that, again under the guidance of the state, should safeguard access to foreign outlets and strategic raw materials.

THE EU: RESHAPING THE POWER PARADIGM?

The EU's identity is rather distinct from that of China. It is often perceived to be a normative actor, founding its policies on values, institutions and cooperation rather than power politics. As such the EU constitutes an effort to reshape the power paradigm to reflect a new kind of power in global politics. As stated in its 2003 Security Strategy the EU aims at the "development of a stronger international society, well functioning international institutions and a rule based international order". The rules underpinning this new international order are to be founded on Europe's liberal political norms, its views of an open global market and its preference for highly institutionalized multilateralism.

Similarly, the relations with the emerging powers are largely constructed from the belief that the latter should adapt their international political norms to the European standards. Normative convergence is thus the starting point for developing relations with emerging countries.

Europe's policy towards China has to date been one of conditional cooperation. The EU is prepared to help the PRC, to invest in the development of the country, but in turn, China must meet a number of standards and demands. This is a rather unique way of dealing with a rising power. In contrast to the United States, Europe is not gearing up for a confrontation if needed. So-called "hard power" is hardly on the agenda. European nations are not taking up bases in Asia to curb Chinese influence in case this might be necessary. Power politics, based on military capabilities and threats with the use of force, seems to have disappeared from the diplomatic handbook all together. On the contrary, Europe wishes to forge a tighter link and strengthen its influence through ever-increasing economic interdependence and shared values. In this process, Europe sees itself as the model China should aspire to. EU policy is based on the belief that "human rights tend to be better understood and better protected in societies open to the free flow of trade, investment, people, and ideas. As China continues its policy of opening-up to the world, the EU will work to strengthen and encourage this trend."

British top diplomat Robert Cooper champions this approach in an often-quoted book, where, he talks about a post-modern security strategy with the emphasis firmly placed on values and international cooperation rather than hard power and control over territories. "Nationalism makes place for internationalism", he writes. "The final goal is the liberty for each individual."

The crucial question is to what extent this approach can be actually successful. Beijing has not put democracy and respect for human rights on top of its list of priorities. In terms of foreign policy, it is unrealistic to think Beijing will comply with Europe's "post-modern" discourse. If one, in accordance with Robert Cooper, distinguishes between "modern states" and "post-modern states", then China is to be categorized as a "modern state", for which "internationalism" is but one modus operandi serving the national interest. The PRC is therefore by no means at a point where it can meet the European expectations. Chinese officials, scholars and pundits all tend to indicate this when talking in private. It is crucial for the EU to be aware what power it has to sway policy in China. An important parameter in the EU's dealings with China will be the strategic weight Brussels will be capable of bringing to bear with Beijing. China perceives the EU foremost as an economic actor, far less as a political actor. One reason why Beijing for example wants the PCA negotiations to focus on trade and economic cooperation might be that it has doubts about the EU's capacity to deliver really in the political domain.

The EU should also be critical of its leverage as a normative actor. China may well recognize the advantages of cooperating with the EU and of learning from it in certain areas, but it is certainly not willing to accept the tutelage of the EU. China is not a prospective EU member, nor does it see itself as a weak nation, depending solely on the EU for support in its political and economic reform process. The most real incentive that the EU has to offer is access to its market. The EU's success with China will to a large extent rest on recognition of common interests, in areas such as the environment and energy, but also in trade and investment. The degree to which China's interests match those of the EU will determine the success of relationship.

As the constellation of world power is changing, the EU's strategy will have to change with it. Europeans must come to grips with the fact that "the West does not enjoy a predestined supremacy in international politics that is locked into the future for an indeterminate period of time. The Euro-Atlantic world had a long run of global dominance, but it is coming to an end." The future is more likely to be shaped by Asia and China in particular. China's mounting power and growing assertiveness poses a challenge to the EU's standing in the international order. The growing economic weight of Asia and China's reemergence is facing Europe with a process of de-centering. As David Kerr observes the "fact that most powers in Eurasia – and China foremost among them – are accumulating sovereignty or the means to stronger sovereignty, not sharing sovereignty as the European experience promotes, means that the European region remains quite exceptional in both its political dynamics and its strategic organization." Even if China will continue to defend its interests in a peaceful way, partially by nourishing its bilateral relations, partially by working via multilateral institutions, its growing capabilities ask the EU to adapt with regard to its policymaking capacity. In order to face common challenges with China and to fill the present strategic void, the EU needs to develop the capability to play a role of importance in the changing global environment. The

EU has to pool the fragmented capabilities of its member states into real levers for exerting influence if it is to be taken seriously as a strategic international actor by Beijing.

TOWARDS A PRAGMATIC RELATIONSHIP

The Sino-European partnership has been going through turbulent times in the past few years. As it stands, the partnership is not strategic, but it has vast strategic potential. The challenge will be to work out a pragmatic consensus on how to gradually turn joint strategic interests into more result-driven cooperation. Given the distinctive identities of China and the EU and their different development paths, this process will inevitably have to be commensurate with the two partners' internal transformation. After a period of difficulties over issues like Tibet, climate change and alleged economic protectionism, both sides are now figuring out how to best position themselves in the future. Beijing is executing an important review of its major relationships and one of the questions is where the EU will fit in. There is growing momentum for synergies with Washington, leading to speculation about a transpacific bargain. But in the multilayered multipolar world it will remain key for China to maintain good relations with the other powers too. For Europe, changes brought about by the Lisbon reform treaty may ultimately halt its descent into strategic redundancy and instigate the EU to assure protagonists like China that it has indeed the ambition to develop solid strategic partnerships.

The years ahead will thus be ones of relation therapy. Europe and China need to define for themselves what they consider to be the main interests driving their partnership. For the EU in particular it is a matter of finding a remedy against the kind of diplomatic schizophrenia in which short-sighted policies of the member states counteracted the proselytizing European Commission. It would be a good start to evaluate the effectiveness of the current instruments for engaging China. More efforts should also be made in bringing member states around the table to deduce a common denominator from their often-diverging national interests. If Europe is to constructively engage China, it will have to engage itself collectively first. Simultaneously, China and Europe have to agree on which interests they will build the pillars of their strategic partnership. One of the main setbacks in the EU-China partnership has always been its obsession with dialogues without a common view on how the new world order actually binds them together. Obviously, the global financial crisis and the subsequent economic recession have confirmed the necessity to reshape our economies. Both countries face an important challenge to combat unemployment, to improve social welfare and to be more efficient in using scarce natural resources. Increased investment in innovation, a secure climate for creative development and a dynamic services sector will be vital for developing new and sustainable sources for growth. This is an individual responsibility, but it can only be successful in a climate of trust and reciprocal openness. Both sides are confronted with similar social challenges: an ageing population, a heterogeneous ethnic society, growing urban complexes and substantial internal economic differences. They have a common interest in enhancing social equality and welfare. While facing different economic limitations, both sides are aiming to make their development inclusive and harmonious. Rather than lecturing each other, this brings the opportunity to exchange lessons learned. The emphasis should not be on differences per se, but on commitment and progress.

China and Europe are both regional powers with broad global interests. As a consequence of increased international engagement and increasing economic interests abroad, Europe and China are geopolitically more proximate than ever before. There is an important joint interest to promote stability and sustainable development in those regions that we share in our extended neighbourhoods. This is particularly the case of the Middle East, Africa, and South-Central Asia. We have to avoid that these regions develop into a belt of insecurity that endangers our development. There is a strong need to work together to enhance security, to guarantee that our policies benefit lasting stability and development, to invest in the safety of our energy supplies, to limit the impact of environmental hazards, to support effective governance, tackle non-traditional security threats, and enhance maritime security. It is legitimate that growing interests bring the need to exert influence, but this should be cooperative and aim at sharing the costs of maintaining security.

We are moving steadily towards a new multipolar world order. In this order the major powers will have to balance between meeting increasing international expectations and persistent strong internal needs. The emerging multilayered and culturally diversified multipolarity will make global governance much more complex and is by no means a guarantee for multilateralism. To be effective multilateral organizations need to reflect the emerging new international order, but effective multilateralism also implies that all parties are committed to overcome diverging expectations and try to reach a pragmatic consensus on how to make foreign policies complementary and mutually supportive. Europe and China could be in the vanguard here as well. As the unipolar moment fades, Europe and China have showed themselves anxious not to slide into another era of great power rivalry. Such contest would severely weaken the two player's chances for sustainable internal development. In spite of all the friction and misunderstanding, both sides need each other if they are to develop an alternative for harsh international anarchy. Successful bilateral cooperation will be key in promoting global peaceful development. It will also give them the scope to strengthen their internal unity, which will be key in boosting positive power vis-à-vis others. If Beijing and Brussels are serious about changing the nature of great power politics, a pragmatic partnership between China and Europe build on mutual benefit, trust and understanding is mandatory.

6

China and the Evolving World Order: A Stakeholder or a Revolutionary Power?

China's rapid rise has raised the question if China is a stakeholder or a dissatisfied revolutionary power to advance its alternative visions. This chapter argues that although China is not a simple rule-taker content to preserve the existing order, it is not yet a revolutionary power discontent with and willing to undermine the existing order.

Not only is China far from the position to overtake US power, it has not articulated distinctive values to underwrite the world order.

With a historical identity as an East Asian empire, China's visions of a sinocentric hierarchical order or *tianxia*(all under heaven) system have been categorically rejected by its neighbors. Embracing the Westphalian principles of state sovereignty while adapting to the emerging transnational norms, China is a reformist/revisionist power, dissatisfied not with the current order but its position in the order.

If China's demands can be accommodated through negotiations with the United States and other powers to increase China's voice and weight in existing institutions and, with adjustments, tweaking some rules, China would not necessarily become a revolutionary power.

CHINA'S EVOLVING ATTITUDES TOWARD THE POST-WWII ORDER

Historically, great powers have been the rule-makers of the world order to reflect their values and interests, weak states the takers, and dissatisfied emerging powers the breakers, pursuing alternative principles to conform to their distinctive preferences. Rising as the hegemonic power after WWII, the United States played a leading role in the construction of the post-WWII order embodied in three institutional arrangements: 1) a multilateral economic system, including the Bretton Woods institutions of the World Bank and the International Monetary Fund (IMF), and the General Agreement on Tariffs and Trade (GATT); 2) a collective security system of a concert of great powers, appealing to both state-centric, system-maintaining instincts and globalist, system-transforming possibilities to replace the old empire system of balance of power, spheres of influence, and secret alliances; and 3) political self-determination, including de-colonization and promotion of self-governing, democratic states to global dominance. As stated in the Atlantic Charter, the post-WWII international system would "respect the right of all peoples to choose the form of government under which they will live" and "see sovereign rights and self-government restored to those who have been forcibly deprived of them."

The start of the Cold War, however, distorted the liberal design of the word order as the United States moved to safeguard a free (Western) world against communism. Becoming the target of US containment, China was a revolutionary state, leaning toward the communist camp against the Western world in the 1950s. But China was not able to articulate alternative values and norms. While the traditional Chinese world order of cultural hierarchy was replaced by Mao's version of Chinese nationalism under the cover of communism, Chinese leaders faced the contradiction between the universal nature of communism and Mao's version of nationalism.

Rejecting the Soviet version of communism, China ironically embraced the Westphalian principles by proposing the five principles of mutual respect for sovereignty and territorial integrity, mutual non-aggression, non-interference in each other's internal affairs, equality and mutual benefit, and peaceful coexistence at the Bandung conference in 1955: "The Five Principles take mutual respect for sovereignty as a core." Chinese leaders embraced the Westphalian principles because the historical memories of victimization during the long century of national humiliation produced a deeply rooted fear among Chinese elites about the possible erosion of sovereignty by imperialist powers. The Westphalian principle that enshrined the norms of state sovereignty was instrumental to China as a relatively weak power to participate in international affairs on an equal footing, manage its own domestic affairs free from foreign interference, and coexist peacefully with other nations.

Entering the United Nations in 1971, China started the struggle to adapt to the transnational norms. During the first two decades, China's attitude toward transnational norms remained very passive and skeptical, and its participation in UN institutions was highly selective and symbolic. It began to gradually converge toward transnational norms only after the economic reform and opening-up brought it unprecedented interdependence with the global economy in the 1980s. Participation in international institutions took place first in low politics issue areas, starting with membership in the World Bank and the IMF in 1980. China became the World Bank's largest borrower in the 1990s. Both the World Bank and the IMF "provided unique opportunities for China to learn from the experience of other countries in a professional and politically neutral international setting." After difficult negotiations, China joined the GATT/World Trade Organization (WTO) in 2001. As a result, China was able to follow the East Asian model of export-led growth and became a key nodal point in global and regional production chains.

But China was reluctant to embrace transnational norms on sensitive security and human rights issues. Gaining membership in international security regimes, including international arms control and disarmament regimes and UN peacekeeping operations, China demanded two preconditions for such operations: endorsement by the United Nations Security Council and consent by the government of the host country, the latter of which could only be omitted in a failed state such as Somalia. China frequently cautioned against integrating human rights monitors, judicial reform, police training, and military restructuring into the remit of a peacekeeping mission. Similarly, "the norm of human rights has not been completely internalized in China and is controversial if it is confronted with the norm of sovereignty."

China's adaptation to transnational norms partially reflected its evolving position in globalization. Because the impact of globalization on state sovereignty varies from one state to the other, determined by the strength and development level of individual states, globalization can represent a significant threat to state sovereignty when China was relatively weak. As a rising power, however, China can now participate in the international institutions on "its own terms and reap the benefits of globalization without an undue loss of autonomy."

CHINA RESPONSIBLE GREAT POWER

It has long been established that great powers have a distinct status given to them through recognition by other members of international society. Such status recognition, however, is contingent upon exercising great power responsibilities. In the broadest terms, Hedley Bull outlined great power responsibilities as twofold: managing relations with each other and providing central direction within international society as a whole. If we think of the latter in terms of exercising leadership in shaping and underwriting the institutions, norms, and rules of international order then the rise of China poses an interesting question: as China's power grows will it continue to seek status recognition as a legitimate great power within the dominant form international order currently takes?; or will it seek to reform order, replacing existing US/Western-determined institutions, norms and rules with China-centred alternatives?

This question has taken on increasing resonance in recent years as observers have pointed to a shift in China's foreign policy approach from generally 'keeping a low profile' to 'striving for achievement'. This shift is mostly associated with China's 'assertiveness' in pursuing its maritime claims in the East and South China Seas. However, it can also be seen in the promotion of new institutional initiatives such as the One Belt, One Road (OBOR), the Asia Infrastructure Investment Bank (AIIB) as well as the BRICS New Development Bank. That the Chinese leadership feels the confidence to propose its own initiatives and assert its 'core interests' in international society has led one scholar to describe China as a 'post-responsible' power. The Chinese leadership no longer feels compelled to frame China's rise through the narrative of a status quo 'responsible power' but rather seeks to actively shape its environment so as to secure its interests.

However, the notion of 'responsibility' of power and governance is long established within Chinese statecraft and therefore was never a purely externally derived concept. Likewise, the role identity of status quo 'responsible power' is one of a number of different role identities China has projected within international society, existing alongside other identities such as 'developing country', 'emerging power' and 'leader of the Third World'. Inherent within these other role identities are ideas of China's responsibility to promote reform of international order rather than merely conform to the expectations of Western powers. Indeed, China has a long history of promoting reform. The PRC and its immediate Nationalist predecessor put forward concrete proposals for building international institutions that took better account of the needs of developing and post-colonial states at Bretton Woods in 1944 and Bandung in 1955. In the 1960s, this responsibility to reform international society became more radical before the emphasis under Deng Xiaoping moved towards domestic reform and adaptation to international society from the late 1970s. Underpinning China's promotion of reform pre-1978 was a search for legitimacy from key constituencies in

Asia and Africa at a time when China was alienated from international society by US-led containment. Could it be that the current leadership is again turning more towards non-Western constituencies in a search for legitimacy and therefore China's responsibility to reform is becoming more salient?

Certainly what has been called China's 'periphery' – the states of Southeast, South and Central Asia – have received more attention both in terms of official recognition within China's foreign policy hierarchy and in terms of their importance within the OBOR and AIIB. For example, the capital and vote share of the AIIB gives China the greatest sway with 30.34 percent and 26.06 percent respectively, but this is followed by India and Russia which hover around the 8 percent and 6 percent range. Germany, France, Australia and the UK all have capital and vote shares of under 5 percent, roughly equal with Indonesia. This represents a reverse trend with respect to the US-European dominance of the Bretton Woods institutions and US-Japanese dominance of the Asian Development Bank. At the launch of the AIIBin January 2016, Xi Jinping stated that "[the AIIB] will enable China to undertake more international obligations, promote improvement of the current international economic system and provide more international public goods". Likewise, China's Finance Minister Lou Jiwei stated that the establishment of the New Development Bank and the AIIB would not only contribute to building global infrastructure but also help reform global economic governance. At the 60th anniversary Asia-Africa conference Xi also made proposals for the improvement of South-South and North-South cooperation and called for reform of the global aid regime. There is, therefore, a clear emphasis on the value of these new initiatives in promoting reform as well as complementing existing institutions. Chinese officials have been keen to assert that they do not challenge existing lenders such as the World Bank and Asian Development Bank but work alongside them with projects being co-financed with the WB and ADB in the initial few years.

The fact that non-Western and even Western states have been keen to sign up to and endorse China's new initiatives shows that China is receiving recognition from key constituencies. However, China's strategy in the South China Sea, which has included island building, harassment of other claimant states' survey vessels, emphasis on bilateral conflict resolution and rejection of 'internationalisation', has raised serious concern amongst Southeast Asian states about revisions to the regional security environment. This is especially so as China is viewed by some as deliberately seeking to divide the Association of Southeast Asian Nations on the issue.

Considering Southeast Asia forms an integral part of China's 'periphery' this has complicated China's search for legitimacy as a reforming power.

In the case of the maritime disputes the primary audience for China's assertiveness is not abroad but rather domestic nationalist constituencies. Related to this is Xi's "China Dream" narrative which speaks of the "rejuvenation of the Chinese nation" and is also part of an effort to boost the CCP's and particularly Xi's legitimacy at home by appealing to nationalism. As part of the "China Dream" discourse has been the development of a model of domestic and world order built on 'Socialism' and 'Chinese civilisation' that can provide an alternative to the dominant Western neoliberal capitalist model.

Of course, for any new model to take effect beyond China's borders it would need endorsement from other states raising the question of whether China's efforts to court nationalist constituencies at home and its neighbours abroad can ultimately succeed considering the competing expectations these constituencies may have.

What seems to be clear at least is that China has shifted from a dominant framework of *responsibility to conform* to a *responsibility to reform* in its effort to court alternative constituencies in its search for legitimate great power status. The challenge will be to develop a coherent agenda for reform which can resonate with non-Western states, be accepted by Western states and also fulfil the expectations of domestic nationalist constituencies.

CHINA'S DIPLOMACY FOR THE 21ST CENTURY

"Doing our own business well first" – this is one of the admonitions left to the Chinese people by Deng Xiaoping, the designer of the improvement and opening up of the contemporary China. It is also the most direct and the simplest expression of "development demand". The half a century history since the founding of New China has proved that if the domestic economic construction and the improvement of the living of the people do not receive enough attention, the foreign policy of peace and independence would often than not remain empty and powerless, without the social base to last. Only when the domestic economy has developed and the political situation and the relations among all nationalities are kept stable, is it possible for diplomatic work to acquire a solid base. The main threat to China's state security comes not from foreign invasion or other wars, but from within, that is, whether or not China itself can maintain a stable, orderly and healthy development.

The "internal weakness" exhibit by Russia in the Kosovo subject has fully testified to this point. The most profound lesson taught by Russia is: first, a country must first of all manage its own affairs well so as to make it hard for potential or realistic enemy or rival to "penetrate" by exploiting the weakness. It is a common sense that flies hover over only rotten eggs. The fundamental destructive factor to the death of a big country lies not in external sources but the inner problems in the deep layers of the society. It is impossible to wipe out a big country. Its decline often starts from within, from the roots, say national separatism or economic stagnation or political turmoil or social disorder, for if a country were thrown into confusion, it would fall apart without being attacked. The Russian arena over the recent decade has exactly been experiencing every process of "national split—economic stagnation—political upheaval—social disorder". The serious "internal weakness" displayed before the nibbling by NATO is due, essentially, to the "internal war" without the smoke of gunpowder. If asked what we should learn from Russians, it is very simple to answer: it should not be soft toward separatists and, even more important, there should be no internal political strife or social disorder; economic development must not stop and the improvement and institutional improvement should not be interrupted. Stability of a country and growing national strength constitute the corner stone for the security of the country and a major source for having a say externally and exert international influence. "The easiest way to capture a fortress is from within". Without internal security, there would be no defending the state security to speak about, let alone safeguarding it.

It should be stressed here that in spite of the grave negative developments like Kosovo crisis, the relations among big powers have become more dependent upon each other while their relations are growing more complicated and delicate. The globalization process of the economy and science and technology has not been slowing down and the global scientific and technological creation is becoming more active than ever before. The economic growth of most countries is still strong. The world's economic aggregates are still growing. What is the most important is that the comprehensive judgment from all features shows that a worldwide nuclear war or a world war with the involvement of all major countries in confrontation could be prevented for a considerably long period of time to come. All countries will seize the time to develop their own economies, science and technology and boost their national strength and make great efforts to improve the living of the people and infrastructure facilities. Recall that during the recent 200 years, China has in most part been in a state of being bullied and humiliated or in an intense period of mobilization for "war and revolution". It did not make any real development and construction until only in the recent 20 years. But the short span of 20 years has brought about a tremendous leap forward: the country walked out of the shadow of exhaustion in the motive forces for economic development; the GDP has ranked among the first ten in the world if calculated according to the exchange rate; till today, the Chinese people are continuing to realize the most massive economic growth in human history (a country with a population of 1.2 billion has expanded its economy at an annual rate of 8% within 20 years). To look forward, even in another 20 years, not to say in another 100 years, if China should maintain the speed of the last 20 years and "concentrate its efforts on economic construction", the Chinese people have every reason to expect that the country will reach the level of a middle-developed country in per capita average and secure a place among the top three in the world in total aggregates. By then, China would have a significant say in the international affairs and the new international political and economic order will be most likely to develop toward the direction we expect.

Before talking about a methodical change in the current international relations or about making greater contributions to the external world, the Chinese people must have a sober estimation of themselves. It should be admitted that, after half a century construction, especially the rapid development over the recent 20 years through improvement and opening up, our comprehensive national strength has ascended a new stair and our international status and influence have grown greatly, China remains a developing country, still trailing behind other countries in many areas and still a far cry as compared with developed countries. This manifests itself not only in the "hardware", such as the per capita GNP, the living standards, development of roads, the modernization of educational facilities and means of information, labour productivity and product quality, and the proportion in the global trade and investment, but also in "software", such as institutional creation, comprehensive quality of services, understanding of the external world by the average people, the attractiveness of the whole country to foreign resources (including materials and intelligence), the general level of theoretical studies and the capability of keeping track with the advanced world levels. The strength of software includes the strength in political and social development and in theory and also the following factors: (1) the domestic political, social and economic system arrangements that are open, stable, lasting, and absorbing; (2) powerful culture, political and ethical appeal and rallying power; (3) theoretical guidance; (4) strategic insight and diplomatic skills; (5) effective domestic and international management, including the effective mobilization of domestic and international resources (especially non-military resources; (6) the populace of high educational level and strong cultural awareness; (7) high level of living standards. It is a long way to go for China to acquire such strength. Economic and military strength cannot substitute for the powerful political and social base". Historically, the contemporary China has not and will not possibly have what it used to experience in the heydays of Han and Tang dynasties. Ever since the modern times, it has been in "tight operation" economically, socially and politically. As the changes in the economic structure advance simultaneously with the changes of the whole social and political system, the awareness of opening up grows together with the growth of the awareness of nationalism. The whole country has grown rapidly, but with problems cropping up one after another and a large number of troubles put on the agenda before the problems left from the old system had not be rooted out, such as bankruptcy of enterprises and workers thrown out of jobs, the regional economic and educational disparities, corruption and the so-called "crises in belief, credit and confidence". The problems in themselves have already restricted its power of influencing the world. If no steps are taken to deepen improvement and opening up, no efforts are made to continue the great development, stopping there, rest contented, the prospects of China and the world would not develop toward the direction in our favour. In this sense, the focus of China's diplomacy for a quite a long period of time to come still remains to be on the creation of a neighbouring environment favourable to China's improvement, development and stability and on meeting the major demands of economic construction. Unless major wars break out not to our liking, there would be no reason to change the priority of this demand.

The above essentials show that what is referred to as "development demand" is much richer and much more extensive in content than what we used to construe or disseminate in the past. For instance, economically speaking, the Chinese people have basically realized a "comfortable living". But when measured by fairly comprehensive standards, China needs more profound political democracy and legal construction and needs the synchronization of the development of spiritual civilization (belief, ethics and values) and material civilization, needs more rational and smooth run-in between the stratification of the society and the various interest groups, needs more Chinese people who have broader and more lenient insight on the world, and needs greater development of the strategic thinking and theoretical nature about China's international relations. The term "Development" covers political development, the development of civilization, social development and development of values. Under the precondition of making economic development the central task, the development in all features mentioned above will greatly help China to raise its status and power of influence internationally in the new millennium and that will naturally provide more solid base for China's diplomacy to display its prowess.

CHINA'S TRADE POLICIES IN WIDER ASIAN PERSPECTIVE

This chapter looks at China's trade-policy developments compared with related trends in India and southeast Asia (the ASEAN countries). The larger backdrop is the historic – but very recent – integration of first China and then India into the global economy; but in between also lies the longer history of southeast-Asian integration into the global economy, which accelerated after the 1970s. Such preliminary observations also raise the question of economic integration *between and among* these different parts of Asia – or the lack thereof – and how that relates to trade policies. Time and space prohibit an even wider comparison with Japan, South Korea and Taiwan, the more developed countries of northeast Asia.

Consider the following questions. How far has economic opening come in China, India and southeast Asia, and how much farther is it likely to go? Where does trade policy in these regions fit in the spectrum between liberalism and intervention? How does it relate to broad trends in domestic and foreign policies? What is China's place in the World Trade Organisation, just four years into accession? What are its negotiating positions and strategies in the Doha Round? How does it interact with other WTO members, particularly the major players? What of China's future in the WTO? How does that compare with India's and the ASEAN countries' longer history in the GATT/WTO and their Doha-Round negotiating positions? What is China's Free-Trade-Agreement (FTA) strategy? Will it become the FTA hub in east Asia? How does that compare with FTA developments in India and the ASEAN countries?

Making a stab at answering these questions will proceed as follows. China, India and southeast Asia in the context of economic globalisation and policy reforms around the world. At their trade-policy frameworks. It summarises recent reforms, links them down to domestic economic policies, and up to foreign policy and trade diplomacy.

The concluding argument of the paper, worth flagging at the outset, is that trade *policy* matters more than trade *negotiations*. There has been huge trade-and-investment liberalisation; but this has happened *unilaterally* for the most part, not through trade negotiations, whether in the WTO or in FTAs. Trade negotiations have distinct and perhaps increasing limitations, and their effects should not be exaggerated. All the more reason, therefore, to rely on the unilateral engine of freer trade, with China setting the late 20th/early 21st-century example much as Britain did in the second half of the 19th century. That will have powerful emulatory effects elsewhere, particularly in Asia. A combined China-and-India effect, with India accelerating liberalisation in response to China, will send even stronger liberalisation signals, not least to southeast Asia.

What makes the crucial difference to economic globalisation today, and probably for next half century, is the dramatic opening of first China and then India. They are the world's second- and fourth-largest economies respectively (at purchasing-power parity): China accounted for 12.5 per cent, and India about 6 per cent, of global GDP in 2003. Together they are home to 40 per cent of humanity (China with a population of 1.37 billion, and India 1.07 billion). With still low levels of per-capita income (China's being 15 per cent, and India's 7 per cent, of US levels, measured at PPP), and huge supplies of cheap, productive labour, they have the potential for stellar catch-up growth rates for decades ahead. Their integration into the world economy, still in its early stages, promises to be more momentous than that of Japan and the east-Asian Tigers, and perhaps on a par with the rise of the US as a global economic power in the late nineteenth century.

Asia was conspicuously absent from the world economy from early modernity to relatively recent times. International economic integration spread from Britain to Western Europe and the British offshoots of Empire, notably north America and Australasia, plus a handful of other lands of recent settlement (such as Argentina). Mostly, Asia came into the fold only in the second half of the 20th century: first with the emergence of Japan in the 1950s (rather its re-emergence after its late nineteenth century rise and then wartime destruction); followed by Hong Kong, Singapore, Taiwan and South Korea; and then the second-generation Tigers of southeast Asia. China and India remained closed during most of this period. Only come the 1980s and 1990s did they wake up and join the fray.

Southeast Asia has a longer history of global economic integration than China or India. This is particularly the case with Singapore and Malaysia: both were tightly integrated into the commercial networks of the British Empire. Notwithstanding vast differences among countries in the region, the older ASEAN members (Singapore, Malaysia, Thailand, Indonesia and Philippines) have integrated further into the world economy since the 1970s, especially through trade and foreign direct investment (FDI) in manufactures. In terms of headline indicators, the ASEAN countries have a combined GDP well below that of China but still ahead of India (at market prices, though below the Indian level in terms of PPP comparisons); a combined population less than half that of China or India;

and an average per-capita GDP that is higher than China's or India's.

The rise of east and south Asia (but not west or north Asia) is one feature of globalisation today; the other is its extremely partial and uneven nature. China, India and southeast Asia figure prominently in that story too. A recent World Bank report identifies 24 "new-globalising" developing countries with a total population of 2.9 billion. Between 1980 and 1997, this group registered a doubling of their trade-to-GDP ratio, a two-thirds increase in real per- capita income, and a one-third cut in average import tariffs. In the same period, the 49 "less-globalised" developing countries in the sample, with a combined population of 1.1 billion, saw a decline in their trade-to-GDP ratio, a rise of just 10 per cent in real per-capita income, and an 11 per cent cut in average import tariffs. The former also registered a better reading on the rule of law than the latter. These figures are, of course, yet further empirical support for the proposition that relatively liberal trade policies and openness to trade, combined with market-oriented institutions at home, lead to higher rates of growth than is the case for economies that remain relatively closed. That is what distinguishes the West, and more recently Japan, the east-Asian Tigers, and now China and India, from most other countries in the developing world. But what is really striking about this group of 24 new globalisers is that, first, Asia makes up 85 per cent of its population, and second, that India and China alone make up 75 per cent.

Now turn to China specifically. Between 1980 and 2003, its real income per head rose by over 300 per cent. Its export and import volumes have grown by 11-13 per cent a year since 1980, and by 35-40 per cent annually in the last few years. Manufactures account for 90 per cent of merchandise exports. China's ratio of trade in goods to GDP, at market prices, now stands at about 70 per cent. This is truly exceptional.

The most-peopled country in the world has, in quick time, acquired the trade openness of a much smaller country (such as South Korea). It is far more open than roughly equivalent large countries like the US, India and Japan, with trade-to-GDP ratios of about 20 per cent. China's share of world merchandise exports was 6 per cent in 2003, up from 1.2 per cent in 1980. China has just overtaken Japan as the world's third-largest trading nation.

China's trade openness is intimately bound up with its openness to inward investment. The stock of FDI in China was over $550 billion in 2004 from $25 billion in 1990. It was about 40 per cent of Chinese GDP, compared with 1.5 per cent for Japan, just over 5 per cent for India and 13 per cent for the US. FDI inflows in 2004, at $60 billion, were over one-third of the total going to all developing countries. The bulk of FDI stock is in manufacturing, and it is estimated that China is home to about 7 per cent of global manufacturing production. Foreign-owned firms generate over 50 per cent of exports (on a par with small, highly open economies like Estonia, Costa Rica and Malaysia) and 60 per cent of imports. The latter figures are especially striking, and bear repetition: *foreign affiliates generate one-half of total exports and an even greater share of imports.*

This astounding combination of trade-and-FDI penetration means that China is already well integrated into the world economy, indeed more so than other developing countries (except highly open, small-to-medium economies, most of them in east Asia), and much more so than the giant rival on its eastern flank, Japan.

China's global integration dwarfs that of India, but the latter has come far by its own standards, especially since the early 1990s. Real incomes have increased by 125 per cent since 1980 (less than half the increase in China). Exports and imports have picked up since the early 1990s, albeit from a very low base. India accounts for less than 1 per cent of world manufacturing exports, putting it in 30th position globally. It has a 1.4-per-cent share of world commercial-services exports, in 19th position globally (though Chinese commercial-services exports are about double the Indian level). FDI has increased from a low base, with an inward investment stock of about $36 billion by 2004. FDI inflows were $6 billion in 2004 – about 10 per cent of Chinese levels.

What about southeast Asia? Its figures mirror China's but not India's. Its trade levels in 2003 were a little ahead of China's but well ahead of India's. Basically, China has been catching up fast with southeast-Asian trade shares; and, with higher growth in trade volumes, it will rapidly overtake southeast Asia. ASEAN countries are highly open to the world economy, with an average trade/GDP ratio of 134.5 per cent, about double that of China. This masks differences within the region: Singapore is at one extreme; Malaysia is also extremely trade dependent; and even Thailand, Philippines and Vietnam have trade/GDP ratios of over 100 per cent. FDI inflows, which have not maintained their pre-Asian-crisis rate of increase, pale in comparison with inflows to China but are still some way ahead of Indian levels.

There are increasing economic links between China, India and southeast Asia, though from a low base. The main link is between China and southeast Asia. China's share in ASEAN exports nearly tripled, and its share of ASEAN imports more than quadrupled, between 1993 and 2003. Trade in manufactures accounted for most of this increase. ASEAN trade with India, though increasing, is about 20-25 per cent of ASEAN-China trade levels.

What do these comparisons tell us about relative specialisation in the current and emerging international division of labour? The main point is that China has clear-cut comparative advantage in labour-intensive manufactured exports; and this will remain the case for some time ahead, given a huge pool of cheap labour pouring from the countryside into the cities, particularly on the coast. Less often mentioned is China's growing exploitation of comparative advantage in labour-intensive agricultural exports such as fruits and vegetables. At the same time, it is sucking in ever-increasing land-intensive agricultural imports as domestic resources shift further to industrial production. It has recently become a net importer of farm produce. Such rapid specialisation is forging complementary trade relationships with agricultural and other commodity producers in Australasia, Latin America and Africa. In manufactures, as China integrates into global supply chains, it is forging very strong links with the USA, EU and other east-Asian countries, including ASEAN. Much of this is in the form of vertically-integrated, intra-industry trade: China imports capital-intensive components for labour-intensive processing and export to the rest of the world. Finally, rising real incomes are driving domestic demand for sophisticated foreign consumer products and services.

The net effect of China's insertion into the global economy is to intensify competition, and with it the need for mutual adjustment and adaptation. More pressure will bear down on low-value, low-wage industries in the West that compete directly with Chinese exports. More pressure is already being felt in developing countries that compete directly with Chinese manufactured exports for third-country export markets. Competition is particularly keen in the global market for clothing.

Now turn to India. China should be the shadow of India's future. With an abundance of cheap labour, India should become a powerhouse for manufacturing exports, occupying low-wage niches (e.g. in textiles and clothing) vacated by China as real incomes rise there. This should apply to labour-intensive agricultural exports too. That is the story of fast-paced, catch-up growth in developing countries in the last half-century.

But this is not happening in India. Its major problem is that only 10 million people are employed in the formal manufacturing sector, out of a total employable population that is rising to 450 million. Industry has a less than 30 per-cent share of GDP, compared with a figure of 50 per cent or more in China and other east-Asian developing countries. External protection, strangulating domestic labour-market regulation, poor infrastructure and other bad business-climate conditions are to blame. Agriculture accounts for 60 per cent of employment but only 20 per cent of GDP. Growth and employment generation are hindered by high external protection, poor infrastructure, other barriers to internal trade, small plots of land, and otherwise pervasive government intervention.

That leaves services, with a share of 50 per cent of GDP (high by developing-country standards and much higher than the share of services in China's GDP). India does have comparative advantage in labour-intensive areas of services, which it is exploiting in business-process outsourcing and software exports.

But this is not the panacea often advertised. IT-related services will generate an extra 1 million jobs and account for 1 per cent of GDP by 2010, according to the most optimistic projections. The jobs created require relatively high qualifications and are well paid by Indian standards. But they are a drop in the ocean compared with the wealth-creation and employment-generation potential in manufacturing and, to a lesser extent, in agriculture.

Where does southeast Asia fit into this comparative-advantage picture? It will maintain strong trade-and-FDI links with the USA and Europe. But its future also seems to lie in complementary trade, especially of the intra-industry manufacturing variety, with China and other parts of northeast Asia (Japan, Korea and Taiwan).

This will bring in associated FDI. Production-sharing arrangements in IT-related sectors figure prominently, with different parts of the value chain in different locations. But, to exploit these niches fully, the older ASEAN countries need to improve infrastructure, education, skills *and* governance in order to compensate for eroded advantage in cheap labour. They also need to liberalise highly protected markets in agriculture and services. The newer and much poorer ASEAN countries (Cambodia, Vietnam, Laos and Myanmar) can exploit comparative advantage in cheap labour, especially as relative incomes rise in China. However, for some ASEAN countries with an eroding labour-cost advantage, there are areas where trade with China is more frictional than complementary, e.g. in agriculture, textiles and clothing. Finally, the older ASEAN countries should be able to export more commercial services to an opening and expanding Chinese market, gain from expanding travel and tourism, and invest in large Chinese infrastructure projects.

ASEAN trade with India is much less developed. Trade-and-FDI links are increasing in services and pockets of manufacturing (e.g. cars and car parts). However, for bilateral trade to really take off, India will have to burst its self-imposed chains in manufacturing. That would lead to much stronger, complementary trade and associated FDI between China, India and southeast Asia in goods and services, and with it a more rational, integrated Asian division of labour. But that appears to be on the distant horizon. In all, China's, India's and southeast Asia's integration into the world economy creates vast opportunities. In China and southeast Asia, catch-up growth based on inward investment and manufactured exports, underpinned by trade-and-investment liberalisation, has massively benefited the poor. That has happened to a lesser extent in India because it has been far less successful in exploiting comparative advantage. The task for public policy is to grasp these opportunities by keeping borders open, or opening them where they are closed, while managing the necessary adjustments. The emerging complementary commercial relationships between China, India and southeast Asia, and between them and other countries, in both developed and developing worlds, will hopefully make this political task realistic and manageable. But protectionist danger lurks behind every free-trade opportunity. These dangers are bound to increase as China's advance gathers pace; and they will increase further if India accelerates its pace of global integration. They will come from declining industries in rich countries and directly competing industries in other poor countries.

Last, the growth story told here masks large and in some cases increasing problems with regional income disparities, environmental pollution, and health, education and social-security systems. That is more the case in China and India, but less so in the richer southeast-Asian countries. Reversing or even slowing down integration into the world economy is not the lesson to draw. That would deprive people of further growth and poverty reduction, and more generally of further improvements to human welfare. Rather the challenge is to bring globalisation's benefits to the parts of these regions they have not yet reached, while devoting more public and private resources to health care, pollution control and other public goods.

THE CHINA CHALLENGE TO THE WORLD ORDER

China's active participation in international institutions came when the post-WWII world order underwent a dramatic transformation. In particular, international treaties, such as the International Covenant on Civil and Political Rights (1976) and the "Responsibility to Protect" (R2P) endorsed unanimously at the 2005 UN High Level Summit, depicted state sovereignty as contingent on fulfilling certain obligations, such as not pursuing weapons of mass destruction (WMD) or committing atrocities. The rise of non-Western powers also contested the post-WWII order because most emerging powers, having suffering historically at the hands of Western imperialism, are dissatisfied with Western dominance in the existing order. Although Western powers would like rising powers to simply accept existing norms in return for a seat and voice in the existing order, emerging powers often diverge from them on the norms, and rules to govern state conduct. In addition: "the Janus-like US attitude toward multilateralism complicates the 'responsible stakeholder' scenario. Since World War II, no country has done more to build institutions of world order. And yet, few have so resisted submitting to norms and rules it hopes will bind others."

As a result, although the United States has been remarkably adept at encouraging and in many cases assisting China's integration into the international system, it is not prepared to see China rising as a contender to US dominance. For example, the US-led negotiations of the Rans-Pacific Partnership (TPP) are not designed to contain China, but the Obama administration presented them in a way that: "If we do not help to shape the rules so that our businesses and our workers can compete in those markets, then China will set up rules that advantage Chinese workers and Chinese businesses." This was interpreted as "the United States is less than welcoming of China's integration."

It is difficult, if not impossible, for the United States to maintain hegemony for long, given the open and competitive nature of the post-WWII order. Free trade and free capital flows tend to diffuse wealth and production from developed to emerging economies. Imperial overextension, such as the costly wars in Iraq and Afghanistan, accelerated the diffusion. It is, indeed, true that the US global order has enabled the rise of China and eroded its own hegemony. However, it is too late to reverse the outcome. Benefiting from this process and rising to the second largest economy, China regards the existing order as favoring the United States and its allies at the expense of China's power aspirations and has become a challenger in many respects.

First, seeing a structural conflict between China as a rising power and the United States as the sole superpower, many in China have worried that the United States has a hidden agenda of pressing on the issues of human rights and democracy to prevent China from rising to what they regard as its rightful place. Beijing has elevated the norm of sovereignty over the human rights principles to which it has formally assented and taken a strong stance against the emerging "responsibility to protect" doctrine and the international human rights order rooted in respect for fundamental liberties and the democratic process.

Second, as its power grows, China has become increasingly assertive in maritime territorial disputes with its neighbors. Submitting the "Nine-Dash Line" maritime boundary based on historical claims to the United Nations to legitimize its far-flung claims, China has refused to take part in an international court case brought by the Philippines under the UN Convention on the Law of the Sea (UNCLOS), which provides not only rules for determining conflicting maritime claims but also legal institutions for impartially applying those rules. Beijing is a signatory to UNCLOS but insists that the court has no jurisdiction, despite widespread consensus to the contrary, and has, thus, eroded existing maritime regimes and rules without either leaving UNCLOS or offering replacements. If China thumbs its nose at an adverse decision and a subsequent determination of the merits of the dispute, it will be in blatant violation of the UN convention obligations that it freely ratified after taking an active part in the long negotiations preceding the treaty. Rejecting peaceful settlement of maritime as well as territorial disputes through international arbitration, adjudication, and other third-party procedures, China is plainly out of step with the practices of other Asian countries and the rest of the world.

Third, Beijing has demanded a capital share and voting rights in global institutions commensurate with its "weight." Criticizing the global economy's dependence on a dollar-based single currency system as one cause of the global financial crisis, People's Bank of China Governor Zhou Xiaochuan proposed China's RMB be included in the basket of key international currencies on which the value of the IMF's Special Drawing Rights (SDR) is based. Gaining the status in 2015 paved the way for Beijing to flex its muscle more in the global economy, a key step in boosting its global role and breaking the dominance of the US dollar, the stronghold of American power. China also proposed to rebalance the voting shares of the IMF in accordance with the growing economic strength of emerging economies at the G20 meeting in 2010. The IMF moved to increase China's voting shares from less than 4 percent to over 6 percent, and the reforms were ratified by all other members but were stuck in the US Congress until 2015. In frustration, China worked with four other emerging economies and co-founded the BRICS (Brazil, Russia, India, China and South Africa) Bank in 2014, a symbolic gesture to create a sort of IMF clone writ small.

Fourth, debating if China should adopt its own "Monroe Doctrine" to establish a sphere of influence and de-

Americanization in the region, China has tried to build regional security institutions without US participation to better accord with its interests and preferences. The Shanghai Cooperation Organization (SCO) is the first regional organization launched by China without US participation. Although the SCO claims that it is not against any third country, China played a leadership role obviously with the goal of balancing US influence in the region. President Xi demonstrated a clear intention to exclude the United States from regional organizations when he announced that Asian security should be "maintained by Asians" at the 2014 Shanghai Summit of the Conference of Interaction and Confidence-Building in Asia (CICA). He invigorated this little-known regional summit that had languished for years because its membership did not include the United States and most American allies and partners, such as Japan, the Philippines, and Singapore.

Fifth, China has competed with the United States for leadership of regional economic architecture. Negotiating the Regional Comprehensive Economic Partnership (RCEP) with ASEAN states as an alternative to TPP, China launched two major initiatives in 2015. One was the Silk Road Economic Belt and Twenty-first Century Maritime Silk Road, known as One Belt One Road (OBOR), which is to bind together 65 countries and 4.4 billion people beyond China's land and maritime borders to provide an outlet for excess industrial capacity, access resources, and strengthen national security cooperation. Aligning with Xi's "China Dream" of national rejuvenation, the perceived ultimate objective of OBOR is to reshape the international system and put China at the center of the world. The second initiative was the Asian Infrastructure Investment Bank (AIIB), officially launched in June 2015 and joined by 49 other founding members. Headquartered in Beijing and headed by a Chinese citizen, the AIIB was perceived "as an alternative to the World Bank and other international development institutions." The United States tried to dissuade its allies from joining the bank but was caught flat when the United Kingdom, followed by other prominent allies, including France, Germany,

Italy, Australia and South Korea, applied as founding members of the AIIB before the deadline of March 31, 2015.

The accession of the United Kingdom and several European countries was regarded as powerful testament to China's role in the reconstruction of the world order. A Chinese specialist held that although the Bretton Woods system led by the United States made contributions to resolving global issues, this old vehicle was tired and needed reform. US attempts to delay the reforms caused complaints from many countries. China, therefore, launched the AIIB to help reduce the tension in the existing system, provide international public goods, and participate in international rule-making.

A Reformist/Revisionist Power

To some observers, the China challenge to the existing world order makes it a revolutionary power, but its initiatives do not amount to replacing the existing order. China is a reformist/revisionist power, demanding reform of global governance and more influence as a rules-maker. Challenging US dominance, Xi had to commit China to "firmly maintain international order and the international system to the purposes and principles of the UN Charter as the core and to maintain and consolidate the fruits of victory of World War II." Fu Ying explained that "China has neither the intention nor ability to overturn the existing order." This is not modesty but a reflection of China's awkward position in the international system.

First, China is far from being able to step into America's shoes any time soon. The United States remains the most powerful nation in the world, using not only its military and economic might but also its soft power to shape the world order. A Chinese specialist admitted that China may one day overtake the United States in the size of economy but may never overtake its influence and leadership role in the world. Another specialist explained that China faced predicaments in devising an international discursive power: using Chinese discourse, people could not understand and would not accept it; using others' discourse, China would lose itself. The traditional Chinese system as a hierarchy was in contrast to the Westphalian principles and could not automatically transform into modern discursive power.

Unable to construct an alternative order, China has insisted on the Westphalian principles, which looked attractive to many countries in an era of intense US interventionism that often ended in chaos and chronic instability within those countries affected. But many of China's neighbors now worry that, as China's relative power rises, China's imperial past may produce undue pressure on its leaders to regain its predominant position and restore the old Chinese hierarchical order. One reporter took a note that at the sixtieth anniversary of the Bandung Conference, the 1955 meeting that gave birth to the five principles of non-intervention, only two notable leaders bothered to turn up. One was Xi, who used the occasion to portray China as the well-meaning leader of the non-western world. The other was Prime Minister Abe Shinzo, who suggested that the threat to the sovereignty of smaller countries no longer came from the West.

Second, even in the Asia-Pacific region, achieving dominance cannot be a serious Chinese objective because of the presence and influence of the United States, Japan, and other regional powers. While China is rising, many surrounding states are also on the rise. China's shift from espousing a peaceful rise to far more assertive behavior has made its neighbors nervous, motivating not only US allies such as Japan and Australia but also countries such as Vietnam, India, Indonesia, and the Philippines, which were once either enemies of or neutral towards America, to realign with the United States and with each other to balance China's power aspirations. The twenty-first century has seen multipolarity rather than Chinese hegemony in the region. While many Chinese blamed the United States for inciting China's neighbors against China, one cool-headed specialist wrote that the difficulties in relations with neighbors were not caused by the United States stirring up trouble but because the great majority of East Asian countries were worried about China. In East Asia, the old rule that economics determines politics lost effectiveness because nearly all these countries closely worked with China economically but aligned with the United States in security and politics and welcomed and even invited the US balance to the growth of Chinese power.

China's institutional initiatives will not play a critical role in its rise but are the consequences of its rise. Historically, to bandwagon with a rising power is common practice due to potentially great relative gains. The most successful rising powers have been precisely the ones that have attracted the greatest number of bandwagoners. It does not serve China's interests to have tensions with many neighbors simultaneously. China cannot rise successfully without winning the support of its neighbors or at least preempt their balancing motives. China's long-term interests depend on relationships with its neighbors as well as with the United States.

Third, China has benefited and continues to benefit from the post-WWII order underpinning stability and economic growth in the world and the region. As one Chinese commentator admitted: "China became the largest beneficiary by taking maximum advantage of globalization...A large part of the world has prospered under such an arrangement (American global leadership)...These nations are essentially free riders, of which China is the biggest and most successful one." Although China is uncomfortable with the United States militarily and strategically engaged in its home region, it benefited from the US security role in the Asia Pacific. Residing in a neighborhood with complicated power competition and historical animosities, Chinese leaders have to be measured and judicious. "The corollary of the decline of the West is not the rise of Asia. It is the erosion of Asia, at least as an idea, as rivalries within geographic Asia overtake the notion of regional cohesion that once bound these countries together."

Beijing's interests will be served best by working with the United States and its neighbors to maintain the rule-based regional order. China often expresses concern over the US–Japan alliance; yet that is part of the regional security architecture that has underpinned the stability in East Asia and prevented remilitarization of Japan. "Imagine what the regional security picture would look like to China if Japan were strategically independent from the United States." Without the US nuclear umbrella, Japan would have developed nuclear weapons a long time ago, prompting South Korea and even Taiwan to develop their own. From this perspective, one Chinese specialist suggested that: "Chinese policymakers and analysts should not believe their own jingoistic rhetoric about a United States in decline. Even if it's true, a weak America isn't good news for China."

Fourth, facing immense internal huddles in its rise, China is a fragile rising power with profound internal causes of concern that have the potential to derail its rise. The internal challenge "is a far bigger issue for China's leaders than sovereignty over some barren rocks in nearby seas." No economy keeps growing at the same pace forever. The era of superior Chinese economic performance is over, exacerbated by the environmental destruction, rampant corruption, a growing gulf between rich and poor, huge local government debt, and looming demographic challenges that are worsened by the fact that it would be the first country to get old before it gets rich. A slowing economy has placed huge pressure on the Chinese leaders as resentment among China's have-nots has the potential to evolve into a concerted challenge to the Communist Party's legitimacy and authority. Pan Wei rightfully suggested, "Nobody can destroy China unless China destroys itself first." China's rise ultimately depends on its own domestic development and much less on what others do. To ensure its further rise, China must put its own house in order first.

Still a Stakeholder

Although China's rising power and the initiatives such as the AIIB and OBOR may give China more leverage as a revisionist/reformist power, it is still difficult for Beijing to rival the existing order before China achieves a level of power comparable to that of the United States in the 1940s-1950s and can present alternative values. Until then, China's initiatives may resemble that of its many antecedents, joining the long list of much-hyped initiatives aimed at transforming the global system but either languished in obscurity or were integrated into the existing system. Still a stakeholder, China's initiatives represent an assumption of responsibility as much as a declaration of privilege.

This is particularly true of China's regional economic initiatives. Although OBOR is driven more by China's strategic ambitions than commercial logic, it is far from clear whether OBOR could support China's ambitions to build a network of non-Western countries in which China plays the dominant role. China would have to secure support from India, Russia, Japan and many others across Central, South and Southeast Asia to buy into its foreign policy, turning their back on the United States, and, in effect, giving China carte blanche to determine outcomes in a world that bears no resemblance to that when the Silk Road evolved. The Silk Road network of land and maritime routes stretching from Europe to Asia's eastern coast, linking diverse cultures, is to connect China's historic and modern roles in the region. But the history of ancient expeditions is complicated, with the backdrop of conflict and the push to spread a sinocentric world order unacceptable in the modern context. In the search for political influence, China may find itself tangled in conflicts for which it is not prepared. As a result, while some in the West characterized OBOR as China's Marshall Plan, Chinese leaders rejected the comparison, claiming it was focusing on economic growth rather than political influence.

In the case of the AIIB, Western commentary once expressed fear that China would use it for narrow political and economic ends. With a diverse group of 50 founding members, however, the AIIB has not become a blatant agent of Chinese foreign policy. While the participation of European governments is testament to China's economic attraction, it comes at a cost to China's control of the institutions; these Western countries with their active and vocal NGO communities would try to pressure the AIIB as they have done to the World Bank, badgering it to impose restrictions on its lending on environmental and human rights concerns. As a result, the AIIB has engaged former officials from other multilateral development institutions to help craft practical policies on the environment, society, disclosure, procurement, debt sustainability, and oversight mechanism. To make it more in line with the principles of the existing institutions, Beijing has pledged that the AIIB will be "lean, clean, and green" and emphasized transparency, accountability, openness, and independence. "The key reason that China adapted its positions and accepted an AIIB different from its earlier design is the role of the international community. The evidence suggests that the existing system also has the power to balance, influence, and shape that challenge, to check China's revolutionary ambitions, and to make China play by the rules."

China is willing to make the AIIB a multilateral and high-standards institution because it could not only prove itself as a responsible stakeholder but also further its strategic agenda by developing mutually beneficial long-term relations with many countries, an admission of the sobering experiences of China's bilateral lending mechanisms such as China Development Bank and the Export-Import Bank of China. Through these agencies, Beijing years ago surpassed the World Bank as the largest global provider of development finance. However, the attempt to use that lending to buy political allegiance and to secure imports of natural resources and export markets for its own goods increasingly revealed that opaque lending to unstable regimes was no guarantee of either a commercial or a geopolitical return. Inviting in more experienced lenders in the AIIB reassures borrowers that this is not just old Chinese lending practices in new clothes.

The AIIB episode reveals that Asian and European countries do not want to choose between China and the United States and want to benefit from working with both Chinese initiatives and America's initiatives such as TPP. One observer argued that the kind of infrastructure financed by the AIIB is the "hardware" of trade and investment, necessary but not sufficient to deepen integration. TPP, on the other hand, represents the "software" of integration, reducing trade barriers, opening up services for trade and investment, and harmonizing various regulatory barriers to trade. The competition between America and China to produce better multilateral institutions will be good for the world. "In doing so, the power struggles between the United States and China in Asia have primarily developed around standard-setting through institution-building, not any direct military arms race or trade friction talks, as a new way to dominate the regional order-creating processes." "A race to the top in corporate governance, and not a race to the bottom, it does not matter whether America wins or China wins. Either way, we will see an improvement in the standards of managing institutions of global governance."

Conclusion

The rise of China has caused concerns in the United States and other parts of the world that China is to assert itself in its region and further afield and become a revolutionary power to undermine the existing world order. But China is far from the predominant position the United States gained after WWII, and is still abiding largely by the established rules of the world order, engaging in reforms to revise rather than rewrite the norms and principles. The differences between China and the United States are not primarily over the principles of the world order but whether China has obtained the prestige and position of authority commensurate with its rising power status. China may remain so if it is given more room as a rule-maker, in conjunction with the other powers, to reform the existing order, better reflecting its enhanced power and interests.

After all, "the distribution of relative power internationally has shifted with the rise of the emerging markets, a prominent one being China. What seemed the natural order of the post-WWII period when the United States accounted for around 35 percent of global gross domestic product is not sustainable when the United States is below 20 percent. This development does not mean that Americans will have lower absolute welfare or less absolute power, but it does mean that institutions and patterns of behavior premised on overwhelming American primacy need to be adjusted to take account of the rise of others. "'Accommodating' their legitimate aspirations for voice in the international system is not weakness or appeasement, it is essential to a stable international order and to maintain American influence." It is in the US interest to assiduously use the institutions, norms, and regulations it and its partners have crafted to meet China's reform demands to a sufficient degree so that the Chinese elite would internalize the norms and values established by the United States.

This outcome would very much depend upon America's continuing ability to enforce the rules while providing China with enough breathing space as a rule-maker. It would also depend upon China viewing the maintenance of the world order as serving its interests while being able to introduce reforms to ensure that it does. In addition, it would depend on Chinese nationalist sentiment not trumping pragmatism as China continues to benefit from its integration into the global economy and the evolution of the current world order. In this case, it is positive that the United States maintains a balance of welcoming China rising to shoulder more international responsibility while constraining Chinese adventurism. As Secretary of Defense Ashton Carter said: "While most Chinese and much of the Chinese leadership are inclined to continue to take advantage of an international system of free trade and openness that has allowed China to develop in its own way, there is another tendency in China, which is to believe that after a century of humiliation, as they put it, it's now China's time to dominate its region. And that is a tendency that we check through our strength in the region and through our allies and partners."

7

Xi Jinping Heralds 'New Era' of Chinese Power at Communist Party Congress

Xi Jinping has heralded the dawn of a "new era" of Chinese politics and power at the start of a historic Communist party congress celebrating the end of his first term in office. Speaking in the Great Hall of the People in Beijing, at the start of the week-long 19th party congress, Xi told delegates that thanks to decades of "tireless struggle" China stood "tall and firm in the east".

Xi Jinping speech: five things you need to know

Now, Xi said, it was time for his nation to transform itself into "a mighty force" that could lead the world on political, economic, military and environmental issues.

"This is a new historic juncture in China's development," China's 64-year-old leader declared in his bold 3hr 23 minute address outlining the party's priorities for the next five years.

"The Chinese nation ... has stood up, grown rich, and become strong – and it now embraces the brilliant prospects of rejuvenation ... It will be an era that sees China moving closer to centre stage and making greater contributions to mankind."

Xi warned that achieving what he has hailed the "China Dream" would be "no walk in the park": "It will take more than drum beating and gong clanging to get there." "[But] our mission is a call to action ... let us get behind the strong leadership of the party and engage in a tenacious struggle."

Xi became the Communist party's general secretary – and thus China's leader – at the last party congress in 2012, and has since emerged as one of China's most dominant rulers since Mao Zedong.

In the surprisingly long speech – titled "Secure a decisive victory in building a moderately prosperous society in all respects and strive for the great success of socialism with Chinese characteristics for a new era" – Xi struck an upbeat tone that contrasted with the grey skies and drizzle outside.

"The Chinese nation is a great nation; it has been through hardships and adversity but remains indomitable. The Chinese people are a great people; they are industrious and brave and they never pause in pursuit of progress," he said.

"The Communist party of China is a great party; it has the fight and mettle to win."

Xi warned that corruption remained the greatest threat to the party's survival despite a five-year war on graft that he claimed had been "built into a crushing tide". "We must remain as firm as a rock ... and secure sweeping victory," he said, warning that "pleasure-seeking, inaction and sloth" were no longer acceptable. "We must ... rid ourselves of any virus that erodes the party's health."

Xi, who has sought to portray himself as a strong and stable international statesman since last year's election of Donald Trump, also painted China as a responsible global power that was committed to tackling shared dangers such as climate change.

"No country alone can address the many challenges facing mankind. No country can afford to retreat into self-isolation," he said.

Without directly mentioning Trump, he noted how China had "taken a driving seat in international cooperation to respond to climate change". He added: "Only by observing the laws of nature can mankind avoid costly blunders in its exploitation. Any harm we inflict on nature will eventually return to haunt us. This is a reality we have to face."

Xi took a harder line on Hong Kong, which witnessed an unprecedented 79-day pro-democracy occupation and the birth of a nascent independence movement during his first term.

He vowed that Beijing would not allow the "one country, two systems" model, under which the former British colony has operated with relative autonomy from the mainland since handover, to be "bent or distorted". Nor would independence activists be tolerated. "We will never allow anyone, any organisation, or any political party, at any time or in any form, to separate any part of Chinese territory from China."

Xi was similarly uncompromising on China's overall political model, offering no hint that democratic reform was on the horizon or that the party was considering loosening its grip on power. "No one political system should be regarded as the only choice and we should not just mechanically copy the political systems of other countries," said Xi, who has overseen one of the most severe political chills in recent Chinese history. "The political system of socialism with Chinese characteristics is a great creation."

Xi insisted China did "not pose a threat to any other country" but his speech chimed with the increasingly assertive – some say domineering – foreign policy that has emerged on his watch. He cited Beijing's highly controversial island-building campaign as one of the key accomplishments of his first term. "Construction on islands and reefs in the South China Sea has seen steady progress."

Beijing did not seek global hegemony but "no one should expect China to swallow anything that undermines its interests".

More than 2,200 delegates have poured into Beijing for the week-long gathering, bringing with them an effervescence of political tributes.

"This is a joyous occasion," Hu Xiaohan, the director of the Congress' media centre, enthused at a reception on Monday night. "Great changes have occurred in China and we are so proud of it," said Xue Rong, a delegate who had travelled to the capital from Henan province. "Xi Jinping is a great man. He is down-to-earth, too. He carries the people in his heart."

Zhao Yongqing, the propaganda chief of the north-western region of Ningxia, said he had been inspired by Xi's opening pitch to the congress. "I feel a big responsibility. As a delegate, I must study and understand Xi's speech thoroughly, and publicise and implement it well when I return home."

The event, which Xi will use to pack the Communist party's upper ranks with allies, marks the official end of what is expected to be the first of his two five-year terms in power.

For some though it has come to represent the advent of a new political erathat could extend well beyond the originally anticipated end of Xi's second term, in 2022.

Chen Daoyin, a Shanghai-based political scientist, said he believed the congress heralded the start of China's third great political epoch since Mao Zedong's communists seized power in 1949. The first epoch was Mao himself, a revolutionary standard-bearer who helped the country find its feet; then came Deng Xiaoping, the reformer who masterminded China's economic opening and helped it grow rich. "Now it's Xi Jinping's turn to usher in ... the Xi Jinping era," said Chen.

XI JINPING THOUGHT ON SOCIALISM WITH CHINESE CHARACTERISTICS FOR A NEW ERA

The Thought consists of a 14-point basic policy, as follows:

1. Ensuring Communist Party of China leadership over all forms of work in China.
2. The Communist Party of China should take a people-centric approach for the public interest.
3. The continuation of "comprehensive deepening of reforms".
4. Adopting new development ideas based on science and for "innovative, coordinated, green, open and shared development".

5. Following "socialism with Chinese characteristics" with "people as the masters of the country".
6. Governing China with the rule of law.
7. "Practise socialist core values", including Marxism, communism and "socialism with Chinese characteristics".
8. "Improving people's livelihood and well-being is the primary goal of development".
9. Coexist well with nature with "energy conservation and environmental protection" policies and "contribute to global ecological safety".
10. Strengthen national security.
11. The Communist Party of China should have "absolute leadership over" China's People's Liberation Army.
12. Promoting the one country, two systems system for Hong Kong and Macau with a future of "complete national reunification"; and to follow the One-China policy and 1992 Consensus for Taiwan.
13. Establish a common destiny between Chinese people and other people around the world with a "peaceful international environment".
14. Improve party discipline in the Communist Party of China.

Views on capitalism

[...] their theory that capitalism is the ultimate has been shaken, and socialist development has experienced a miracle. Western capitalism has suffered reversals, a financial crisis, a credit crisis, a crisis of confidence, and their self-conviction has wavered. Western countries have begun to reflect, and openly or secretively compare themselves against China's politics, economy and path.

—Xi Jinping, the CPC General Secretary, on the inevitability of socialism.

The CPC don't believe that they have abandoned Marxism. The party views the world as organized into two opposing camps; socialist and capitalist. They insist that socialism, on the basis of historical materialism, will eventually triumph over capitalism. In recent years, when the party has been asked to explain the capitalist globalization occurring, the party has returned to the writings of Karl Marx. Marx wrote that capitalists, in their search for profit, would travel the world in a bid to establish new international markets – hence, it is generally assumed that Marx forecasted globalization. His writings on the subject is used to justify the CPC's market reforms, since nations, according to Marx, have little choice in the matter of joining or not. Opting not to take part in capitalist globalization means losing out in the fields of economic development, technological development, foreign investment and world trade. This view is strengthened by the economic failures of the Soviet Union and of China under Mao.

Despite admitting that globalization developed through the capitalist system, the party's leaders and theorist argue that globalization is not intrinsically capitalist. The reason being that if globalization was purely capitalist, it would exclude an alternate socialist form of modernity. Globalization, as with the market economy, therefore does not have one specific class character (either socialist or capitalist) according to the party. The instance that globalization is not fixed in nature, comes from Deng's insistence that China can pursue socialist modernization by incorporating elements of capitalism.Because of this there is considerable optimism within the CPC that despite the current capitalist dominance of globalization, globalization can be turned into a vehicle supporting socialism. This event will occur through capitalism's own contradictions. These contradictions are, according to party theorist Yue Yi from the Academy of Social Sciences, "that between private ownership of the means of production and socialised production. This contradiction has manifested itself globally as the following contradictions; the contradiction between planned and regulated national economies and the unplanned and unregulated world economy; the contradiction between well-organized and scientifically managed Transnational Corporations (TNCs) and a blindly expanding and chaotic world market; the contradiction between the unlimited increase of productive capacity and the limited world market; and the contradiction between sovereign states and TNCs." It was these contradictions, argue Yue Yi, that led to the dot-com bubble of the 1990s, that has caused unbalanced development and polarization, and widened the gap between rich and poor. These contradictions will lead to the inevitable demise of capitalism and the resultant dominance of socialism.

CHANGE OF POWER STATUS AND THE SPEED OF CHINA'S RISE

Entering the 21st century, there are more and more predictions about when China will become a superpower. Some guess that China will be as strong as the United States in the coming decade, some bet that in 20 years and some predict its rise in year 2040. In spite of those disagreements among scholars, the forecasts were all based on the speed at which China's total power has been growing in recent years, without any consideration of the influences of the other powers' growth. As we are aware that China's power status is related to that of the other states, when forecasting China's future power status, we should not only take account of the speed of China's power growth but also the growth of the other states' power. To foresee the future change of China's power status, we should clarify the conditions for ascent and descent of international power status.

Conditions for Ascent and Descent of Power Status

As a state's power status is determined by quantitative comparisons of powers among states, the change in power status of a state depends on the difference in power growth rates between two states in a given period of time. Based on the afore-mentioned formula of a state's power status, the expression for the change of a state's power status should be $Sc = A(1 + Ra)/B(1 + Rb)$ " A/B, (here Sc refers to the result of a change in power status of two states A and B;

where *A* and *B* indicate the original power for State A and State B respectively; while *Ra* and *Rb* indicate the actual growth rates of the two states, respectively). The expression shows that the change of a state's power status depends entirely upon the power growth rates (*Ra* and *Rb*) of the two states over a certain period of time. That is, the state with a faster power growth rate will rise, and the other will fall, and the statuses remain unchanged if the growth rates of the two state powers are the same. Over a fixed time period, the difference in power growth rates for the two states may result in three possibilities for change of a side's power status: rising, falling or unchanged. The three scenarios may result from 13 different situations, in which there are five for ascent, five for descent and three for no change.

It will be a political issue if a state is able to rise to a superpower in a few decades, but only an historical issue if a state rises to a hegemon over hundreds of years. As the atrophy of a state's power is a significant factor for the rapid rise of other states' power statuses, it creates an important scenario for a shift of power between two states. Therefore, power atrophy is an important political issue deserving more attention than power growth. A state's power increases in most years, decreases occasionally and very rarely has zero growth. Thus, the probability of the 10 scenarios of power-status change varies. Often both states enjoy positive power growth simultaneously; it is less common for one state to have a positive power growth while the other has a negative one; it is rare for both states to have negative power growth and is even less common that one state incurs zero power growth. When two states simultaneously have positive or negative power growth, it takes a longer time for their power gap to change and their power statuses to shift, and the probability of power-status shift is small. If one of the two states incurs zero power growth, their power gap will change relatively rapidly and there will be a higher probability for their power status to shift. However, the fastest change in the two states' power gap or their power statuses will occur when the two states have opposite power growths, i.e. one state's power increases and the other's decreases ($Ra > 0 > Rb$ or $Ra < 0 < Rb$). Because national power grows in most years and opposite power growths of two states tend to shift power statuses easily, the factors leading to power atrophy are more significant than the factors enhancing national power in terms of changing the power gap and power status between states.

Political turbulence can cause a state's comprehensive power to diminish severely and rapidly, and it alters a state's power status at a faster rate than does economic development. Being defeated in a war, state disintegration, civil war, social turmoil and political movements all work effectively in shifting power status. The shift of power status between China and the Soviet Union after the Cold War serves as a typical example.

In 1991, prior to collapse, the Soviet Union was the only competing superpower in the world rivalling the United States, and its power status drastically differed from that of China. However, as the succeeding state of the former Soviet Union after its collapse, Russia's comprehensive power endured a drastic fall and as a result its geographical area was reduced by about 24%, its population reduced by 48%, its economy decreased by 11%, and the size of its military was cut by 33.7%. At that time Russian comprehensive power was still greater than China's, however, its power status fell into the same class that China belonged to.

The power gap between them was only in degree and no longer in character. Thereafter, Russia's economy declined for years, its military capability was severely weakened, and its political power was diminished internationally. Even though it is hard for us to figure out in which specific year the power-status shift occurred, we are quite certain that China's comprehensive power surpassed that of Russia during the 1990s. Up to 1999, sustaining only military superiority over China, Russia fell far behind China in aspects of political power and economic power. In 1999, Russia's GDP accounted for only one-fourth or one-third of China's GDP of $1 trillion.

Economic crisis can cause a nation's power to decrease rapidly and it works as a faster agent than economic development in changing the power gap or power status between two states. The East Asian Financial Crisis during 1997–98 widened the power gap between China and the Southeast Asian countries and meanwhile reduced the disparity of economic power between China and Japan. The East Asian Financial Crisis decreased China's annual economic growth rate to 7% from 9% prior to the crisis while it caused negative and zero economic growth, respectively, for Indonesia and Japan. Indonesian GDP fell to $50 billion in 1998 from $190.3 billion in 1995 (in 1998 its currency exchange rate fell to US$1:IDR7500 from $1:IDR2321 in 1996) and it recovered to $208.3 billion in 2003, with only a 9.5% increase from its GDP in 1995. In that period, Japan's GDP reduced from $5083.1 billion in 1995 to $4326.4 billion in 2003, a total reduction of 15%. During the same period, China's GDP (by currency exchange rate) doubled from $704.1 billion in 1995 to $1409.9 billion in 2003. Therefore, in the eight years from 1995 to 2003, the economic gap between Indonesia and China had been widened from 3.7 times to 6.8 times, while the economic gap between China and Japan narrowed from 7.2 to 3.0 times. In terms of PPP, China's economy even surpassed Japan's, causing a shift in their economic power rankings.

Political Factors Determining the Fluctuation of China's Power Status

According to the principle that opposite power growths among states tend to change power status between states easily, we come to realize that in 10 years (by 2015) whether China can sustain the existing power status will be determined mainly by the likelihood of political crisis that may cause China's power status to descend. Since its foundation in 1949, China's power status has undergone a spell of four rising and three falling periods. During 1950–58 China's power status had been rising. During that period, the Korean War tremendously raised both China's military power status and her domestic and international capabilities of political mobilization. Between 1952 and 1958, China's GDP increased by as much as 1.9 times. During 1959–63 China's comprehensive power atrophied severely. The Anti-Rightwing Movement led the Chinese government to adopt the policies of 'Great Leap' and 'People's Commune', which resulted in an overall economic crisis. It was not until 1964 that China's economy recovered to the same level of 1960. In 1959, Sino–Soviet relations began to deteriorate and China was facing joint pressures from both the United States and the Soviet Union. During 1964 and 1965, China's national power enjoyed a brief rising period but fell again during 1966–76. In May 1966, the Cultural Revolution occurred and the country was immersed in turbulence and chaos when the government's ability to maintain order was severely hampered, economic activities stagnated, and the military weakened. However, in the same period of time, many Asian states such as Japan, South Korea and Singapore had industrialized their countries and their power status was rising rapidly in relation to China's.

From 1978 to 1988 was a period when China restored its social order, increased its domestic mobilization capability and normalized relations with the United States and the Soviet Union. Consequently, China had again enhanced its international political capability, and its economy sustained an average annual growth as high as 10.2%. The political events of 1989–93 slowed China's economic growth, and dramatically reduced its domestic and international political mobilization capabilities.

Thus, China's power status fell as her political power diminished in such a drastic manner. From 1993 to 2004 was the third period when China's power status ascended. During this interval, China gradually emerged from the international isolation which had started in 1989 and its capabilities of domestic and international mobilization once again increased. During 1993–2004, China's economy sustained an annual growth of 9.2% and the 1997 East Asian Financial Crisis accelerated the ascendance of China's economic power status. Ever since the founding of the People's Republic of China, each of the three major descents of China's power status was traced back to a political crisis rather than wars or economic difficulties. Therefore, we can believe that as long as there is no future political crisis, China will be able to avoid a fall in its power status.

Based on the principle that national power usually sustains growth in the majority of years, the author argues that the major external elements affecting the speed of rise of China's power status will be: (1) US military commitments and an increase or decrease of its international mobilization capabilities, and (2) the pace of political integration of the European Union (EU). According to the current growth of the comprehensive strengths of major powers, the author assumes that no other single nation, except the United States, could have larger comprehensive power than China in the next 10 years.

Although each individual European state has smaller comprehensive power than China, the EU as a unified power will have a superior status to China's. If the political integration of the EU results in an international player with national character in the next 10 years, our references for judging China's future power status should include both the United States and the EU. Some people suppose that China's future power status would fundamentally depend upon China's economic growth. They obviously have neglected the political and military powers of the United States and the EU. China possesses a huge supply of low-paid labour, therefore in the next 10 years China's economic growth will be faster than that of the United States and the EU. It is also quite possible for China to narrow its economic gap with the United States and the EU. Nevertheless, there is uncertainty with regard to the development of the military and political powers of China, the United States and the EU in next 10 years.

In 10 years from now, China may narrow its military gap with the EU but the change of its military gap with the United States will depend on its military containment against Taiwanese secessionists. A favourable security environment will constrain the EU from large military expenditure.

Therefore, in the next 10 years, China's military strength will grow faster than that of the EU and will reduce the military gap between the two. Nevertheless, the change of military disparity between China and the Unites States will be determined by the rates of military investment of the two sides. As a result of the pro-independence group introducing a timetable for Taiwan to achieve legitimate independence by 2008, the Chinese government will inevitably enhance its military capability to contain Taiwanese secessionists. If the Chinese government was to launch a military attack against Taiwan's independence, it would be possible for China to narrow its military gap with the United States. If the United States continues to wage wars against smaller states while China has no need to attack Taiwanese secessionists militarily, the US military budget will increase faster than that of China's, thus the military power gap between China and the United States would be enlarged.

In the coming decade, China will probably reduce the disparity of its political power with that of the United States, but in the meantime her advantageous political power with relevance to the EU may diminish. In the 1990s, global democratization and marketization increased the US international mobilization capability to a historical peak. With little resistance from the UN Security Council, the United States obtained UN authorizations on waging the Gulf War in 1991, the Somali War in 1996, the war in Kosovo in 1999 as well as the war in Afghanistan in 2001.

Many countries provided military and economic support to the United States during these wars. However, the United States current unilateral policy caused its international political mobilizing capability to fall sharply from 2003. Without any UN authorization, the United States waged war in Iraq under the excuse of alleged Iraqi possession of weapons of mass destruction. The US action encountered strenuous objections from many traditional European allies, headed by France and Germany. As no weapons of mass destruction have been discovered in Iraq, US international influence has been seriously weakened. In the next 10 years, hegemonic position will drive the United States to continue its unilateralist foreign policy. Meanwhile, China will maintain its multilateral diplomacy to harmonize relationships with her neighbours, the EU and the developing countries of other regions.

Their opposite foreign policies will reduce the political power disparity between China and the United States. Presently, China has greater political power than the EU because China is a single state while the EU is a regional organization with inconsistent foreign policies adopted by its member states. In 1999, the EU introduced the Euro which entered circulation in 2002 and finally established a single currency system on the EU market. In the year 2004, the political leaders of EU member states signed the European Constitution laying a legislative foundation for the EU to become a single state entity. If the EU constitution is approved by its member states, it will establish its own three-in-one entity of administrative institutions including a council, a committee and a foreign ministry. Future political integration of the EU will enhance its character as a large national state, which may help it to narrow its political power disparity with China.

Based on the above analysis, if we assume that both the United States and the EU act as single states, the comprehensive national power gap between either China and the United States or the EU and China will probably be narrowed by the year 2015. China's comprehensive power status may rank third in the world. In 10 years and beyond, it may be possible for China to reduce its economic power disparity with the United States and the EU even though its economic power may still be smaller than theirs. China will narrow its military power gap with the EU but its overall military strength will still be weaker than that of the United States or the EU. In terms of political power, China will narrow the gap but still cannot catch up with the United States. China may maintain her political power superiority over the EU but the disparity between the two may be reduced by further political integration of the EU if all its member states ratify the EU Constitution before 2015.

We have discussed why China enjoys the leading power status among the major powers with the exception of the United States. Based on the principle that a nation's power status ascends in accordance with a faster growth rate, we may presume that China will strengthen its power superiority over Japan, Russia and India within the next 10 years. If the EU becomes a single state entity by 2015, Britain, France and Germany will no longer be regarded as individual international players. Thus, we only assess here the power status between China and three other states: Japan, Russia and India.

With regards to economic power, low-cost labour and a rapidly expanding domestic market will ensure China a faster economic growth than Japan and Russia in the next 10 years. According to World Bank data based on PPP calculations, Japan, Russia and China have GDP per capita in 2001 of $26,940, $8230 and $4580, respectively. This indicates that China's labour wage level was less than 18% of Japan's and 56% of Russia's. Low-cost labour guarantees foreign investors long-term high profits in China. At the end of 2005, China adopted a floating exchange rate according to World Trade Organization regulations and the Renmenbi (RMB) will appreciate continuously over the next 10 years. The increase in RMB exchange rate will make China's economic growth appear even faster. Although it enjoys the same advantage of low-cost labour as China, India is far behind China in aspects of opening-up to foreign investment as well as other economic reforms. Therefore, the Indian economy will continue to grow at a slower pace than that of China.

In terms of military power, it is anticipated over the next decade none of the three states, namely Japan, Russia and India, will be involved in military conflict with the United States. Therefore, the military spending of these states will increase slower than China's. Even though India and Russia are both faced with the threat of separatism in Kashmir and Chechnya, respectively, they do not face direct military protection of these separatists by the United States. As a result, the threat to Russia and India, from the separatists in these two regions, will not be comparable to that caused by the Taiwanese secessionists.

Japan is under US military protection, hence its military investment will not increase as fast as that of China. The Japanese government has decided to reduce its 2005–09 military expenditures to $233 billion, i.e. 3.7% less than its average annual military spending in the previous five years.

As a result of the danger of Taiwanese independence, China is faced with potential military clashes with the United States in the Taiwan Straight. China's military spending in the next 10 years will increase much faster than that of Japan, Russia and India. This will in turn reduce the military disparity between China and Russia and at the same time make its military superior to Japan and India.

In terms of political power, China's endeavours in East Asian regionalization will effectively enhance its ability for political mobilization over the next 10 years. China will have the opportunity to further improve its relations with the EU and that will strengthen China's influence on global affairs. India, Russia and Japan, however, will have few chances to further enhance political influence in their own regions.

Although India has already been a leading nation in South Asia, the South Asian regionalization has much less momentum than the East Asian. The Eastern expansion of the EU is constraining Russian political influence in East Europe and the former Soviet Republics. To sustain its special relationship with the United States, Japan has adopted a policy undermining the establishment of the East Asian Community. This policy is similar to that adopted by Great Britain with regard to the EU. Japan's policy against East Asian regionalization may ultimately weaken its political influence in East Asia. In terms of global affairs, both India and Japan may have the opportunity to become permanent members of the UN Security Council but they will have little chance of obtaining the power of veto. What they actually obtain may only be a position of permanent/non-permanent membership without substantially increased power. Russian political impact on global affairs will further diminish as it is still trapped in a regressive inertia following the collapse of the Soviet Union.

COMMUNIST RULE OVER A MARKET ECONOMY

All of this economic activity is occurring under a communist party government which, since the introduction of market reforms in 1978, operates a system it describes as 'socialism with Chinese characteristics'. These 'Chinese characteristics' are a common theme in the country's adaptation to the modern world.

After China was rendered the 'sick man of Asia' as a result of European and Japanese imperial aggression, revolutionary forces turned to the then modernizing philosophy of Marxism to revive their nation. A poor match for the Marxist requirement that a state should industrialise before being ripe for revolution, agrarian China pursued a different path under the leadership of Mao Zedong.

Chinese communism took on 'Chinese characteristics', allowing the peasants rather than the proletariat to become the vanguard of the revolution in the early 20th century.

The formula succeeded in bringing Chinese Communist Party (CCP) rule and releasing China from internal chaos and a 'century of humiliation', as the Chinese often express it. After Mao's death in 1976 it became apparent that China needed not only an able new leader but a new formula for strengthening itself for the modern world. The command economy was not releasing China's huge potential for growth and power but had kept it backward in comparison to Japan and other developed economies.

The stage was set for veteran politician Deng Xiaoping to rise to the top and implement his ideas of reform. It was under Deng's leadership that China decoupled the economy from politics, allowing a command economy to transform into a market-based one. Politics, however, remained under the tight control of the CCP, as the crushing of the 1989 Tiananmen Square student uprising demonstrated. The failure of democracy to take root in China did not adversely affect China's economic growth. Thus, just as Chairman Mao could proclaim in 1949 that China had stood up, so too market forces - or capitalism - allowed communist China to rehabilitate itself to the point where the rise of China is becoming a serious issue of consideration for 21st century international relations.

History and Culture

Specifically, the question is whether China will rise to become once again a major political, military and economic power, just as it had been during its Middle Kingdom period of tribute-trade relations in the traditional East Asian world order. It was a world which came to an end after two millennia as a result of dynastic China's gradual weakening, lack of technological innovation and finally defeat in the Anglo-Chinese (or 'Opium') wars of the 19th century. As *The Economist* has observed: 'In fact, China was the largest economy for much of recorded history... [and in] 1820 it still accounted for 30% of world GDP.' Historian Arnold Toynbee marveled at China's record as a force for stability, commenting that it brought to its world 'long-lasting unity and peace'; while Mark Borthwick cites China's enormity as significant in its own right for the Middle Kingdom having been a centre for gravity in world affairs: 'The largest political unit of Asia has been and remains China,' he notes. 'Its combined population and physical domain have not been equaled by any other nation.' Add to this impressive physical dimension the activating spirit of civilisational power, and it is not difficult to see why China was able to exercise a stabilising effect through the soft power of attraction, which was more reliable and hence sustainable than the hard power of threat and physical coercion.

Indeed, China has been well equipped with the philosophical resources for socially constructing peace through Confucianism, Daoism and Buddhism. In all, the rise of China could represent an alternative to American global dominance. Whether this alternative is a form of complementary balance like the Chinese yin-yang symbol, or a dangerous competition for global hegemony, has remained a matter of debate. The yin-yang perspective is not without persuasion, though there are problems still complicating the hoped for harmony. Perhaps greatest amongst them is the problem not of physical power but the soft power of values: how attractive is a China that lost Confucianism to Communism, and is still trying to find its way back again to Confucian humanism without sacrificing the politics of control. Domestically, too, there are costs in China's economic success with the growing divide between the wealthy coastal region and the poorer interior. Internal weakness does not bode well for external resilience, as China's history has shown. Hence China's rise as a global power - while probable given its present trajectory of growth - must still navigate a minefield of hazards and uncertainties.

To understand this phenomenon of the emergence of China, it is important to establish what it takes to be a global power in the contemporary world.

CHINA'S COMMUNIST PARTY CONGRESS - ALL YOU NEED TO KNOW

He predicted Xi would be remembered as the leader who made China a strong and powerful nation: "Being strong first of all means being a global power: being a world leader and therefore leading the world. It also means that the Communist party must be strong, and that it must maintain one-party rule."

Elizabeth Economy, the director for Asia studies at the Council on Foreign Relations, said she also considered Xi a transformative figure who saw himself in the same tradition as Mao and Deng.

"I don't think there's a lack of confidence in Xi Jinping," said Economy, who is writing a book on the Communist party leader called The Third Revolution.

"I think he believes that in order to reclaim China's historic greatness, its centrality in the world, that China needs a strong leader – and he is the person for the job."

Economy compared Xi's bold political vision to a pyramid: "Xi Jinping sits on top of the Communist party, the Communist party sits on top of China, and China sits on top of the world."

Since you're here...

... we have a small favour to ask. More people are reading the Guardian than ever but advertising revenues across the media are falling fast. And unlike many news organisations, we haven't put up a paywall – we want to keep our journalism as open as we can. The Guardian is independently owned. That means we don't have a billionaire owner funding us but it also means we increasingly rely on contributions directly from our readers.

The Guardian's independent, investigative journalism takes a lot of time, money and hard work to produce. But we do it because we believe our perspective matters – because it might well be your perspective, too.

XI JINPING LOOKING STRONG BUT CHINA'S CHALLENGES REMAIN

Without once changing his direction, flipping his political message or sending a single tweet, China's president Xi Jinping has entrenched his position as a powerful leader at home and an influential force overseas.

At the 19th Communist Party congress in October, in the Great Hall of the People in Beijing, Xi made a 3½-hour speech in which he outlined the blueprint for consolidating the party's grip on power.

By the congress's end, he had been elevated to "core" leader of the party, a status that placed him on a par with former strongmen leaders Mao Zedongand Deng Xiaoping. He had chosen the other members of the elite standing committee of the politburo and enshrined himself in the party constitution.

Despite the strong position he holds heading into 2018, analysts and scholars speaking to *The Irish Times* say Xi faces challenges at home and abroad.

He has to make good on promises to improve the environment and to implement the rule of law, while also providing better access to healthcare and education, reforming the unpopular "hukou" residence permit system and making economic growth meaningful to everyone, not just an urban elite.

"Yes, Xi has consolidated his power and position, and is genuinely now very powerful. But like the regime itself, his power is brittle – hard and strong as far as it can be seen, but not necessarily without its Achilles' heel," says Steve Tsang, director of the Soas China Institute in London.

Recent months have seen widespread clearing of migrant workers, the urban "underclass", in Beijing. While this operation has proven unpopular among ordinary Beijingers, including the middle classes on whose support he relies, it is expected to continue next year.

The National People's Congress in March will be watched for signs of Xi anointing a successor. Although the duo haven't yet made it to the standing committee, speculation continues that Guangdong party chief Hu Chunhua may be appointed vice-president and Chongqing party boss Chen Min'er vice-premier.

This is of particular interest to Ireland as Hu visited this year.

External forces have done much to burnish Xi's credentials as a stable and responsible leader. He moved quickly to establish China as a champion of globalisation in the gap left by US president Donald Trump's isolationist moves.

"Xi has remarkably become a source of stability, responsibility and predictability. But China's challenges remain as fearsome as they did in the era of Hu Jintao," says Kerry Brown, professor of Chinese studies at King's College, London.

"There is the need for fundamental reforms in the administration, finance sector, in central and provincial relations, and in the way that Chinese people participate in decision-making," says Brown.

David Kelly, research director at the China Policy analysis firm in Beijing, believes Xi has established himself at the top of the hierarchy, and that he is unchallengeable for now.

"He has lots of popular support through anti-corruption. The strategy has been to compensate for local setbacks with international successes, which we label 'the China Solution'," said Kelly.

The central government faces challenges such as the gap in communication between the central government and local authorities, the rural-urban divide and the gap between state-owned enterprises and the free market.

"Xi doesn't need any financial setbacks, or a shortage of labour leading to inflation," said Kelly. "He's not as secure as he'd like to be."

With projects such as the Belt and Road Initiative (BRI), a massive infrastructure programme aimed at expanding China's reach, Xi has taken a risk because of high levels of debt in the public coffers and because some of the BRI partners are less reliable than desired.

International successes

"The risk-taking is not paying off uniformly. All the international successes, such as G20 and the BRI, are being aggressively tied to one figure. You concentrate the gains, but you also concentrate the risks," said Kelly.

One of the main external events is the Korean nuclear crisis, simmering just across the border.

North Korea is an ally, although relations are strained over Kim Jong-un's nuclear programme, and China has come under pressure to do more to help secure a solution.

Trump in particular has been on Xi's back, and following the successful testing of a missile that can reach the US mainland, pressure is unlikely to diminish.

Viewed more broadly, however, Xi has no real interest in rushing to become the world's biggest superpower and Beijing is unlikely to take a more proactive role in North Korea. It sees the problem chiefly as one for the US. Unless Trump issues an ultimatum, Beijing will keep its distance.

James McGregor, president of the greater China region for the consulting firm Apco, believes Xi is standing tall in a world looking for leadership and predictability.

"But his stature could diminish if Chinese policies continue to be very different than the official rhetoric. Now that he seems to be in charge of everything he also could face blame for anything that goes wrong. Maintaining power in China is a difficult exercise," said McGregor.

CHINA RISES FROM THE ASHES OF IMPERIAL PLUNDER AND HUMILIATION: THE CHINESE COMMUNIST REVOLUTION

The rise of modern China to become the second largest economy in the world was made possible only through the success of the Chinese communist revolution in the mid-20th century. The People's Liberation 'Red' Army defeated first the invading Japanese imperial army and later the US imperialist-backed comprador led Kuomintang "Nationalist" army. This allowed the reunification of China as an independent sovereign state. The Communist government abolished the extra-territorial privileges of the Western imperialists, ended the territorial fiefdoms of the regional warlords and gangsters and drove out the millionaire owners of brothels, the traffickers of women and drugs as well as the other "service providers" to the Euro-American Empire.

In every sense of the word, the Communist revolution forged the modern Chinese state. The new leaders then proceeded to reconstruct an economy ravaged by imperial wars and pillaged by Western and Japanese capitalists. After over 150 years of infamy and humiliation the Chinese people recovered their pride and national dignity. These socio-psychological elements were essential in motivating the Chinese to defend their country from the US attacks, sabotage, boycotts, and blockades mounted immediately after liberation.

China: Reformers and Compradors

Contrary to Western and neoliberal Chinese economists, China 's dynamic growth did not start in 1980. It began in 1950, when the agrarian reform provided land, infrastructure, credits and technical assistance to hundreds of millions of landless and destitute peasants and landless rural workers. Through what is now called "human capital" and gigantic social mobilization, the Communists built roads, airfields, bridges, canals and railroads as well as the basic industries, like coal, iron and steel, to form the backbone of the modern Chinese economy. Communist China's vast free educational and health systems created a healthy, literate and motivated work force. Its highly professional military prevented the US from extending its military empire throughout the Korean peninsula up to China 's territorial frontiers. Just as past Western scholars and propagandists fabricated a history of a "stagnant and decadent" empire to justify their destructive conquest, so too their modern counterparts have rewritten the first thirty years of Chinese Communist history, denying the role of the revolution in developing all the essential elements for a modern economy, state and society. It is clear that China 's rapid economic growth was based on the development of its internal market, its rapidly growing cadre of scientists, skilled technicians and workers and the social safety net which protected and promoted working class and peasant mobility were products of Communist planning and investments.

China 's rise to global power began in 1949 with the removal of the entire parasitic financial, compradore and speculative classes who had served as the intermediaries for European, Japanese and US imperialists draining China of its great wealth.

China's Transition to Capitalism

Beginning in 1980 the Chinese government initiated a dramatic shift in its economic strategy: Over the next three decades, it opened the country to large-scale foreign investment; it privatized thousands of industries and it set in motion a process of income concentration based on a deliberate strategy of re-creating a dominant economic class of billionaires linked to overseas capitalists. China 's ruling political class embraced the idea of "borrowing" technical know-how and accessing overseas markets from foreign firms in exchange for providing cheap, plentiful labor at the lowest cost.

The Chinese state re-directed massive public subsidies to promote high capitalist growth by dismantling its national system of free public education and health care. They ended subsidized public housing for hundreds of millions of peasants and urban factory workers and provided funds to real estate speculators for the construction of private luxury apartments and office skyscrapers. China 's new capitalist strategy as well as its double digit growth was based on the profound structural changes and massive public investments made possible by the previous communist government. China 's private sector "take off" was based on the huge public outlays made since 1949.

The triumphant new capitalist class and its Western collaborators claimed all the credit for this "economic miracle" as China rose to become the world's second largest economy. This new Chinese elite have been less eager to announce China 's world-class status in terms of brutal class inequalities, rivaling only the US .

8

Xi Plans to Turn China Leading Global Power by 2050

President Xi Jinping warned of "severe" challenges while laying out a road map to turn China into a leading global power by 2050, as he kicked off a twice-a-decade party gathering expected to cement his influence into the next decade.

In a speech that ran for more than three hours on Wednesday, Xi declared victory over "many difficult, long overdue problems" since he took power in 2012. He said China would continue opening its doors to foreign businesses, defend against systemic risks, deepen state-run enterprise reform, strengthen financial sector regulationand better coordinate fiscal and monetary policy.

"Right now both China and the world are in the midst of profound and complex changes," Xi said. "China is still in an important period of strategic opportunity for development. The prospects are very bright, but the challenges are very severe."

The speech signaled that Xi would prioritize extending the influence of the Communist Party in China over the next five years, raising questions over his commitment to implementing tough reforms and expanding the role of the market. While economic growth has surprised on the upside in recent quarters, inefficient state-owned enterprises and ballooning corporate debt pose threats to stability. S&P Global Ratings last month cut China's sovereign rating for the first time since 1999.

He also devoted significant time to defining China's place in the world, calling for a strong military while also saying it would never seek global hegemony. Xi is seeking to boost China's global clout with infrastructure spending and avoid a conflict with U.S. President Donald Trump over North Korea.

"The focus is on strengthening the Party as an instrument to lead China to the promised land," said Steve Tsang, director of SOAS China Institute at the University of London. "Politics will remain the focus of his next five years. The Party will direct the economy and economic reforms."

XI JINPING'S AND ECONOMY OF CHINA

Since the heady days of Mao Zedong's dictatorship, the president of China has been limited to two five-year terms. No longer. The Chinese Communist Party announced that a proposal to scrap that rule Sunday, setting the stage for current president Xi Jinping to rule beyond the end of his next term in 2023.

In other words, China seems to be morphing from a one-party state to a one-man state. This change—which is accompanied by other constitutional revisions that strengthen Xi's power—has been rumored for a while, but it's still a radical move. The collective governance system that has kept China remarkably politically and economically stable since the early 1980s is out, replaced by Xi's personal fiat.

Whether you view Xi's dictatorial coming out as a net good or a net yikes for China's economy depends somewhat on your diagnosis of its biggest challenges—and, in turn, whether overcoming those challenges requires more state power or less.

Most China experts agree that to sustain long-term growth, the Party must cede its control over the economy, allowing markets to determine prices, encouraging competition, and putting wasted assets to productive use. Without these reforms, the country will continue to amass debt and encourage capital outflow, leading ultimately to economic catastrophe (most likely in the form of a long period of slower growth).

But it's not so easy to become a more free market—particularly because China's growth model has warped its economic institutions.

The stunning pace of China's development relied on amassing and deploying huge sums of wealth to fund industrialization. Pulling this off required sweeping state control over resources from savings deposits to mining rights to real estate. Party officials who happened to be granted bureaucratic control over that process also gained control over the resources. Extravagant rent-seeking resulted, building family dynastiesentrenched by deeply rooted patronage networks.

The reforms needed to expand China's productive capacity would also require elites to cede control of resources to markets. Unsurprisingly, they resist.

At the same time, the credit-fueled growth model that enriched these elites has produced ever-diminishing returns on investment. The slowing of household income growth has made starker the ill-gotten gains of the Party spoilage system. When Xi took office as president in 2013, the masses seethed with resentment toward "corrupt" officials, threatening the Party's legitimacy.

Xi has positioned himself in opposition to those interests, launching a far-reaching crackdown on "corrupt" officials. At the same time, he touted the importance of market reforms and opening up China's economy. And so his fans might see his power grab as a necessary move to break elite opposition. In addition, with limitless power, Xi buys time to push through market reforms that, though vital to the country's long-term growth, will be painful in the short term as China writes down losses, recapitalizes its banks, and suffers slower—or even negative—growth.

Since this inevitable messiness ups the risk of political strife, pulling this off by 2023, when Xi's term was previously slated to end, would be tricky, as Julian Evans-Pritchard and Mark Williams, economists at the research firm Capital Economics, note. Extending Xi's window of time for forcing through these changes and leading the country through an economic slump makes it likelier that China might weather these changes without a political or social crisis, goes the logic.

That said, while Xi has paid market reforms plenty of lip service, he has yet to deliver on them, as noted by Victor Shih, a professor of political economy at the University of California-San Diego. "From everything we've seen, despite his rhetoric about reform and opening, Xi Jinping heavily favors a strong state sector," says Shih. That raises another possibility: Perhaps China's chief economic woes stem from Xi's having too much power, rather than too little.

"Whatever biases he has will continue to be reflected in the Chinese government's policies for the duration of his tenure, which now will likely stretch well into the next decade," says Shih.

Xi has some good biases—for instance, his seeming commitment to cleaning up air pollution in northern China. But he also has a bias toward heavy state intervention into the economy, as is evident in his efforts to fix problems like dangerous debt levels and deflationary overcapacity—the latter via much-touted "supply-side reform." During Xi's tenure, the government took action to control the stock market, bond market, and foreign exchange markets, as well as the supply of coal, steel, and cement, Shih points out.

Now, without checks and balances on his power, Xi will command more personal authority over policy than any individual has since the chaotic reign of Mao Zedong. "For lower-level officials, it is now abundantly clear that there are no alternative centers of power to appeal to, and that waiting for Xi to pass from the scene is also not an option," says Yanmei Xie, analyst at GaveKalDragonomics, a research firm, in a note. "To survive and thrive in the current political climate therefore requires demonstrating loyalty to Xi."

And loyalty to Xi means loyalty to his policies and his targets. The thing is, those targets often reflect "inherently self-conflicting goals," says Shih.

For instance, officials who meet the goals of Xi's deleveraging campaign will find themselves struggling to reach China's growth target (which, when it's announced next week, is expected to be "around 6.5%").

Thanks to this notorious GDP growth target—and the way China ignores losses in its GDP calculations—officials have long invested in projects that don't make enough money to pay off interest on their loans, as Michael Pettis, a finance professor at Peking University, explains at length. As a result, a good deal of apparently new lending actually goes toward servicing interest payments—such that it takes increasing amounts of credit to create a yuan worth of GDP growth.

While the point of deleveraging is in part to dodge a crisis, it's also, in theory at least, to halt this pattern. That entails shifting credit toward companies that will invest in profitable projects, and away from wasteful investments that plunge the country deeper into its cashflow hole.

Xi's refusal to abandon GDP growth targets—now combined with personalization of such policies—directly counters this goal. So while Xi might be applauded for his commitment to curbing financial risk, the fact that cracking down on lending risks throttling GDP growth bodes ill for the results.

Of course, with loyalty measured in target-meeting, officials have every incentive to massage their reported numbers—which, as GaveKal's Xie notes, could "lead to more rather than less falsification of data." Distorted data will make it harder and harder for Xi and his experts to know how the economy is actually doing, amplifying the destructive magnitude of ill-thought policies.

This dynamic has plenty of precedent—most notoriously during Mao's Great Leap Forward program of the late 1950s and early 1960s, aimed at rapidly collectivizing agriculture and industrializing the countryside.

When one of his ministers criticized the plan, Mao purged him. Political incentives encouraged local officials to fudge their official crop yields. Grain shortages led to a famine that killed between 30 million and 50 million people. Obviously this is an extreme case, adds UCSD's Shih, and no one expects anything so catastrophic to happen today.

Still, Mao's intensely destructive Cultural Revolution, launched a few years after the Great Leap Forward, is a key reason his successor, Deng Xiaoping, instituted the term-limit rule in the first place, in 1982, deliberately to prevent the the future emergence of another Mao-style personality cult.

There are also foreboding economic implications for the constitutional fiddling for China's already flimsy rule of law. The ease with which Xi has changed the Constitution will likely give investors pause as they realize rules can change with the party chairman's whim, notes Shih.

The confidence problem goes for Chinese residents too. The announcement has sparked more of a popular outcry than the Party probably expected, based on social media response.

It seems unlikely that nationalist propaganda will distract Chinese people from the glaring truth: Xi has dismantled the collective-rule system responsible for this unusually stable and prosperous period in China's history.

XI JINPING'S RISE TO POWER

Chinese President Xi Jinping is aiming to show the world's second largest economy who's boss. The country's top leaders are gathered in Beijing this week for the National Congress of the ruling Communist Party, an event that takes place just twice a decade and is the peak of China's political calendar.

For Xi, it's a chance to tighten his already strong grip on power as he prepares for a second five-year term. During his first five years, he made it clear that the Party's interests take precedence over market forces — and many experts expect that to continue.

"If there's a clash, the market has to be subordinate," said Yanmei Xie, a Beijing-based analyst at research firm Gavekal.

Xi's first term was full of drama: a far-reaching anti-corruption campaign that swept up business leaders and top officials; a stunning stock market crash that wiped out many people's savings; and sharp plunges in the Chinese currency that contributed to fears of a collapse of the country's economic growth.

Despite the turmoil, the economy has managed to keep chugging along, expanding at a rate that many Western nations can only dream of. But experts say Xi's government has failed to move quickly enough to deal with the bigger issues that threaten China's long-term economic health, such as soaring debt and bloated state-run companies. Can he do better over the next five years?

Heavy hand of the state

Xi has spent the past five years opening up some parts of the Chinese economy, but retaining the government's firm grip elsewhere. Aidan Yao, senior emerging Asia economist at AXA Investment Managers, points out the government has made China's currency more market-based and now allows foreigners to invest in the local stock market.

The International Monetary Fund endorsed China's yuan as a reserve currency two years ago — putting it in an elite club that includes the U.S. dollar and British pound. But the heavy hand of the state has remained evident. Government agencies clumsily intervened when the stock market crashed in 2015 and triggered alarm in global markets by devaluing the yuan without warning.

Meanwhile, foreign companies frequently complain that Chinese authorities ensure preferential conditions for domestic firms.

'Bird-caged Economy'

A last-hour surge by some of China's biggest companies kept the nation's benchmark stock index in the green. The Shanghai Composite Index ended 0.3 percent higher, despite almost three stocks falling for each that rose. The onshore yuan was little changed against the U.S. dollar and 10-year bond yields held steady near the highest level since late 2014.

"We have a fairly clear blueprint of Xi Jinping's political economy, with incredibly robust, strengthened state-owned sector playing a large role in propping up growth," Jude Blanchette, engagement director at the Conference Board's China Center, said in a Bloomberg Television interview. "We're moving into a sort of China Inc. 2.0, a real upgraded version. That, sure, has markets and they're going to play a really important role in this, but this is all within a birdcaged economy."

Xi's speech — officially known as the party work report, China's most important policy document — included sections on politics, the economy, national defense, foreign policy and Hong Kong and Taiwan. He reiterated the goal of attaining "moderately prosperous society" by 2020, which has helped drive economic policy over the past five years.

Xi also laid out an ambitious plan to make China a "great modern socialist country" over two stages in the following 30 years — part of what he has called the "Chinese dream."

By 2050, he said, China will become "a global leader in terms of comprehensive national strength and international influence" with the rule of law, innovative companies, a clean environment, an expanding middle class, adequate public transportation and reduced disparities between urban and rural areas.

"Chinese people will enjoy greater happiness and well-being, and the Chinese nation will stand taller and firmer in the world," Xi said of his vision for 2050. He said China "is approaching the center of the world stage."

Xi painted China's governance system as a unique development model while hailing signature policies like his Belt-and-Road infrastructure initiative and anti-corruption campaign, which has ensnared some 1 million officials since 2012 and sidelined many of his would-be rivals.

Xi affirmed the Communist Party's supremacy and said that China shouldn't copy the political systems of foreign nations, repeatedly emphasizing that the country had entered a "new era of socialism with Chinese characteristics." He called for the rejection of the "Cold War mentality" in addressing global challenges, and said China would never seek global hegemony.

Xi said the Communist Party will strive to fully transform the People's Liberation Army into one the world's top militaries by 2050, and emphasized the need to modernize its combat capability.

"A military is built to fight," he said. Throughout the week, more than 2,000 delegates to 19th Party Congress will discuss and approve Xi's report and revisions to the party charter. They will also appoint a new Central Committee, which will elect the party's Politburo and its Standing Committee — China's most powerful body — the day after the congress ends on Oct. 24.

'Get Rich'

Xi is set to emerge as one of the country's top three leaders along with Deng Xiaoping and Mao Zedong, who founded the People's Republic of China in 1949. He'll be looking to secure a majority of allies on the new Standing Committee, which may potentially include possible successors who could rule until 2032.

The Communist Party has been adept at changing course and finding ways for its citizens to make money, according to Fraser Howie, co-author of the books "Red Capitalism" and "Privatizing China."

"The bargain certainly in the past 25 years plus has been forget political freedoms, we will allow you to get rich," Howie said in a Bloomberg TV interview. "Keeping power has been of absolute paramount importance to the party, and that's the focus of what these meetings are about."

THE REGULATORY SUPERPOWER

Both European integration and European foreign affairs have been characterized by the setting and institutionalization of standards to provide predictability and reliability. The EU is known as a "regulatory superpower". The EU has the world's largest single market, and most multinational corporations. This of course includes some of China's leading (state-owned) companies, which have a strong interest in accessing it. The EU conditions require such companies to comply with regulatory standards and this therefore impacts on other countries' rules regulations with regards to economic competition, data protection and privacy, product quality, labor law, social standards, and environmental guidelines. The EU's accession process and neighborhood policy means that it is well accustomed to laying out conditions for engagement with outside countries. An EU that meets China united can use its regulatory competences to develop a sustainable, durable and rather cheap policy (insisting "only" on existing standards) that serves its own as well as the world's interest in fostering a predictable and reliable China.

Never before has the world needed Europe's regulatory competence more than at a time when China aims to redraw international affairs and the U.S. is retracting from global governance.

THE INCREASINGLY SIGNIFICANT "CHINA FACTOR" IN AMERICAN POLITICS

Compared to European nations, the U.S. choice between economic interests and human rights is neither as wavering as that of France and Germany, nor as clear as that of Britain, which has placed economic interests above all else from the start. If we say that one huge purchase order can change the EU's approach to China, then the attitude of U.S. political circles toward China is, comparatively speaking, complex and longstanding, and a large volume of purchase orders cannot fundamentally change it. For example, on September 8, 2009, during Wu Bangguo's visit to the U.S., China presented the U.S. with a $12.4 billion trade agreement. Two days later, the U.S. slapped tariffs on Chinese steel pipes and tires. This outcome plunged the patriotic angry youth in China into deep gloom, and an essay titled "Ten billion U.S. dollars worth of purchase orders buy U.S. sanctions; purchase order diplomacy is truly a disgrace for our people," spread like wildfire over Chinese websites.

China not only makes use of "purchase order diplomacy" to manipulate and modify such unprincipled European foreign policy that is subordinate to economic interests, but also derides the "hypocrisy of human rights diplomacy."

Compared to the EU, the channels by which China influences U.S.-China policy are much more complex. Up until the 2009 China visit of the Obama government's Secretary of State, Hillary Clinton, who made it clear that the U.S. would not allow human rights issues to affect economic relations between the two nations, the U.S. had maintained its criticism of and concern for the human rights situation in China. As for China seeking to influence U.S. policy decisions through highlevel U.S. officials and business people, the U.S. has kept up its vigilance on this point.

In late April 2009, the U.S.-China Economic and Security Review Commission held a hearing targeting mainly China's use of foreign dignitaries and the media to advance its propaganda strategies. But all precaution to the contrary, what is undeniable is that the "China factor" has already become a major element of U.S. politics at this juncture. U.S. political circles and their think-tanks have divided into factions—the so-called Blue Team and Red Team—due to their differing stances on China.

To draw a broad distinction, the Blue Team holds that China's actions in international affairs have been a serious threat to American interests, and its main points are China's ideological and human rights problems; and the Red Team follows its own wishful thinking in its firm belief that China's abrupt rise will be a stabilizing force in East Asia and the world, and its main point is the enormous economic stake China has in a stable world.

Following the shift in the center of gravity in Sino-U.S. economic and trade relations, and the emergence of a new generation of U.S. politicians, the members of the Red Team and the Blue Team are no longer divided along party lines, but rather by the interests of their electoral districts. In recent years, the most important "discovery" by Chinese authorities was that those members of Congress whose attitudes were hardening because of damage to the interests of their electoral districts were not, after all, the old-school "anti-China faction" members who had previously hated Chinese Communist ideology—and that therefore all sorts of "appropriate" tactics could be employed to soften their positions, such as strengthening economic cooperation with companies in their electoral districts, for instance.

In fact, in China, a country which practices media and thought control, it is simply impossible for someone who has never lived in a totalitarian state to recognize the truth based on a ten-day junket.

The following are the chief ways China influences the U.S. by towing the profit line:

1. Launch lobbying efforts through various channels. During the Mao Zedong era, Chinese authorities understood U.S. politics according to the political logic of totalitarian states and were eager to carry out diplomacy at the level of heads-of-state. They thought the U.S. was also a "one man show" and the top leader could have the final say. In this respect, Deng Xiaoping slavishly followed the precedent. Not until the turn of this century did the Chinese government begin to realize that U.S. politics were not entirely dominated by the "leadership core" at the White House, but that the 535 members of Congress on Capitol Hill could, whenever they wished, "create trouble," big or small, for the White House and for all manner of foreign governments, corporations, and community organizations. Thus, lobbying Congress is a method essential to realizing China's national interest. At present there are some two dozen public relations companies and law firms advising China. Two law firms—Patton Boggs and Jones Day—have been hired directly by the Chinese embassy in the

U.S. Jones Day's main job is to brief China on the issues of Taiwan, Tibet, religious freedom, trade, and exchange rates, and to act as liaison with the U.S. Congress and the executive branch.

2. Invite members of Congress on cursory exchange junkets to China. Beginning in 2004, China's National People's Congress and the U.S. Senate established a formal exchange mechanism. According to a memorandum signed by both parties, they agreed to exchange visits once every two years and establish a fixed meeting mechanism between them, whereby each country sends 12 senior members annually to take part in meetings to take place alternating in Washington and Beijing. At present, three China-related "China Congressional groups" have already been established within the U.S. Congress, of which the bipartisan "U.S.-China Working Group" is the most conspicuous. The group was founded in June 2005, and by the following year it had nearly 40 members. Co-chairs Rick Larsen and Mark S. Kirk have said on many occasions that "we should cross the river hand in hand with the Chinese people." Larsen's other famous line is: "The best way for Congress members to understand China is to go to China." In fact, in China, a country which practices media and thought control, it is simply impossible for someone who has never lived in a totalitarian state to recognize the truth based on a ten-day junket. Moreover, the Communist Party of China has accumulated several decades of experience with the "culture of inspection" and is very good at presenting its best face to foreigners and high-ranking leaders. From the July 1944 visit to Yan'an by the "U.S. Army Observer Group" to the succession of U.S. politicians who visited China following Nixon's visit, the impression of China is often a good one. For James R. Lilley, former U.S. ambassador to China, the biggest headache in his life was discussing China issues with these "China hands" who had been to China a few times or made a brief stop there.

3. Lobby U.S. political circles through U.S. multinational corporations with investments in China. The broad interests of multinational corporations investing in China make them an important link in Sino-U.S. political and economic relations. Over the years, in order to achieve and safeguard the profits from their investment in China, multinational corporations have engaged in a lot of lobbying of Congress. They have professional lobbyists in Washington, and have formed alliances.

   China's behaviour in Africa is "new colonialism," or "economic imperialism," aimed at plundering African energy resources while disregarding Africa's environment and ecology.

   Prior to China's accession to the World Trade Organization (WTO), they were keen to appeal to the U.S. government to extend China's Most Favored Nation (MFN) status unconditionally. Faced with China's poor human rights situation and authoritarian politics, their main arguments in lobbying Congress were: "China is moving further along the road to Western-style democracy"; "economic development will spur political reform in China"; "the spread of the Internet will bring freedom of the press to China," and so on. The Chinese government greatly benefited from a number of these lobbying activities. For example, in 2000, prior to the vote on China's MFN status, Boeing and hundreds of other U.S. multinational corporations banded together to launch a massive lobbying operation in Congress. Participants included the companies' experts in government relations, lobbying mechanisms of trade federations, as well as the lobbying firms they jointly hired. Over a period of about a year, they organized a large number of lectures and discussions to impress on Congress the idea that opening up trade with China would give American companies enormous business opportunities, and their efforts were ultimately successful. This collective lobbying cost a total of $112 million. Prior to this, the record for U.S. business community's collective lobbying effort was for the enactment of the North American Free Trade Agreement, which cost less than $30 million.

In 2006, the United States issued a proposed rule, *Revisions and Clarification of Export and Reexport Controls for the People's Republic of China (PRC); New Authorization Validated End-User*, increasing the number of products subject to export restrictions by 47 items, but in the end, what prompted the U.S. to reduce restrictions was not the protest by the Chinese government, but the lobbying by U.S. multinational corporations Boeing, United Technologies, and others.

4. China's Africa strategy: mutual tolerant alliances with tyrants who oppose human rights. As of today, of the 53 sovereign nations in Africa, 49 have established diplomatic relations with China (the remaining four maintain "diplomatic relations" with Taiwan). In global terms, compared to other areas, China's penetration and influence in Africa has been its most successful.

China's current Africa strategy commenced in 1995, when China completely abandoned the "anti-colonial, anti-hegemony" ideological strategy of the Mao era, broadened the scope of its exchanges from single-purpose (ideology-export) to multi-purpose, and, in economic terms, moved from pure economic aid to an emphasis on the mutually beneficial "win-win" approach to resource development. Especially when it comes to their joint resistance to criticism from the international community of the human rights situation in China and Africa, China and some African dictatorships have formed alliances of interests.

There are two distinct characteristics of Sino-African relations during this period: 1) Summit Diplomacy became the basis for bilateral relations; for example, in 2007 Hu Jintao led a delegation of 130 to Namibia, boosting economic cooperation between the two countries; 2) China's investment in and development of strategic resources constitute the essential relationship of Sino-African cooperation. China is now Africa's second- largest trading partner. However, this strategy constitutes an attack on the existing international order, and the strength of China's political influence is clearly growing by the day. In particular, China's protection of nations that violate human rights and its disregard for issues of governance and transparency in African nations have become topics of concern in the international community. Such criticism centers on the following three aspects.

a. China's behaviour in Africa is "new colonialism," or "economic imperialism," aimed at plundering African energy resources while disregarding Africa's environment and ecology. China imports mainly energy and raw materials and the damage of this sort of extractive industry to the environment is relatively large, leading to criticism and protests from a number of African governments and non-governmental organizations. China's economic developments in Africa are mainly in oil exploration, timber extraction, and dam construction. African scholars and NGOs are very critical of China's oil exploration and dam construction. Western companies are subject to supervision from civil society and do not dare to engage in resource extraction in Africa that goes against human rights and ethics. For example, Austrian and Canadian companies, under pressure of public opinion, abandoned their oil exploration rights in Sudan. But Chinese, Malaysian, and Indian oil companies, due to the lack of intervention by civil society, bought up these rights. PetroChina requisitioned a large land area, destroying the local traditional livelihood, causing displacement of the northern Upper Nile residents and showing disregard for their southern counterparts. Intellectuals in Sudan and Mozambique have strong views on China's dam construction in Africa; the director of the London and Khartoum-based Sudanese Piankhi Research Group, Ali Askouri, wrote an article critical of China's forced relocation of the population from the oil-producing region and also referred to the fact that China's participation in the Merowe Dam construction forced three ethnic groups to relocate, affecting the lives of many.

b. China's economic development projects in Africa have not in fact brought many employment opportunities for Africans. Some Chinese companies, taking into account cultural differences, the language barriers, and costs, have opted for bringing laborers from China, which was undoubtedly a blow to the African labor market. In addition, the fact that these Chinese companies have frequently brought work models from China (long hours, excessively low wages, and poor working conditions) over to Africa, has created an adverse effect. Moeletsi Mbeki, deputy chairman of the South African Institute for International Affairs, feels that for South Africa, China's economic development is both an attractive opportunity and a frightening threat.

...[T]he "soft power" China is peddling to the world is vastly different from the soft power (cultural values) recognized by the international community. China's "soft power" in European countries takes the form of purchase order diplomacy; in Africa, natural resource diplomacy, along with conditional economic aid. Moreover, the impact of its genuine soft power—its cultural values—is extremely limited and mostly negative.

c. China disregards human rights and supports dictatorships. There are three reasons why the harm created by China's method of providing aid to Africa has come in for criticism: 1) China's non-interference in internal affairs and failure to attach any conditions to its aid break the Western countries' model of aid with political conditions attached, and allow some African countries to exercise autocratic power with impunity. Richard Dowden, director of the British Royal African Society, points out, "The Chinese government likes to deal with undemocratic governments." China's support for Zimbabwean President Robert Mugabe has also been criticized by the international community. The result of the economic cooperation between China and Sudan is largely the great amount of oil-drilling in Sudan. And according to the latest report of the United Nations Environment Programme (UNEP), the main cause of the Darfur crisis is environmental degradation. The resistance of Sudan and other countries to the international community's criticism of the human rights situation in the two countries is even more the result of the alliances of interests. 2) Figures on China's aid to Africa are not transparent. At the present stage, the Chinese Ministry of Commerce is responsible for China's aid to Africa, but every province and city, and every ministry and committee, has its own projects. When high-ranking leaders visit, they are provided with loose estimates, and the multi-pronged aid method makes it difficult to determine the total amount of aid. 3) China's aid is in the form of national loans to help African countries in economic construction. But due to the general lack of management capacity in African countries, not only is it difficult for China's various loans to Africa to help the normal development of the continent, the loans in fact increase the recipient countries' heavy debt burden and have a negative impact on their political development.

China's aid to Namibia and the related procurement scandal are a vivid illustration of the enormous corruption risks encountered when China links its overseas aid with corporate interests. China conditioned its low-interest loan to this small African country by its purchase of $55.3 million worth of Chinese container scanners, to "help fight smuggling." The supplier of these scanners was the Tongfang Weishi Technology Stock Company, which was headed by the son of the CPC General Secretary and China's President Hu Jintao. One could say that the Tongfang Weishi Company corruption case in Namibia caused serious damage to the "China model" in the eyes of the African people.

In sum, the "soft power" China is peddling to the world is vastly different from the soft power (cultural values) recognized by the international community. China's "soft power" in European countries takes the form of purchase order diplomacy; in Africa, natural resource diplomacy, along with conditional economic aid. Moreover, the impact of its genuine soft power—its cultural values—is extremely limited and mostly negative. In recent years, the issue of the quality of products "made in China" has caused the international community to be even more convinced that China is a society that has lost its moral compass. For many China-based "China experts," "Chinese characteristics" in fact means "corruption." Thus, "soft power" diplomacy with "Chinese characteristics" frequently leads to the breaking of the rules of the game and corruption. Extended to international investment, trade, and political relations, the "Chinese characteristics" leave a profound mark—that of rampant corruption. In recent years there have been endless corruption scandals involving multinational corporations investing in China: Lucent, Dell, IBM, Hitachi, and Siemens have all engaged in bribery of high Chinese officials. And even in so pure a body as the Nobel Prize Committee a scandal has broken out involving suspected bribery of several committee members by the Chinese government. One can say that the "interest"-led soft power that China exercises in the international community will result in the "spiritual pollution" of the world. If not taken seriously, the world will suffer the consequences of the corrupting power of this "spiritual pollution."

XI MAY SCARE ASIA BACK INTO WASHINGTON'S ORBIT

One thing seems certain about Xi Jinping's move to establish himself as China's dictator for life: The bolder and more openly assertive foreign policy he has pursued since taking power five years ago is here to stay. The conventional wisdom is that the U.S., its Asian allies, and the broader international order are thus in for a rough stretch, as China demands its place in the sun. "Xi's consolidation of power," writes my Bloomberg View colleague James Stavridis, "will make China an even more formidable competitor." Less appreciated, though, is that this approach could also end badly for China, because Xi may be overplaying his country's hand.

What's indisputable is that Xi's approach to foreign affairs marks the culmination of a break with Deng Xiaoping's famous maxim that China should "hide our capabilities and bide our time." The basic idea was that China's neighbors and the U.S. would seek to contain a rising power that too openly displayed its geopolitical ambitions. To discourage foreign hostility, and to ensure access to the trade and investment, Beijing should therefore keep a low profile and avoid picking fights when possible.

Through the 1990s and early 2000s, Beijing followed this strategy with remarkable fidelity, achieving enormous gains in what Chinese analysts called "comprehensive national power" while provoking remarkably little international resistance.

Yet more recently, China has been moving in another direction. The process started in 2008-09, before Xi assumed power, when the global financial crisis led Chinese officials to conclude — prematurely — that America had been dramatically weakened, and that Beijing could accelerate its bid for primacy in the South China Sea, East China Sea and elsewhere in the Asia-Pacific. The shift has accelerated significantly since Xi took over.

Over the past five years, Xi's steady accumulation of authority at home has been mirrored by his bid to make China a recognized and respected great power on the global stage. Under his leadership, China unilaterally declared an Air Defense Identification Zone in the East China Sea and undertook a remarkable campaign to build and militarize artificial islands in the South China Sea. Beijing has pushed projects — such as the Belt and Road Initiative, Regional Comprehensive Economic Project, and Asian Infrastructure Investment Bank — meant to draw neighboring countries into China's economic orbit and weaken U.S. influence.

Chinese commentators have also talked up the concept of "Asia for Asians" — code for a regional order from which America is excluded — and the Chinese military has ostentatiously displayed "carrier-killer" missiles and other weapons meant to keep Washington at arm's length.

And since late 2016, China's quest for international power and leadership has gone into overdrive. At the Davos World Economic Forum in early 2017, Xi depicted China as a global leader on trade and climate issues, in unsubtle contrast to U.S. policies. At the 19th Party Congress in October, Xi declared that China could now "take center stage in the world" — as explicit a repudiation of the "hide and bide" strategy as one can imagine. The message Xi is sending is that China is no longer willing to wait indefinitely for its geopolitical moment. The time to make China great again is now.

The reasons for this insistence are both personal and geopolitical. By all accounts, Xi has a strong sense of his own destiny, and wants to be the leader who restores China to its historical statute and prominence. And with the U.S. in political disarray and its president expressing ambivalence about the country's longstanding global role, Xi senses that China's window of opportunity has opened.

The U.S., its allies, and other countries that are nervously watching China's rise are thus in for a prolonged geopolitical challenge, as a country of 1.4 billion people throws its weight around on the global stage. Xi is determined to "rebuild an Asian order with China at its center," says Australia's Hugh White, a gambit that will put great strain on the regional order the United States has constructed. Yet there is also great danger for China, because Xi's agenda risks triggering the international resistance previous leaders sought to avoid.

This is an old story in international affairs. In the late 19th and early 20th centuries, the Kaiser's Germany might have become Europe's dominant power had it simply prioritized economic growth and avoided antagonizing its neighbors. Yet by pursuing an aggressive foreign policy and starting a naval arms race with Great Britain, it provoked the hostility of the coalition that would eventually defeat it — with American help — in World War I.

Today, China confronts a similar dilemma. For reasons of history and geography alone, most of China's neighbors are naturally more inclined to resist than to welcome Chinese hegemony. The fact that Beijing remains a one-party, Leninist dictatorship only increases the fear that it inspires among many democratic neighbors. The basic logic of geopolitics suggests that these countries will move to counter China's rise — as many of them are already doing.

Even before Xi took power, Chinese coercion in the South China Sea and East China Sea was squandering much of the regional goodwill Beijing had won through its "smile diplomacy" in earlier years. And over the past decade, regional powers such as Japan, India and Australia have tightened or modernized their relationships with Washington, invested in new military capabilities, and sought greater security cooperation among democratic countries in the region.

Vietnam and Singapore have pursued deeper defense relationships with the U.S., and Indonesia and Malaysia are showing interest in doing likewise.

Many of these trends predate Xi's rise, but they are intensifying as he makes his agenda clear. Beijing's behavior has shattered any remaining illusions that China can rise without causing severe strategic turbulence, so its neighbors are looking for ways of containing the dragon.

Yet they will only be successful in doing so if they have the full backing of the U.S., and here the signals are mixed. On the one hand, Chinese ambitions are rapidly awakening responsible U.S. national security professionals to the rising danger in the East, and thereby catalyzing the same balancing tendencies we are seeing within the region. The Trump administration's National Security Strategy described China as a dangerous, revisionist power; the Pentagon has now produced a defense strategy and a defense budget that are geared toward an intense political-military competition with Beijing.

On the other hand, the Trump administration has handed China a great strategic gift by withdrawing from the Trans-Pacific Partnership, which would have offset Beijing's economic influence by linking an array of Asia-Pacific countries more closely to Washington. The president himself also seems torn between condemning China as a geoeconomic rival — see his recent steel and aluminum tarrifs — and buddying up to Xi, who cuts the strongman figure Trump seems to so admire.

The crucial strategic question, then, is how strongly the U.S. will support the front-line countries that are increasingly alarmed by what they see in Beijing. After all, a committed superpower with lots of friends and allies in China's backyard can still make life plenty difficult for Beijing.

Xi's foreign policy boils down to a gamble that Trump's America will not be up to this task. If he is right, the geopolitical payoff for China will be immense. If he is wrong, the geopolitical blowback could be severe.

POWER SHIFT AND PEACEFUL CHANGE

Seen in this light, the rise of China need not lead to a volcanic struggle with the United States over global rules and leadership. The Western order has the potential to turn the coming power shift into a peaceful change on terms favorable to the United States. But that will only happen if the United States sets about strengthening the existing order. Today, with Washington preoccupied with terrorism and war in the Middle East, rebuilding Western rules and institutions might to some seem to be of only marginal relevance. Many Bush administration officials have been outright hostile to the multilateral, rule-based system that the United States has shaped and led. Such hostility is foolish and dangerous. China will become powerful: it is already on the rise, and the United States' most powerful strategic weapon is the ability to decide what sort of international order will be in place to receive it.

The United States must reinvest in the Western order, reinforcing the features of that order that encourage engagement, integration, and restraint. The more this order binds together capitalist democratic states in deeply rooted institutions; the more open, consensual, and rule-based it is; and the more widely spread its benefits, the more likely it will be that rising powers can and will secure their interests through integration and accommodation rather than through war. And if the Western system offers rules and institutions that benefit the full range of states — rising and falling, weak and strong, emerging and mature — its dominance as an international order is all but certain.

The first thing the United States must do is reestablish itself as the foremost supporter of the global system of governance that underpins the Western order. Doing so will first of all facilitate the kind of collective problem solving that makes all countries better off. At the same time, when other countries see the United States using its power to strengthen existing rules and institutions, that power is rendered more legitimate — and U.S. authority is strengthened. Countries within the West become more inclined to work with, rather than resist, U.S. power, which reinforces the centrality and dominance of the West itself.

Renewing Western rules and institutions will require, among other things, updating the old bargains that underpinned key postwar security pacts. The strategic understanding behind both NATO and Washington's East Asian alliances is that the United States will work with its allies to provide security and bring them in on decisions over the use of force, and U.S. allies, in return, will operate within the U.S.-led Western order. Security cooperation in the West remains extensive today, but with the main security threats less obvious than they were during the Cold War, the purposes and responsibilities of these alliances are under dispute. Accordingly, the United States needs to reaffirm the political value of these alliances — recognizing that they are part of a wider Western institutional architecture that allows states to do business with one another.

The United States should also renew its support for wide-ranging multilateral institutions. On the economic front, this would include building on the agreements and architecture of the WTO, including pursuing efforts to conclude the current Doha Round of trade talks, which seeks to extend market opportunities and trade liberalization to developing countries. The WTO is at a critical stage. The basic standard of nondiscrimination is at risk thanks to the proliferation of bilateral and regional trade agreements. Meanwhile, there are growing doubts over whether the WTO can in fact carry out trade liberalization, particularly in agriculture, that benefits developing countries. These issues may seem narrow, but the fundamental character of the liberal international order — its commitment to universal rules of openness that spread gains widely — is at stake. Similar doubts haunt a host of other multilateral agreements — on global warming and nuclear nonproliferation, among others — and they thus also demand renewed U.S. leadership.

The strategy here is not simply to ensure that the Western order is open and rule-based. It is also to make sure that the order does not fragment into an array of bilateral and "minilateral" arrangements, causing the United States to find itself tied to only a few key states in various regions. Under such a scenario, China would have an opportunity to build its own set of bilateral and "minilateral" pacts. As a result, the world would be broken into competing U.S. and Chinese spheres. The more security and economic relations are multilateral and all-encompassing, the more the global system retains its coherence.

In addition to maintaining the openness and durability of the order, the United States must redouble its efforts to integrate rising developing countries into key global institutions. Bringing emerging countries into the governance of the international order will give it new life. The United States and Europe must find room at the table not only for China but also for countries such as Brazil, India, and South Africa. A Goldman Sachs report on the so-called BRICs (Brazil, Russia, India, and China) noted that by 2050 these countries' economies could together be larger than those of the original G-6 countries (Germany, France, Italy, Japan, the United Kingdom, and the United

States) combined. Each international institution presents its own challenges. The UN Security Council is perhaps the hardest to deal with, but its reform would also bring the greatest returns. Less formal bodies — the so-called G-20 and various other intergovernmental networks — can provide alternative avenues for voice and representation.

THE TRIUMPH OF THE LIBERAL ORDER

The key thing for U.S. leaders to remember is that it may be possible for China to overtake the United States alone, but it is much less likely that China will ever manage to overtake the Western order. In terms of economic weight, for example, China will surpass the United States as the largest state in the global system sometime around 2020. (Because of its population, China needs a level of productivity only one-fifth that of the United States to become the world's biggest economy.) But when the economic capacity of the Western system as a whole is considered, China's economic advances look much less significant; the Chinese economy will be much smaller than the combined economies of the Organization for Economic Cooperation and Development far into the future. This is even truer of military might: China cannot hope to come anywhere close to total OECD military expenditures anytime soon. The capitalist democratic world is a powerful constituency for the preservation — and, indeed, extension — of the existing international order. If China intends to rise up and challenge the existing order, it has a much more daunting task than simply confronting the United States. The "unipolar moment" will eventually pass. U.S. dominance will eventually end. U.S. grand strategy, accordingly, should be driven by one key question: What kind of international order would the United States like to see in place when it is less powerful?

This might be called the neo-Rawlsian question of the current era. The political philosopher John Rawls argued that political institutions should be conceived behind a "veil of ignorance" — that is, the architects should design institutions as if they do not know precisely where they will be within a socioeconomic system. The result would be a system that safeguards a person's interests regardless of whether he is rich or poor, weak or strong. The United States needs to take that approach to its leadership of the international order today. It must put in place institutions and fortify rules that will safeguard its interests regardless of where exactly in the hierarchy it is or how exactly power is distributed in 10, 50, or 100 years.

Fortunately, such an order is in place already. The task now is to make it so expansive and so institutionalized that China has no choice but to become a full-fledged member of it. The United States cannot thwart China's rise, but it can help ensure that China's power is exercised within the rules and institutions that the United States and its partners have crafted over the last century, rules and institutions that can protect the interests of all states in the more crowded world of the future. The United States' global position may be weakening, but the international system the United States leads can remain the dominant order of the twenty-first century.

CHINA ASCENDANT: IS CONFLICT INEVITABLE?

Thucydides' purpose in his great epic was to account for "what led to this great war falling upon the Hellenes." He acknowledged that what we know as the Peloponnesian War was produced by many different disputes and depicted them masterfully, laying bare their specificities. But, in the opening pages, he warns us that dwelling on the particulars obscures "the real reason" for carnage that ruined Hellas. "What made war inevitable," he tells us early on in his masterpiece, "was the growth of Athenian power and the fear it caused in Sparta." He might have added, for his account makes it abundantly clear that such was the case, "and in Sparta's closest allies as well." Among the lessons offered by Thucydides is that we ought not to dwell on the trees and risk missing the lines of the forest—the larger trends that drive politics and war.

Thucydides' epic has inspired many explorations of what in international-relations scholarship is referred to as "power transitions." Not a few of these studies conclude that these mega-shifts are among the most perilous periods in the politics among nations. Why? Because the established, dominant power fears that, even if it is has not yet been surpassed and may not be anytime soon, the margin of its advantage over an ascendant rival, which it has long watched uneasily, is diminishing—and will likely continue to do so. The rising power, having lived under a political-military-cultural-institutional order that reflects the preponderance of the reigning hegemon, and that therefore protects and advances its interests, grows in confidence. Eager to demonstrate to itself and others that a new era is nigh, it begins to probe and to push so as to assay the reaction and explore the possibilities.

Shifting circumstances and the attendant uncertainty make power transitions hazardous. The leaders of the dominant power whose position is being eroded feel that they must show that their side is still supreme. That impulse arises from the need to retain legitimacy among their citizenry and to show the challenger that they still have plenty of power and resolve and should not be underestimated. The leaders of the ascendant rival, on the other hand, are no less eager to show their own people, the hegemon, and the latter's allies, that a new arithmetic of power is emerging. One side's fear and the other side's hubris produce a volatile mix. The result need not be, as it was in Hellas, a catastrophic war. A shifting balance of power could instead create a more benign context, though one conducive to apprehension, limit-testing, crises, misperceptions, and strategic reassessments prompted by uncertainty and fear.

The latter denouement is worth keeping in mind when one assays the origin and significance of recent events involving the assertion of China's power in East Asia. One of these was Beijing's proclamation on November 23 of an Air Defence Identification Zone (ADIZ) extending into the East China Sea and covering islands that Japan and South Korea control but that China claims. An ADIZ is standard practice and thus hardly an illegal or belligerent act, but China's version is more stringent than is customary. It requires aircraft passing through to file flight plans with the Chinese authorities and to be under the guidance of Chinese air-traffic controllers, even if the plane is not heading to China. Moreover, it overlaps with Japan's ADIZ, covering the Senkaku/Diaoyu islands, which both China and Japan claim.

The United States, followed by Japan and South Korea, flew military aircraft through the Chinese ADIZ to demonstrate that they didn't accept its legitimacy; but various commercial airlines (Singapore Airlines, Qantas, Korean Airlines, Asiana Airlines and American air carriers, as per an FAA directive), in an understandable decision designed to ensure their passengers' safety, agreed to comply with China's stipulations. South Korea subsequently expanded its ADIZ, extending it into China's, to underscore Seoul's claim to (and control of) the Ieodo (Suyan Rock in Chinese parlance), which is disputed by Beijing. Yet these defiant gestures by Washington, Tokyo, and Seoul do not change the reality that has emerged, which is that China's action, taken from a position of unprecedented confidence and capacity stands. The question is whether Beijing will follow up with an expansive ADIZ to back its claims in the South China Sea.

The ADIZ decision is but one example of China's determination to stake its maritime claims. As far back as 1974, it defeated Vietnamese forces, taking control of those parts of Paracel/Xisha archipelago that it did not occupy already. More recently, China has continually dispatched naval patrols into the waters surrounding the Senkaku/Diaoyu islands and staged naval exercises in nearby waters, prompting Japan to follow suit. Beijing has also taken a tough line on the Spratly/Nansha Islands, asserting its legitimate ownership, rejecting the competing claims of Taiwan, Vietnam, and various other Southeast Asian states, combining tough rhetoric and actions (patrols in disputed waters, surveillance), notably against the Philippines over Huanyang Island/Panatag (Scarborough) Shoal, but not just there.

That the disputes over these various island groupings—many of them uninhabited rocks—in several instances pits

China against allies of the United States or countries with longstanding and close ties to Washington hasn't deterred Beijing. To reassure its partners, the United States has dispatched diplomatic luminaries, issues statements of solidarity, and conducted naval exercises with some of China's coclaimants. None of these steps has made Beijing any less hesitant to assert its claims. Its uncompromising stance has created doubts in the region about whether American protection is now worth what it once was. The standard explanation of what motivates China in the quarrels over these islands and their surrounding waters invokes the importance of sea lanes essential to Northeast Asia's trade and defence and bountiful offshore oil and gas deposits. While scarcely irrelevant, these considerations don't explain why China has been acting with particular assurance in recent years, the latest example of which occurred on December 5, when a Chinese naval vessel and an American warship nearly collided when the former crossed in front of the latter at close quarters in the South China Sea.

The islands' economic and strategic value is not new. What's different is that China now wields unprecedented economic and military power, thanks to the breakneck pace of its economic growth and technological modernization since 1978, its purchases of an array of manner of advanced Russian armaments, and its progress in across-the-board military modernization. China has long been determination to erase the humiliation it endured with the onset of nineteenth century. Having been a center of cultural splendor and wealth for centuries, it became a plaything of the Western imperial powers and of Japan, enduring more than a century of exploitation, coercion, humiliation and occupation. The memories of this dark period are ensconced in the minds of Chinese, both rulers and the ruled. Part of Beijing's swagger in East Asia stems from the determination to bury this painful past and to ensure that it never repeats itself. That enterprise necessarily entails challenging Washington's long-held primacy in region. It's not, therefore, just about energy, strategic outposts, waterways and other such tangibles. It's as much, if not more so, about casting off the burdens and demons of the past.

This helps explain why nationalism has sidelined Marxism/ Maoism as Beijing's legitimating ideology. The latter has little to offer when it comes to the managing and modernization of a twenty-first century economy, and may even be an impediment. Besides, for the well educated, tech-savvy, and materialistic members of Chinese middle class and intelligentsia, especially the younger individuals among them, regaining respect and righting wrongs has a resonance that chiliastic programs devoted to revolutionary transformations and utopia simply lack. The Mao suit is now a sartorial curiosity, the Red Book a dusty relic, another victim of the Internet's richer offerings. If there's one group that's more nationalistic than the Chinese leadership, it's China's educated young urbanites, who take to chat rooms and websites to issue denunciations and demands for toughness whenever China's pride is injured.

There are two trends that bear on China's role in the world and that therefore have consequences for America and its allies and friends. The first is that, over the past two decades in particular, China has raised the risks that Washington will have to assume to protect, or even reassure, states that have relied on preponderant American power for protection. Russian arms sales to China, which cover just about every category (including surface ships, submarines, fighter jets, air defence and anti-ship missiles, surveillance and fire control radars, and helicopters) and have amounted to $31 billion between 1992-2012. They have played a pivotal part bringing about this change, and the projected sale of the Su-35 multirole fighter will extend Beijing's capacity to patrol the vast South China Sea and to project power with greater effect. Washington's allies and friends still believe that America can be relied upon to defend them in an-all out war with China. But when it comes to skirmishes, the controlled application of force, and displays of power designed to intimidate, the value of the American connection as a counterbalance to China is diminishing. States in the region understand that the United States will risk confronting China only under exceptional circumstances and so the cumulative effect of carefully calibrated displays of strength, and the accompanying disregard for American power, will inevitably have psychological repercussion across East Asia that work to China's advantage.

Those who insist that a unipolar world abides compile charts and graphs showing that the United States has vastly more economic power (its GDP in 2012 was nearly twice that of China: $15.7 trillion versus $8.3 trillion) and military might (a defence budget of $682 billion compared to $166 billion in 2012 current dollars) than China tend. But such statistics miss this point. In a remarkably short time, China has forced the East Asian states that have trusted in American primacy to wonder how reliable it is now—and, more so, what its value will be two decades hence.

From a global vantage point, we are a long way from witnessing Pax Americana yielding to Pax Sinica, and Walter Russell Mead's recent claim, in his "The End of the End of History," that a latter-day Triple Alliance comprising China, Russia, and Iran is remaking the international order exaggerates both the reach and versatility of these countries' power, and more so their long-term prospects for unity. In East Asia, however, a power shift is underway, and no region matters more to China. That the United States can still prevail over China in "a force-on-force" war there is true for now but also beside the point because it is an unlikely scenario. What Beijing has done, and with considerable success, is to reset the calculations of risk, thereby casting doubt on Washington's capacity to provide reassurance and protection during lesser contingencies at a cost it deems acceptable. Beijing's East China Sea ADIZ and its tough words and deeds relating to islands and bodies of water it claims are all about creating this new context. China challenges. Washington offers symbolic reassurance. Regional states realize on each such occasion that the ratio of relative power is shifting.

The second trend, still only dimly discernible, is closely connected to the first. It has to do with the strategies that the states that feel most exposed to Chinese power will adopt to adjust to the eastern power transition. Through its still-nascent "Look East" policy India, whose security depends on China not having free rein in East Asia, has begun to beef up strategic cooperation with states in that region that are adjusting to China's surging power. New Delhi formed a "strategic partnership" with Indonesia and bilateral ties have grown, including in the military sphere. India has been intensifying security consultations with Japan and Australia, deepening defence cooperation with Vietnam, and participating in naval exercises with the United States, Japan and Australia. And it has revamped its relationship with the United States: the suspicion and intermittent hostility that marked the Cold War era have given way to a gradual strategic convergence. No matter what the two proclaim publicly their new course is in large part a reaction to China's rise.

JAPAN

Japan is slowly rethinking its generation-long military minimalism for the same reason. It is common to read that cultural constraints (a legacy of the atomic bombardment, defeat and occupation endured at the end of World War II) rule out a change in Japan's national security strategy. This conclusion overlooks the extent to which the attitudes and norms within countries that relate to national security, while important, are reshaped by what happens beyond their borders. Besides, Japan's choice is not binary: sticking with status quo despite the adverse effects that increasing Chinese power could have on its security or ramping up military spending recklessly, flexing its newly-acquired muscles, and scaring the neighborhood. With defence spending that's long averaged barely 1 percent of GDP, cutting-edge technological capabilities, and the wherewithal to manufacture an array of major armaments, Japan can increase its military strength selectively without sowing panic, especially if it retains the alliance with the United States and forges alignments with other states rattled by China's rising power.

Among the challenges Japan faces in creating new alignments is its troubled relationship with Russia and South Korea. Opening a new chapter with Russia will require reaching a compromise on the territorial dispute over the South Kurile/ Northern Territories island cluster, perhaps by using the ultimately unsuccessful 1956 formula as a baseline. Mending fences with South Korea presents a far bigger challenge given the legacy of Japanese colonization and the simmering dispute over the Takeshima/Dokdo islands. But inimical countries have redefined their relationships before. China and the United States moved from enmity to alignment after 1969 in response shared anxiety over the expansion of Soviet power. China and the Soviet Union, divided by ideological polemics and disputes over their vast border from the late 1950s till the latter part of the 1980s, forged a strategic partnership in 1996. The United States and Vietnam have—in large part due to the growth of China's power—embarked on military cooperation, and port calls by US naval vessels are now routine. These examples hardly establish that a new relationship between Japan on the one had and Russia and South Korea on the other will be easy, let alone inevitable, only that it ought not to be dismissed as impossible.

RUSSIA

Russia's choices are even more complicated. On the one hand, increasing flows of Russian oil and gas to China, China's massive purchases of Russian arms (the volume has diminished as China's military modernization has advance), and compatible worldviews (created by a belief in the sanctity of sovereignty, the opposition to humanitarian intervention, and the distrust of America's power and motives) have created an entente of sorts. But, if China's ascendancy is not interrupted by political instability and economic crises (neither can be ruled out), Russia will be overshadowed and risks becoming Beijing's adjutant. In Central Asia, which Russia has dominated for over 150 years, China's influence, especially in the economic realm, is already displacing Moscow.

Given the vast Sino-Russian border, and the Russian Far East contains a mere 7 million people (perhaps fewer) and adjoins four Chinese provinces that alone contain more than 130 million people, China's power is proximate. Its centers of power in its northeast, while Russia's are in its European regions, thousands of miles from its Far Eastern extremity. Russia's vulnerability will bring about a strategic adjustment. The most likely one, which perhaps seems implausible given the sparks that fly between Moscow and Washington these days, will result in a reconfigured Russian-US relationship with the substance that the Obama administration's vacuous "reset" lacks.

Despite the Sino-Russian strategic partnership, Moscow has no illusions about Beijing, something its military exercises in its eastern regions and the distribution of its military forces makes clear. The two giants' relationship has undergone several twists and turns since the mid-nineteenth century, and some Russian commentators have warned that a strong China will eventually make Russia less secure and even draw it into its orbit. This raises the question of whether the (admittedly lucrative) business of building up China's military capabilities serves Russia's long-term interests, not only because Chinese arms could eventually compete with Russian weaponry in the global arms bazaar, but also because China could turn into an adversary some day. Seen thus, the Washington's current spats with Moscow ought not to be extrapolated into the future.

None of the realignments I have discussed need happen if China wields it increasing power lightly and wisely, reins in its rising confidence so that it does not beget callousness, and uses noncoercive forms of power adroitly to coopt and divide its neighbours so that they do not coalesce against it. The problem is that power tempts and memories of past injustices generate patterns of behaviour that seem justifiable to those who engage in it but provoke and threaten those who observe or experience them. Some respected experts, Henry Kissinger among them (in his recent book, *On China*), imply that the wisdom and self-assurance bequeathed by a great and ancient civilization will help China's leaders to avoid this timeless trap. Perhaps so. But history suggests that such confidence may prove misplaced. Sinophilia is no less a barrier to clear thinking on China than Sinophobia.

It's not just the arrogance that expanding power tends to breed that could make China overreach. The discourse of nationalism could as well. The Chinese leadership will crank it up during internal crises and instability or external confrontations because it appeals to the pride and sensibilities of millions of Chinese citizens. But the recourse to nationalism will create problems for China's leaders. A nationalistic Chinese public expects them to stand tall in defence of the country's interests, and they will have limited room to back down, let alone yield, during confrontations. The continuing advances in social media (hundreds of millions of Chinese now use cell phones, the blogosphere, chat rooms, and the homegrown version of Twitter) and the rising pace of urbanization will make popular mobilization easier, enabling public pressure to manifest itself more rapidly and dramatically. These social and technological changes could increase the danger that regional crises that pit China against its neighbours could become more frequent and also harder to tame because they are more likely to feature such gambits as chicken, tit-for-tat, and one-upmanship.

The power shift that occurred between Athens and Sparta culminated in a devastating war. The one now unfolding between China and the United States in East Asia will not. China's focus is on economic development and its post-1978 economic reforms—call them the Deng Xiaoping Revolution—has enmeshed in the global economy, giving it a big stake in stability making it averse to crises and conflicts that rattle markets and unnerve investors. Still, there are other impulses than those that motivate *homo economicus*: pride, passion, the quest for respect and standing, the desire for revenge. Thucydides' masterpiece is chock-full of examples of how powerfully these sentiments shape political decisions, particularly in times of uncertainty and apprehension. The challenge in East Asia—for China and for others in the region—will be to manage the consequences of the power transition so that it produces a new and stable equilibrium.

THE RISE OF CHINA AS A GLOBAL POWER

China's population of 1.3 billion renders it the most populous nation on earth, accounting for a fifth of the world's population; while at almost 10 million square kilometres it is the third largest country after Russia and Canada. Its 2.25 million troops form the world's largest armed force. China's reputation as a major military power is crowned by the possession of nuclear weapons that are capable of all ranges and delivery modes. Economically, it is the world's fourth largest trading nation, having risen from 32nd in 1978 and 10th in 1997. Its GDP at 13% of world output (at purchasing power parity) is second to the US. China, inheritor of 5,000 years of civilisation, is also the world's fastest developing economy in the present age, having grown an average of 9.5% annually for the past 20 years. Such high growth rates, low labour costs and a huge emerging market, have attracted the world's highest levels of foreign direct investment. Since China joined the World Trade Organisation in December 2001, it has also become one of the most open economies in the developing world, with average tariffs dropping from 41% in 1992 to 6% after accession to WTO.

CHINA'S NEW ROLE IN THE WORLD: AGGRESSIVE OR RESPONSIBLE

During his report to the 19 National Party Congress of the Communist Party of China (CPC) in October 2017, President Xi outlined China's new international role, stating that: "*the Chinese nation ... has stood up, grown rich, and become strong – and it now embraces the brilliant prospects of rejuvenation ... It will be an era that sees China moving closer to center stage and making greater contributions to mankind.*" He further described the PRC a, "*mighty force*" in international affairs and emphasized that the Chinese military: "*must regard combat capability as the criterion to meet in all its work, and focus on how to win when it is called on.*" In an analysis of Party

Congress speeches over the last 20 years, a *New York Times* study found that no party leader has referred to China as a "great power" or "strong power" more often than Xi had in his opening address. Nevertheless, Xi also stressed that China neither intends to become an imperial power nor does it seek international dominance. Conversely, the PRC will behave as a "responsible great power". All this leaves international observers puzzled: Some believe that China will remain a "responsible" status quo power while other see China's nationalism as another sign of its revisionist ambitions in the 21 century.

Becoming a Great Power

Traditionally, China has viewed itself as a center of world civilization. However, from the mid-19 to the mid-20 century, it experienced semi-colonization, military defeat, internal turmoil and civil war. According to the official historical narrative of the CPC, this 'century of humiliation' finally ended with the Communist Revolution of 1949. Along the same narrative, Mao Zedong united the country and safeguarded its independence, then followed by Deng Xiaoping, who opened up and enriched China once again. Now, Xi Jinping aims to be the leader who completes China's road to "national rejuvenation" and make it a great power again.

Coupled with the reform to the structure of the People's Liberation Army (PLA), many Western journalists and observers fear a nationalist and self-interested China willing to do anything to push its own interests in world affairs. Most prominently, U.S. Secretary of State Rex Tillerson accused the Chinese of undercutting the, "rules-based world order", while the Chinese Party Congress was still in session. Although China's rise and Xi's self-confidence will no doubt lead to changes in global affairs, it would be cynical for Western countries, which have long shaped international institutions and affairs, to deny that same right to China. More crucially, such fears overlook three significant points made in Xi Jinping's speech at the Party Congress.

The Face of Chinese Power

China's increasing investments around the world are literally "buying" the country international influence. However, these investments also increase China's interest in peace and stability, and thus make China a more predictable international actor. In order to ensure the sustainability of its international investments and influence, Beijing needs to provide public goods globally which will in turn promote international stability. The Belt and Road Initiative (formerly "One Belt, One Road") is a perfect example of this policy drive. As a global infrastructure development scheme, the Belt and Road was in part introduced to export economic surpluses (like cement and steel) through heavy investment in politically unstable countries such as Pakistan.In doing so, the PRC's interest in a stable, prosperous and reliable Pakistan has substantially increased. Given these interests, it is very likely that China's regional engagement policies will change.

President Xi made the point that the PRC will never seek to "dominate" the world, indicating that the CPC leadership is well aware of the widespread perception of a "'China threat" and understands that the country has to carefully consider the interests of its international partners. Therefore, China is attempting to tread carefully to not just follow its own interests but seek out win-win scenarios. During his speech, Xi said that China will not pursue a "China first" policy, emphasizing that: *"no country alone can address the many challenges facing mankind. No country can afford to retreat into isolation".* According to the CCP leadership under Xi, Beijing intends to stick to its international commitments such as the Paris Climate Change Accord or the Iranian nuclear deal.

Beijing has repeatedly emphasized its respect for the principle of non-interference in the internal affairs of other states. This appreciation for state sovereignty, which China shares with most developing countries around the world, can be understood in light of China's 'century of humiliation'. Thus, international institutions which involve themselves in the internal affairs of states may come under pressure from Beijing in the future. However, given that China has risen to international prominence under the present international order, Beijing may be hesitant to attempt to comprehensively strengthen state sovereignty at the expense of existing international institutions and international law. Overthrowing a system which it is profiting from is surely not in the PRC's interest.

Additionally, China has to reassure its international partners of its reliability. China can only do so if it proves a minimum degree of commitment to international rules and institutions. This is particularly important for weak partners who fear the overwhelming power of the PRC if China insists on bilateral cooperation without any international legal frameworks at all.

At the same time, though Chinese-led institutions are less comprehensive compared to liberal institutions that have been established under U.S. hegemony. For example, many Western observers consider the Asian Infrastructure Investment Bank (AIIB) to be undermining the liberal agenda of the Western-dominated World Bank. However, when it comes to governing style, structure, resource acquisition, and operative implementation, the AIIB displays striking similarities to the World Bank. While it may undermine U.S. leadership, the AIIB does not break with the most fundamental rules of multilateral investment banks. Therefore, China is not advocating abandonment of a "rules-based" international order altogether, but rather seeks to reform the system.

9

China's New Economic Commission and Xi Jinping's Grasp on Levers of Power

China's Central Economic and Financial Affairs Commission convened for the first time on Monday with President Xi Jinping as the chair, marking the official start of a new command chain in running the world's second biggest economy. The new commission, which plays a similar role to the US National Economic Council, offers a permanent institution for Xi to drive through his economic policies, such as measures to defuse a debt bomb, analysts said.

The meeting, which was also attended by Premier Li Keqiang and Vice Premier Han Zheng, concluded that local governments and companies, especially state-owned enterprises, need to reduce their leverage ratio "as quickly as possible".

Donald Trump's trade endgame said to be the opening of China's economy

The body has been elevated from a standing group under the Central Leading Group of Economic and Financial Affairs and its new role follows a major revamp of China's ruling apparatus to give the party a more prominent role in public affairs.

A statement said Xi had stressed the need to implement his policies such as cutting debt, reducing pollution and eradicating poverty. The official news agency Xinhua paraphrased Xi's message as: "Financial risk management matters to national security... and the safety of people's property."

China's four-decade route to the world's No 1 economy

Zhou Hao, an economist with Commerzbank in Singapore, said the new body was an official way of implementing the view that "the party manages the economy". The institutionalisation of the commission and could help the outside world to have a better understanding of China's policy direction, he added.

"In the past, we didn't know whether or when the top leaders had meetings on economic affairs, and there was confusion even about basic issues such as whether China wants to spur growth or to cut debts," Zhou said. "Now everyone knows Xi is in absolute control... so if Xi said the priority is to cut leverage for China, we know China will do it."

Xi's plan to centralise the decision-making powers of the party actually started five years ago, an article published by Xinhua over the weekend disclosed for the first time.

At the first meeting of the team convened by Xi on April 17 2013, he decided to change the role of the team from a consulting group to a "decision-making" one – an approach that would be different from the days of his predecessors of Hu Jintao and Jiang Zemin.

The 2013 meeting had been kept as a secret until last Saturday, as were the following four meetings of the leading group under Xi, which took place on a quarterly basis in July, September and December of 2013 and March 2014, covering issues of urbanisation, fiscal reform, water supply security and food supply security.

There were few public reports about the leading group's activities before Xi's accession. Previously the State Council, or the central Chinese government, took the front-stage role in economic policy. For instance, when the global financial crisis hit China's growth, it was at a regular cabinet meeting that the then Premier Wen Jiabao decided to launch a massive stimulus of 4 trillion yuan. China began to publish the central economic team's meetings in June 2014 as it became increasingly clear that Xi, assisted by his top economic aide Liu He, had the final say over the world's second biggest economy.

ONE-MAN RULE ISN'T GOOD FOR THE ECONOMY EITHER

China's defenders are putting an optimistic spin on the country's tilt toward one-man rule. Now that President Xi Jinping has set himself up to remain in power indefinitely, they suggest, he will have the runway to see through painful but necessary economic reforms that have long been resisted by various actors within China's political system. In other words, even if last weekend's scrapping of term limits for the presidency dooms hopes for political liberalization, it increases the prospects for economic liberalization.

Such faith is misplaced. Xi's economic agenda has been clear for a while — and it doesn't include the type of marketizing reforms that would structurally improve Chinese growth. In fact, his power grab makes such reforms less likely, not more.

Xi reiterated his priorities at a Communist Party congress last October, when he stressed that deepening "supply-side structural reform" should be the government's central focus. That edict was even added into the Party's constitution — a document that supersedes the official state constitution when it comes to governing China.

The supply-side program has provided the overarching economic policy framework in China since late 2015, when it was first introduced. Given Xi's recent championing of the strategy, it will continue to do so for the foreseeable future. The architect of supply-side structural reform, Liu He, is Xi's top economic adviser and is widely expected to become the county's most powerful economic official at the annual meeting of the National People's Congress next month.

The program has several goals. They include reducing risks in the financial system (and eventually deleveraging);

consolidating and cutting capacity in upstream industrial sectors such as coal and steel; reducing housing inventories; lowering administrative costs for businesses; and fixing the economy's "weak links," which include barriers to trade and investment between provinces.

These are worthy priorities, and significant and important progress has been made in several areas. The financial system saw interbank leverage decrease by over 3 trillion renminbi in 2017 — the first such decline since 2010. Efforts at eradicating subpar production in steel and coal have reduced air pollution and boosted profitability in the industrial sector, as prices have risen by 111 percent and 153 percent, respectively, since the beginning of 2016. China's 40 to 50 biggest cities are now trying to build property inventories back up rather than running them down.

The fact that economic growth accelerated last year for the first time since 2010 has reassured officials that they're on the right course. The problem is that while these developments are positive in the short run, they do nothing to address the fundamental, long-term challenges that China's economy faces: the institutional impediments to sustainable productivity growth.

When most Western economists talk about the "reforms" China needs, they have in mind productivity-enhancing adjustments such as genuinely improving the governance of state-owned enterprises, hardening budget constraints, and fully marketizing pricing mechanisms. Such changes aren't on the table. Even as they laud the valued role of the market, policymakers seem to believe their more interventionist supply-side strategy will reduce risks enough that the economy can continue to grow without being opened up further.

What's more, moving toward one-man rule in China will make any kind of liberalizing reforms harder. To be effective, such reforms would require strong regulatory institutions that are backed by the rule of law. Cleaning up state-owned enterprises, for example, would require managers to focus on their fiduciary responsibilities and legal dividend requirements over strategic Party imperatives — and to be held accountable if they don't. Reducing local-government spending would similarly require provincial cadres to fully respect both the letter and the spirit of recent updates to the budget law. Neither of these critical areas is seeing much, if any, progress at present.

Already, most asset managers cite the lack of legal clarity as a key reason for avoiding portfolio investment in the mainland. And the uneven legal and regulatory environment is a well-documented headache for foreign companies that have no choice but to try and serve one-fifth of the world's consumers.

That lack of confidence is being reflected in weaker capital flows to the mainland: Growth in foreign direct investment in 2017 was a dismal 4 percent. Even as foreign capital would help to sustain China's economic engine, it'll continue to be less forthcoming — thanks in large part to the unsure legal environment.

Xi's administration has often spoken about its desire to improve legal mechanisms. But those efforts are fundamentally undermined by moves to bend or change the law to comport with immediate political concerns. Even if China's leaders did have a secret master plan to liberalize the economy, their recent political decisions would pose one big hurdle to implementing it.

GLOBAL POWER IN TODAY'S WORLD

The term *global power* is a more contemporary term for *great power*, as traditionally employed in the International Relations (IR) literature, and a better fit for 21st century conditions than *superpower*. *Superpower* was the creation of the politics of 20th century nuclear weapons technology, even though the coining of the term in 1944 did not take the nuclear dimension into account but rather the global reach of a nation. As the Cold War became more entrenched, that which distinguished a nuclear *superpower* from a 19th century *great power* was possession of the power of ultimate destruction and the strategic doctrine of nuclear deterrence that emerged from it. The processes of globalization that characterize the present century mean that 'great' power needs more than nuclear superpower capability. Indeed, it needs to broaden out to the more traditional *great power* attributes of maintaining sufficient diplomatic, economic, and military resources for preserving the international order in which *great powers* presume themselves to be the main actors. Beyond being merely 'great', or only 'super', they must now be 'global' and attain transnational competencies that permit interaction with non-state actors, regional forums and the instruments and institutions of global governance. In short, a*global power* needs to promote international order; possess formidable military capability and the communicated will to use it; and engage productively in transnational projects such as global justice, as well as deal effectively with transnational threats such as militant religious extremists.

Such is the meaning behind the term *global power* as used in the present discussion. Its meaning will be further elaborated on China's capacity to match these criteria of not only being (a) a *great power*in the traditional sense and (b) a militarily outstanding one, but also (c) a transnational performer.

Is China a great power *in helping to maintain the world order?* A *great power*, according to Hedley Bull's classic 1977 work, *The Anarchical Society*, belongs to a society of states that maintains a balance-of-power to prevent a global dictatorship emerging through imperial conquest. Besides the balancing-of-power in maintaining this socially constructed system, *great powers* also engage in the order preserving mechanisms of *international law*, *diplomacy*, *concerting* (or joint management of the system), and *war* when it acts to preserve (or defend) the system rather than destroy it.

As a member of the United Nations Security Council, the People's Republic of China (PRC) belongs to the elite club of recognized *great powers*. It is involved in more than 1000 international governmental organizations that deal with issues ranging from drug trafficking to the environment; and it is an ardent supporter of the United Nations and international law, warning against the exercise of military power when peaceful methods of diplomacy ought to be given greater scope for realization. This was especially notable with regard to China's reaction to American military interventions in the post-Cold War era, indicating China's understanding of the need for great powers to critique one another in the interests of a balanced state system. Even before its economic rise and military modernisation, China was a vocal critic of superpower conduct in world affairs. Indeed, China's role during the Cold War was one of balance in the strategic triangle (comprising the US, Soviet Union and PRC), whereby China pursued a policy of 'leaning to one side' (either the Soviet Union or the United States) from within a posture of strategic independence.

Even with the collapse of the Cold War structure, and the clear military and economic superiority that now rests with the remaining superpower, the United States still supports the prevailing state system and is sensitive to balance-of-power as well as concerting behaviour. Thus China may continue to exercise its role of superpower critic as the need arises. China is not alone in its balancing efforts, as the failure of the US to gain UN support for its war on Iraq in 2003 demonstrated. In this sense, the European Union (EU) and its member states, Russia and others act as both a concerting and balancing force. China, too, acted in concert with the US in its campaign against state-defying terrorism. But alongside other states, including France, Germany, Russia, and Turkey, it opposed the US war on Iraq. Even though the US went ahead regardless, it still returned to the UN to gain a mandate to continue in the aftermath of the war and to involve other nations. This indicates that the American hegemon is aware of the need to maintain its power through legitimacy, as well as reducing its foreign policy costs in material terms, in the rate of casualties, and hence in domestic public opinion terms. Another 'Vietnam' - both at home and abroad - would not be countenanced by the American public.

Unlike the characteristically unipolar structure of the state system over which Washington presides coupled with US unilateralist management tendencies, China has been a strong advocate of multipolarity and, of late, multilateralism. This would suit China in view of its subordinate power status in comparison to the US; a view which would suggest to some observers that if China surpasses the US and becomes the dominant state, it would behave in a similar fashion to the US. This is the 'strong states cast long shadows' proposition. Such a proposition supports the China threat thesis if (a) one is opposed to the emergence of an Oriental hegemonic power in the state system preferring an Occidental one, or (b) if one is opposed to unipolarity, preferring a closer semblance of balance-of-power in bipolarity or multipolarity. The first pertains to cultural affiliations and Samuel Huntington's 'clash of civilizations' thesis; the second has an aversion to hegemonic systems. In light of increasing opposition to US hegemonic leadership in the aftermath of the Iraq war, China may garner some support for its rise as a serious balancer to the US. However, the US would need to entrench itself in world-defying, self-aggrandising behaviour to warrant such an adversarial image. Indeed, the US would need to lose its hegemonic legitimacy and China to gain it.

THE PURSUIT OF GREAT POWER LEGITIMACY

It is unlikely the US will persist in such a self-destructive path of loss of legitimacy but it is possible that China will capitalize on it tactically in order to make strategic gains in its own legitimacy enhancement. To gain legitimacy of the order exercised by the US, there would need to be an acceptance of an Oriental superpower, the issue of dissent in its various forms (Tibet. Xinjiang, Taiwan, Democracy, human rights) would need to be addressed, China's championing of international law and diplomacy would need to be maintained and visibly supported, as would a consultative management style global affairs. And this is only in the political field. There is economic and military strength to consider too. However, it is in the political field that legitimacy comes to the fore; such legitimacy equates with 'honour' in ancient Greek or Occidental thought and 'virtue' in the classical Chinese or Oriental equivalent. Legitimacy, honour and virtue are indeed precious moral resources for a great power to cultivate and they apply to aspiring states across the East-West civilisational spectrum. Thus the acquisition of legitimacy may overcome 'clash of civilisations' objections, particularly if deployed along multilateralist rather than unilateralist lines. This, China appears to be doing. Ironically, it was China who acted as an imperial power in its hierarchical international tribute relations until the 19th century, and the United States that disdains imperial ambitions in its 'freedom and democracy' rhetoric.

China's consolidation of its role as a great power in a sovereign state system was evident in its socialist state persona when it emphasized the equality of states principle, criticized the superpowers for putting their own strategic competition ahead of global welfare, safety and justice and, since the Cold War's end, its assiduous cultivation of diplomatic relations with a host of nations and regions. Of interest are its more positive relations with traditional rivals Russia and India. With the former it is engaged bilaterally in a 'strategic partnership' that has developed into a Treaty on Good Neighbourly Friendship and Cooperation (2001), and the establishment of a mechanism of bilateral security consultations (2005) inclusive of joint military exercises - the first being planned for August 2005, as well as multilaterally through the Shanghai Cooperation Organisation. With the latter, now a nuclear power in its own right, China has not only worked to dispel threat perceptions but also supports India as a candidate for a permanent seat on the UN Security Council. According to Chinese State Councillor Tang Jiaxuan, during his visit to India in October 2004: 'India is a major country in Asia... China fully understands India's position and endorses its aspirations... We also hope to see India play a greater and constructive role in the UN Security Council.' Also of consequence is China's interest in promoting peace on the Korean peninsula through its hosting of the Six-Party Talks on prevent the nuclearisation of the Korean peninsula, and a planned common economic future with

Southeast Asia. The end of this decade will see the emergence of a regional free trade agreement between China and the Association of Southeast Asian Nations (ASEAN). Tariffs are to be reduced to between 5% and zero and investment barriers removed. This trade region will create an integrated market of 1.7 billion people, forming what will become the world's most populous free trade zone. At the same time China has committed itself to a code of good conduct over the contested ownership of seabed resources in the South China Sea.

ECONOMIC AND MILITARY DIMENSION OF GREAT POWER

The issue of energy resources in the South China Sea, while seemingly contained within a code of conduct that is not legally binding but which appeals to China's honour and legitimacy, does not remove doubt in the minds political realists who see China's need for energy as an overriding concern, driving diplomacy as well as military expansion. 'China's appetite for energy resources,' notes Jeffrey Robertson, 'threatens to outweigh the trend toward great power responsibility epitomized by its dealings with Russia and India.' How strong are China's appetites in relation to its spirit and reason - or its traditional notion of power in terms of virtue?

The Economist of 2 October 2004 dedicated its *Survey of the World Economy* to China and the United States. It notes that China is the world's largest consumer of steel, copper, coal and cement, the world's second largest consumer of oil (after USA), and that in 2003, China consumed 40% of the world's coal and 30% of its steel. In 20 years (2024), it was projected that China's energy requirements would quadruple but its per capita use of energy would remain half that of the US.

The implication in China's growing appetite is whether it will seek what it wants with a carrot or a stick - with the soft or hard power option - or what combination of both? A classical source of Chinese strategic culture, Sun Tzu states that 'All warfare is deception'. How deceptive is China's military power? How soft is China's hard power? - as in (a) *vulnerable* and (b) a *disguise for soft power*? How hard is China's soft power? - as in (a) *compelling* and (b) a disguise and means for the *acquisition of hard power*? These combinations speak to a realist strategic culture which some commentators view as the natural outcome of China's rise to global power. As the November 2004 issue of the IISS Strategic Comments states, China has 'sought to promote a variety of new institutional arrangements that exclude the United States... [in Eastern Asia] where China can exercise a natural leadership role' and that its need for energy and raw materials has extended its resource diplomacy to Central Asia, the Middle East and Africa. Indeed, many of China's gains are in direct relation to American interests.

It is estimated that China's proven oil reserves will be depleted by 2018. China has been importing oil since 1993. Its dependence on oil imports has led it to energy investments in countries which are not only resource rich but also at polar extremes in terms of friend or foe in the American strategic spectrum. Thus, Australia - a firm US ally - won a AUS$25 billion contract in 2002 to supply liquid natural gas (LNG) to China. It was described by Australia's foreign minister, Alexander Downer, as 'the beginning of a long-term strategic partnership in energy'. As to oil imports, a fifth of China's imports (14 percent from Iran and 6 percent from Sudan) come from countries governed by what the US would regard problematic regimes. The imposition of sanctions on these and other 'rogue' countries would impinge on China's energy sourcing. Why would China choose to invest in such politically risky energy producers? The answer largely lies with the benefits to be gained by entering regions that are prohibited to American business interests. As China specialist Drew Thompson has remarked, '...China's presence in the energy and infrastructure sectors of Sudan, Iran and Syria is largely the result of longstanding sanctions that have largely marginalized multinationals and the "supermajor" oil companies...' It may be concluded that China pursues an opportunistic and pragmatic approach in relation to its energy needs, and as long as there are willing suppliers there is no reason for China to exercise military means for energy acquisition. For example, it is unlikely that China's expanding naval capability is directed to the forcible acquisition of the contested Spratly Islands in the South China Sea. It is more likely that it is a demonstration to Taiwan - an internal not international affair, as far as Beijing is concerned.

Nuclear Superpower Status

With regard to the China threat theory - the fear that China will grow into a military superpower, China's leadership deliberately adopted a policy of good-neighborliness (see above) under the concept of *heping jueqi*, meaning 'the peaceful emergence of China', also known as its 'peaceful rise'. This entails the non-hegemonic stance of China, the emphasis on development and the view that China's economic growth will benefit other nations, not hurt them. Indeed, 'peaceful rise' was replaced with 'peaceful development' to further emphasise the non-threatening nature of China's growth. If China's is a peacefully rising power, how does one explain its armory of over 30 intercontinental ballistic missiles (ICBMs), 110 intermediate-range ballistic missiles (IRBM) as well as its submarine-launch missile capability (which is still small)? While this nuclear force is by no means comparable to that of the US which has over a thousand nuclear missiles, or Russia with its 635 ICBMs, and its newly announced plan for nuclear modernization, China's nuclear force does bestow upon it the prestige and deterrent power sought by others in recent times - including India, Pakistan and even North Korea in its formative stages of becoming a nuclear power.

It may be argued that with its minimal deterrent force China is hardly a nuclear superpower to be taken seriously. On the other hand, China does have global reach - how many nuclear warheads are needed to constitute a threat and to be deemed a credible deterrent? Moreover, China's nuclear arsenal is not designed to compete (as occurred during the Cold War between the USSR and US in the accumulation of ever greater numbers and sophistication of nuclear warheads and delivery systems), but to deter threats to China. It does not have a strategic alliance system to defend or an umbrella under which allies shelter - as is the case with the US and its defence partners. Thus China can claim nuclear superpower status without arousing undue suspicion. The suspicion which it does arouse concerns Taiwan - and this is precisely what Beijing intends: to deter a Taiwanese bid for formal independence.

ECONOMIC EMERGENCE AND POLITICAL CHANGE

Seeds of economic change have long been embedded in the liberal system that North America and Europe together constructed after the Second World War. Indeed, as more of the world adopted liberal market-oriented strategies, the club of developed countries widened, and the international system evolved as a result. This has not always been a seamless process; shifts in the economic balance of power invariably alter relations among states, and in so doing generate no small degree of friction. China's explosive economic emergence, however, promises the greatest shake-up ever of the reigning post-war economic order. It will invariably alter international relations and, by extension, North American-European relations in profound and perhaps unanticipated ways.

China, however, is hardly a new economic power. Prior to the closing of its borders in 1500, its emperors presided over the world's largest and most sophisticated economy. Although modern Europe moved quickly to catch up and ultimately surpass China over the ensuing centuries, it still generated 32% of the world's wealth in 1820. (Hale and Hale) The forced reopening of its borders at the hands of colonial powers marked the beginning of China's return to the world stage; yet colonialism, anarchy, warlordism, nationalist reaction, world war, occupation, civil war and communist revolution rendered this an exceedingly fitful and terribly painful process.

It was only with the 1978 reforms launched by Deng Xiaoping that Communist China began to develop in a more organic fashion. Oddly enough, this reform commenced in the countryside when the state suddenly allowed peasants to adopt market structures in order to encourage production and boost income. Since 1994, however, China's economic revolution has been largely an urban and industrial phenomenon. Growth along the Eastern coast has far outstripped development in the countryside. Between 1978 and 2003, China's per capita GDP grew by 6.1% a year, registering a 337% increase over that period. (Wolf) Large swathes of China's vast hinterland have however been left behind in this process.

China has very quickly moved from a communist ownership model, in which the state possessed virtually all the means of production, to a far more complex system in which private ownership increasingly overshadows state ownership. It has also advanced rapidly up the production scale, moving from very simple assembly to ever more complex manufacturing processes.

The area for autonomous action by the individual in China generally has also been expanding, despite persistent, regrettable and ultimately counter-productive limitations on political freedom. The Chinese people now enjoy unprecedented freedom of movement, information flows are far more developed and open today, and young Chinese possess ever-greater control over their destiny despite the real political constraints they confront. In the words of one western analyst, the Chinese at least enjoy the freedom not to engage in politics. This is hardly the same thing as democracy, but it suggests an important evolution away from the totalitarianism of the Cultural Revolution when the Chinese were compelled to live and breath politics.

Yet, within parameters defined largely by the Communist leadership, China's economic boom is providing an outlet for the country's long pent-up commercial energies and the aspirations of its people for a better life. The possibility of achieving this has certainly diverted some of the political passions that spilled onto Tiananmen Square in 1989, (Hutzler) although repression has done its part as well. China's huge student population certainly has its share of aspirant democrats, but many have simply abandoned politics to focus on their careers. Recent polls suggest that the Chinese are tremendously optimistic about the future; particularly the well educated, who are best positioned to benefit from China's economic expansion and global integration. (Giles)

China's civil society has grown more complex and articulated since 1989 and this too is shaping both the aspirations of its people and the likely manner in which future political change will unfold. Many people today recognize their growing stake in the preservation of civil order. This does not mean that democratic reform will not come, rather it points toward new modalities for pushing for these changes-strategies in which pressure comes from both within the governing elite and from an ever-more articulated civil society. In the words of the historian Lanxin Xiang, the Chinese have embraced Perestroika (restructuring) but have no desire to push for glasnost (openness). (Meeting with Lanxin Xiang) The great threat to the current order may come not from the kind of students who were targeted during the Tiananmen crackdown, but rather from the millions of disenfranchised Chinese, many living in the country's vast interior, who have not benefited from economic reform and growth. China's elite is aware of this and clearly hopes that by easing conditions in the vast hinterland, the regime will be better positioned to defend the political status quo and the stability needed to generate economic growth. But even this offers only a temporary solution to the longer-term problem of China's lack of democracy.

Several years ago after the high technology stock bubble, American economists were ringing their hands over the question of which country might possibly serve as the engine of a global economic recovery. Europe, it was said, was hopelessly over-regulated and increasingly uncompetitive; the United States was heading down a path of rising government and consumer debt, corporate accounting scandals and investor uncertainties; and Japan's economy remained mired in a deflationary recession. Two bright spots, India and China, it was then claimed, lacked the economic weight for their high growth rates to have any significant spillover impact on global growth. Such forecasts, it seems, were made under the old assumption that the global economy and OECD member countries, with a few important caveats, were more or less the same thing.

That assumption proved false. According to a recent Economist survey, China now accounts for 13% of world output in purchasing power parity terms (second only to America's) and will soon be the world's third largest exporter after the United States and Germany. Its domestic demand has been the single greatest factor in Asia's recent recovery, and it is a major underwriter of American deficit spending through its purchase of US treasury bills. The IMF has suggested that if China proves able to implement much needed banking reform, the country will continue growing over the coming decade at 7-8% per annum, a rate which could push the country's GDP above that of the United States by 2020 in purchasing power parity terms. (The Economist, October 2, 2004.) China is thus crossing a threshold. Its economy can no longer be judged as a mere potentiality. It is now an integral player in the global economy, and its international economic weight has grown extraordinarily consequential. Over the last year, the world economy grew by 5%. The two engines of that growth were an American economy unleashed by loose monetary and fiscal policies, very low savings rates and a high propensity to import, and Chinese producers, who are orchestrating one of the greatest economic expansions in recent memory. Yet, China remains a developing country. This accords it a rather unique place in the world economy, one that is perhaps rendered all the more paradoxical by the fact that this ever more economically liberal society is still administered by a Communist party.

THE GEOPOLITICS OF CHINA'S EMERGENCE AND ITS TRANSATLANTIC IMPLICATIONS

China's economic emergence is laden with geo-strategic implications, many of which cannot but recast crucial elements of the transatlantic relationship. It is not yet a truly global power, certainly not in the way the United States is. China is, however, a major power in East Asia and its reach is extending. It is, of course, a nuclear state possessing intercontinental missiles; it has a very large military establishment in possession of ever more sophisticated weaponry, it is a permanent member of the UN Security Council; and its global economic weight is increasing by leaps and bounds. One would therefore be utterly remiss to look at China simply in static terms. It is an ascendant if somewhat contradictory world power, and its growing presence on the global stage is altering the strategic and economic map.

At the same time though, China has dramatically abandoned the revolutionary ideology which once inspired its foreign policy. It is increasingly understood as a status quo power, with a deepening interest in sustaining a global and regional economically liberal order that its leaders now embrace as the key to national prosperity, internal stability and continued party hegemony. It has also altered its foreign policy at least tactically. Where China once considered the developing world as its greatest foreign policy priority, now its relations with the United States, Japan and Europe receive pride of place, followed by its regional neighbours, and then by the developing world. (European Policy Centre Conference, Remarks by Xinning Song) China's recent accession to the WTO and its clearly expressed goals within that body reinforce the view that it has become more of a status quo power dedicated to the preservation of an open trading order. This approach has eased China's relations with developed countries, most of which enjoy improved and fruitful economic relations with China. Yet tensions persist over issues like human rights, China's military ambition, Taiwan, Burma and arms sales. Although Taiwan is certainly the region's most likely strategic flash point, there are other dangerous regional security challenges including North Korea's attempts to manufacture nuclear weapons and China's alarmingly poor relations with Japan. Accommodating an ever more powerful and wealthy China was invariably going to pose challenges to the world's other great powers. (Schwarz)

Since 2003, China has hosted four rounds of the six-party talks among Japan, North Korea, Russia, South Korea, and the United States. It considers itself to be a mediator between

North Korea and the United States in negotiations over the burgeoning North Korean nuclear programme. China crafted the framework for the negotiations. The United States has commended China for its broad efforts to facilitate the six-party talks, but has criticized China for not using all its influence to convince North Korea to commit to Complete, Verifiable, Irreversible, Dismantlement (CVID). China provides North Korea with approximately 40% of its food and 90% of its oil and is North Korea's sole formal military ally. Prior to the recent agreement, some US officials and experts had speculated that China prefers to keep this nuclear issue unresolved because it counterbalances US policy in the Taiwan straits. China has a strong interest in preserving stability in North Korea, which it views as a buffer state, and it resisted threatened use of sanctions or force to resolve the North Korean problem. The United States has now applauded China's role as mediator in the six-party talks, which appear to have resulted in an arrangement that will end North Korea's nuclear programme.

The level of hostility between Japan and China has risen in recent months, in part because Japanese Prime Minister Junichiro Koizumi has paid several visits to the Yasukuni shrine where war criminals, who were responsible for terrible atrocities in China during the Second World War, are buried. Japanese owned businesses in Shanghai were attacked earlier this year after the introduction of a history textbook in some Japanese schools that glossed over Japanese atrocities during World War II.

Mr Koizumi, however, recently apologized for the wartime invasion and declined to visit the shrine this year. (People's Daily Online, August 15, 2005) The creation of a bilateral panel of historians to review the legacy of the occupation could also help ease tensions. But difficulties in the relationship persist. Japanese recent endorsement of the American view that China's Taiwan policy represents the greatest threat to regional stability at a recent "two plus two" bilateral security meeting raised alarm bells in Beijing. (Briefing by Lanxin Xiang) Tension is also arising out of the fact that Chinese economic power is threatening to eclipse that of Japan. Managing this shifting relationship is proving difficult. Finding ways to accommodate the new China while delineating what cannot be given up in the process poses a genuine intellectual and political challenge for the entire western community. (Brzezinski)

Perhaps the most apparent manifestation of how China's evolution might alter US-European relations has been the recent transatlantic tension over a European push to lift its long-standing arms embargo imposed after the military crackdown on demonstrators in Tiananmen Square. In December 2004 EU leaders announced their intention to replace that embargo with an export code of conduct. This would include provisions on arms brokering and technology transfers and supposedly would trigger no increase in quantity or quality of weapons sold to China. But it would also be non-binding, and as such might not constrain members eager to sell more sophisticated systems to the Chinese. (Financial Times, January 22, 2005.) Over the past year, American officials communicated to their European counterparts that lifting the embargo would seriously complicate transatlantic defence trade and cooperation. American leaders strongly oppose any move by Europe that might help tip the delicate balance in the Taiwan Straits. European advocates of lifting the embargo maintain that they have no intention of doing so; but this has hardly quelled US concerns.

American officials and many in Europe strongly oppose lifting the embargo for a range of strategic and political reasons including the fragile military balance in East Asia, the possibility that Western weapons might be used by China in a possible confrontation with China, and the fact that China's political system remains fundamentally undemocratic and unaccountable. Washington is committed to helping Taiwan defend itself in the event of a Chinese invasion; but it is engaged in a delicate balancing game. The Americans have helped arm Taiwan to the point where its self-defence capability is credible, but not sufficiently to tempt it to declare full independence. US officials welcome dialogue and negotiation as the best means of preventing a military conflict. The Americans do not generally share the view of those in Taipei who would abandon the single China ideal, although they are committed to deterring a Chinese military intervention.

American policy should be understood in terms of a classic balance of power politics. Historically great powers have never welcomed the rise of new powers and often work to impede that rise. (Mearsheimer) Several Chinese analysts, including Lanxing Xiang, have suggested, however, that there are risks involved in pursuing this course as well. Xiang uses an historical analogy to point out that Britain's tough policies toward an authoritarian Wilhelmine Germany helped make conflict between the two powers a preordained conclusion. Xiang worries that a policy of aggressive containment toward China might have the same effect, contributing to a climate of suspicion and tension and adding to the risk of miscalculation. (Lanxin Xiang, "Survival", Autumn 2001.)

American officials are somewhat divided on all of this. Those focused on commercial matters have a different view than those responsible for managing strategic-military issues. The US navy, for example, foresees a future Chinese "blue water" naval challenge (Kaplan) although the Chinese currently express an ambition to develop naval assets that would only advance their navy from a posture of coastal defence to a posture that would allow its fleet to exercise some suasion power in the China Sea. At this point, the building of a genuine "blue water" navy is beyond the means of the Chinese, who recognize that they are prepared neither to match American naval power nor to challenge America's overall geopolitical superiority. (Jisi) The US navy will therefore exercise ultimate control of the sea-lanes that are vital to Chinese commercial and energy needs for some time to come. (Mallet, Financial Times) China's growing energy concerns certainly inform its evolving strategic orientation, but so too does its focus on the Taiwan question. The recent Chinese-Russian military exercises included an amphibious assault of the kind that could one day be used in Taiwan. That exercise was coupled with a joint Russian-Chinese demand that the United States abandon bases in Central Asia - something that certainly raised the level of concern in Washington.

China's National People's Congress recently adopted a law that explicitly states that a Taiwanese declaration of independence could be met with a Chinese military response. Chinese officials who met members of this Committee in Beijing insisted that this law has been misinterpreted in the West and that Americans and Europeans do not seem to understand how central Taiwan is to Chinese identity. The Taiwanese government's flirtation with independence has raised a red flag in China. According to the Vice-Chairman of the Foreign Affairs Committee of the National People's Congress, Wang Yingfan, and a number of Chinese foreign policy experts, no Chinese leader could ever concede to the establishment of a separate Taiwanese nation; to do so would be seen by the Chinese people as an act of treason. Ambassador Yingfan asserted to this Committee that China "would pay any price" to preserve what it sees as its territorial integrity and admitted that the law does imply the existence of a military option. (Meeting with Wang Yingfan, July 2005) Ambassador Yingfan suggested that the new law expresses China's desire to resolve the Taiwan question in a peaceful manner, while calling for the tightening of already substantial links between the island and the mainland. The law has certainly not been seen in such a benign light either in the United States or in Europe.

Indeed, the newly promulgated law on Taiwan certainly provoked second thoughts in Europe about revoking the arms embargo. For example, four parliamentary Committees in the British House of Commons - Defence, Foreign Affairs, International Development, and Trade and Industry - expressed strong reservations last spring about lifting the embargo without first clarifying how the European Council will ensure that this does not result in any qualitative or quantitative increase in arms sales to China. The Committees were alarmed by the ongoing human rights problem in China and felt that to lift the embargo would send the wrong political signals to Beijing. They also expressed concern that lifting the embargo could poison armaments cooperation and broader diplomatic relations with the United States. (House of Commons Report.)

Indeed, if not properly managed, trans-Atlantic fall-outs on China policy, like the recent spat over arms sales to China, could collectively weaken the recent efforts of some European and American leaders to deepen trans-Atlantic defence industrial cooperation. It is worth noting that the mood in the US Congress in recent years has not been particularly receptive to open trans-Atlantic defence markets. Secretary of Defence Donald Rumsfeld and other officials have actually fought some of the more restrictive bills coming from Capitol Hill. There is a sense now that were the European Union to end the embargo without stringent controls, the Department of Defence could no longer defend the very notion of a transatlantic defence market in the halls of Congress.

While the United States has long enjoyed a privileged relationship with the Chinese both because of its extensive economic links to that country and because it too is a key power in the Pacific, Europe's relationship with China has expanded rather dramatically. In 2004, Europe passed the United States as China's largest trade partner. (Kynge) Some in Europe now suggest that Europe and China share common views on a range of questions like the central role of the UN Security Council in dealing with international crises and in the desirability of a multi-polar as opposed to a unilateral global order. The Chinese themselves have picked up on this and have recognized the potential economic and strategic value of developing stronger ties to Europe. There is indeed a certain symmetry in Chinese and EU global ambitions. They are both powerful regional actors playing important, if not hegemonic, global roles. They see each other as potential partners with a common need to bolster their respective global influence and prosperity. This symmetry is certainly one of the sub-texts in the battle over the arms embargo, and it likely presages the rise of other transatlantic tensions that will involve China. The European Union defines its relationship with China as a "strategic partnership", a status it accords to its most important partners including the United States, Canada, Russia and India. (European Policy Centre Conference, Remarks by Dirk Sterckx) At the recent EU-China summit, both sides reaffirmed their commitment to building an effective multilateral order.

Not surprisingly, some European and North American Atlanticists see this thinking as a direct challenge to the primacy of the NATO alliance. This is one reason why it may be an opportune moment to develop a nascent NATO-China dialogue. There have already been informal diplomatic contacts in Brussels; the Chinese have participated in several NATO seminars and were invited to observe a NATO exercise. Several NATO officials have also visited Beijing in recent months. Given China's participation in a number of peacekeeping activities, there is clearly ample room for dialogue. Zhang Yesui, China's Vice Foreign Minister recently told a NATO PA delegation that his government is closely following NATO's transformation and that his country warmly welcomes NATO's role in peacekeeping. He also indicated that NATO's presence in Afghanistan has contributed to regional stability. Yet China and Russia have also called for the closing of American bases in Central Asia, so its position is nuanced if not somewhat contradictory. The public's view of NATO is equally ambiguous; the bombing of the Chinese Embassy by US planes operating in a NATO mission over Belgrade provoked a strong nationalist outcry in China and this event, according to Mr. Yesui, is not entirely forgotten

Notwithstanding the improving European-Chinese relationship, there are also tensions between the two. These include China's policy toward Burma, its relationship with Taiwan and human rights issues in general. Europe's central bankers had expressed displeasure with China's foreign exchange policy of tying the Renminbi to the falling dollar and so welcomed the recent decision to allow the Renminbi to appreciate. At the same time, a range of groups worry that Europe's less traditional manufacturing competitive sectors could be overwhelmed by Chinese imports. In recent months, trade tensions with China have risen with Brussels and

Washington alike seeking to limit Chinese imports and investments in sensitive sectors like textiles.

The Chinese see the EU model of regional integration as a way to build a more stable and prosperous East Asia. (Perlez) China is currently not a member of The Association of South Eastern Asian Nations (ASEAN), but it has struck up an important dialogue with that regional body through what has become known as the "ASEAN plus Three" process in which both Japan and South Korea are also engaged. Recently China and ASEAN agreed to negotiate an ambitious trade liberalization agreement, and China has negotiated bilateral deals with a number of ASEAN countries. Intra-Asian trade is growing explosively, placing six regional players into the ranks of the world's ten fastest growing economies. (Baucus) China's new tactic of extending its influence through trade policy and cooperative multilateralism, rather than by simply brandishing its military muscle, points to its growing international maturity and sophistication. It has learned to extend its influence through win-win and not just confrontational approaches, and this is opening new doors. (Xiang "Survival" Summer 2004) Yet China has hardly forgotten the importance of military power; and it is embarked on a major military modernization effort. Moreover, it is not reluctant to brandish this power when it feels key national security interests are at stake.

CHINA'S ECONOMIC AND FINANCIAL DEVELOPMENT

To understand China's economic reform and development since 1978 one may conveniently divide the topic into its domestic and international aspects even though the two are closely related. It is the purpose of this essay to examine the international aspects as China has taken part in the process of world economic globalization, a salient feature of world history today. The Chinese leader Deng Xiaoping who initiated and directed economic reform from a planned to a market economy understood the importance of globalization and adopted what he called an "open-door policy" as an essential part of the reform program. The term globalization refers to the crossing of national boundaries. It means the flow of goods, capital, information/technology and people across national borders. China practiced globalization in the Han dynasty (206BC-220AD) when trade took place between the Han Chinese and neighboring people in the North-west through the Silk Route.

During the Tang dynasty (618-901) trade flourished and the Silk Route expanded as Chinese traded with the Romans. However, in the Qing Dynasty and in the period of the PRC up to Deng Xiaoping's open-door policy China tried to close its doors and resisted globalization. We will survey the accomplishments of globalization for China's economic development and clarify some controversial issues concerning globalization.

Foreign Trade

First consider foreign trade or the flow of goods across national borders. Since 1978 China has encouraged free trade and abolished trade restrictions step by step. The government has changed its policy from the administration of foreign trade by the Ministry of Foreign Trade, to giving provincial governments much autonomy in foreign trade and to allowing private enterprises to engage in foreign trade. The total volume of foreign trade or the total volume of exports and imports increased from 20.64 billion US dollars in 1978 to 620.8 billion in 2002, accounting for 65 percent of GDP and was growing at the rate of 35 percent per year. In 2004, the trade volume reached 1.1 trillion US dollars, and had a growth rate of 30 percent. China became the third largest trading country in the world, next to the United States and Germany.

Today exports from China can be found all over the world. In terms of US-China economic relations exports from China have benefited many Americans in providing them with high-quality consumer goods at low prices, but have also generated resentment and resistance by some American manufacturers and workers. Chinese exports to the US may hurt some US industries producing similar products. US workers in these industries may suffer temporarily, but in the long-run the labour market is able to adjust as new industries are developed to hire the displaced workers. In the long run, the aggregate unemployment rate (now at 5 percent) has not been visibly affected by the American imports of foreign goods. Note also that exports from China, in fact about 60 percent of them, are produced by foreign invested enterprises in China and some are American companies.

Outsourcing of jobs such as having someone in Asia read X-ray or answer phones has also created resentment in the United States. From the economic point of view, outsourcing of jobs as illustrated above is the same as import of services from China. The effects are the same as for the import of goods produced in China that I just talked about. Such imports are good for China and for US although some workers may be displaced temporarily. Although this point is valid, Professor Greg Mankiw of Harvard and at the time Chairman of the President's Council of Economic Advisers got into trouble when he made this valid point in a Congressional hearing in 2004 because such a viewpoint can be unpopular for American workers and politicians.

As an importer China provides a large market for foreign manufacturers and has gained economic power as a result. Demand for imports to China propels economic growth of other countries in the world.

China first took a mercantilist stand in the restriction of imports, but after the rapid expansion of Chinese exports, the table has turned as some developed countries including the US are considering the imposition of restrictions on imports from China. The imposition of quotas on textiles from China is an example.

In 2001 China joined the World Trade Organization. Membership in WTO required China to lower its tariffs for manufacturing as well as agricultural products. The lowering of tariffs helped increase competition for Chinese manufacturers and farmers and provide cheaper products for Chinese consumers.

Foreign trade has helped economic growth in China in three aspects. First international specialization that takes place as each country produces the goods for which it has a comparative advantage in producing will enable the country to obtain more goods than by domestic production alone. Second, exports are a part of aggregate demand and an increase in aggregate demand helps increase the country's national output. Thirdly, trade together with foreign investment has brought in modern technology and method of management that has increased productivity in China.

TRANSFER OF INFORMATION AND TECHNOLOGY

Together with the flow of goods and capital is the transmission of information and technology. This has benefited China by upgrading its technology. So far China has mainly been an importer of technology but it will soon be an important exporter as it is already an exporter of technology to some less developed countries. In recent years the Chinese government has spent a large amount on higher education and Chinese universities, especially the top ones, improved rapidly.

As of today, China has already helped many developing countries in Asia and in Africa by investing in these countries, providing them with technology, labour and assisting them in economic development in general. China seems to have done very well in this regard, in view of the fact that it has its own poor regions to develop also. Chinese diplomacy is based on mutual respect, treating a small country as equal and trying to help solve its problems if it is feasible. The effort of the Chinese government in assisting the developing countries and its diplomatic posture as a friendly country are doing as much in increasing China's influence in the world scene as its rising economic power.

Returning to China as an importer of technology, we know that the import of technology from the US to China is good for China, but is it good for the US? A part of the answer is yes. The main reason for capital and technology to move from US to China is to get a higher return to capital. It raises US GNP as I have explained and that is good for the US. In the very long run, however, one can make a case that this transfer of technology might be bad for the US although it is not necessarily so. To make the case, the transfer may enable China to improve its technology in the future to a point when it will overtake the US in the industries in which the US now has monopoly power. To illustrate, when the Japanese took over much of the monopoly power of the US automobile industry in the 1950s and 1960s, the US lost is comparative advantage in producing automobiles. One can argue that the transfer of technology in producing automobiles from the US to Japan was bad for the US.

This above argument that the US may lose economically by transferring technology to China is different from the fear of military threat from China after it acquires the technology. The fear of military threat can justify restricting the transfer of military technology to China.

ECONOMIC GROWTH

First and most fundamentally, China has enjoyed rapid and sustained economic growth since 1978, when Deng Xiaoping initiated the current era of economic reform. Indeed, before the Asian economic crisis erupted in 1997, this growth was so rapid that some analysts, using optimistic but not unrealistic assumptions, predicted that China's GNP—evaluated in terms of purchasing-power parity— would surpass that of the United States by 2006.2 Yet while China has escaped the immediate brunt of the region's financial crisis, the Asian economic slump has exposed and highlighted some weaknesses in the Chinese economy as well as in the "Asian model" of economic development in general.

Despite large "pump-priming" efforts by the government over the past several years, the Chinese growth rate has been slowing down. According to some measures, prices have been falling as well, which suggests the existence of excess productive capacity. China also faces serious economic challenges not only with respect to its stateowned enterprises (SOEs), many of which have been losing money as they encounter increased competition from the private sector and from imports, but also with regard to its banking sector, which is burdened with the large nonperforming loans that are required to keep many of the SOEs afloat. Thus, the key question for the immediate future is whether the private sector can grow fast enough to absorb those workers who would inevitably be laid off in the course of restructuring China's SOEs and reforming its banks. This reform process is likely to be accelerated when China is admitted to the WTO, thereby bringing matters to a head more quickly.

China's economic prospects for the next decades thus depend largely on whether its leadership has the political will to back economic reforms that are in the short run likely to lead to the bankruptcy of some SOEs or, alternatively, whether China will opt instead for a Japanese-style policy of putting off hard decisions. In the first two decades of economic reform, the Chinese leadership exhibited a talent for "muddling through"—i.e., for implementing enough reform to keep the economy moving forward while for the most part avoiding major shocks to the political system. However, the urban inflation of the late 1980s, which was closely linked to the public dissatisfaction underlying the 1989 Tiananmen protests, offered one instance in which the leadership's ability to strike this balance was sorely tested and ultimately found lacking. Whether China's leadership will prove capable of juggling these competing economic and social/political requirements remains an open question. This analysis proceeds on the assumption that it will, but it must be recognized that China's economic prognosis may be less optimistic than it now appears.

Technological Modernization

China's economic reform program of the past 20 years has included rapid if selective technological modernization. Nevertheless, China's level of technological sophistication is likely to prove a more significant obstacle to its achievement of great-power status than its overall economic development. Starting as it has from a very low level, China's technological progress—while relatively rapid in some areas— has a long way to go. In eight of nine technologies deemed critical for military purposes, Chinese production capabilities have been found to be significant yet limited. The exception is biotechnology, with respect to which China has good basic research but poor production capability. Although China has access to "all but the most advanced dual-use technologies" and is able to assemble many high-tech products, it remains largely dependent on imported high-tech equipment. Nevertheless, urrent capabilities... reflect a significant improvement over the past two decades. When China's economic reform program began in the late 1970s, Chinese industrial technology was universally obsolescent. Now, while China is hardly a high-tech powerhouse, some sectors are relatively modern.

The key question for the future is the extent to which China will be able to develop a technological base sufficient to support advanced weapon production. Although China purchases some advanced weapon systems on the international market, primarily from Russia, Chinese leaders are unlikely to remain content to base their military power entirely on imported equipment. Indeed, on two occasions— in 1960 and 1989— China suffered an abrupt cutoff of foreign arms transfers from the Soviet Union and the West. Thus, putting aside questions of national prestige, China will not want to remain dependent on foreign suppliers in the future. A RAND assessment of China's future technological capability insofar as it affects the country's military potential asserted that, China's prospects for technological progress are moderate.... By many measures China's potential for technological progress looks comparable to that of South Korea or Taiwan in the 1970s. In terms such as absolute numbers of scientists and engineers or total spending on R&D, however, China already vastly surpasses smaller countries like South Korea or Taiwan. Thus, average technological levels in China in 2020 are likely to be comparable to those of South Korea or Taiwan today, but China's greater size suggests that the number of areas in which China possesses state-of-the-art capabilities will be larger than is currently true in those countries.

It was thus concluded that, while China can expect to make significant technological progress in coming years, it is impossible that China will catch up to, much less "leapfrog," the United States... for the foreseeable future. By many measures, China's prospects ... appear comparable to those of Taiwan or South Korea in the 1970s.... Thus, it seems likely that, by 2020, *average* technological levels in China will be roughly comparable to those in Taiwan and South Korea. There may be a difference, however, due to China's scale.... [South Korea and Taiwan] have become very competitive in particular technological niches. If China follows a similar development path, its huge size... means that the number of these niches will be far greater. Thus, while China will on average still be significantly behind the United States... technologically, its technological capabilities could be very competitive in a significant number of areas by 2020.

THE FUTURE IS NOW FOR CHINA'S CHALLENGES AND XI JINPING'S AMBITIONS

Chinese President Xi Jinping is on a roll. In October, the Communist Party he dominates used its national congress to accord him even more authority for his second term, embedding his core position and "thought" in its constitution.

The party's Politburo is now stacked with Xi loyalists, and two important players on foreign policy, State Councillor "Tiger" Yang Jiechi and party doctrine-shaper Wang Huning, have been elevated to support their leader's ambitious global agenda. This month Xi powered serenely through a series of high-level diplomatic meetings, including a summit parley with US President Donald Trump. Despite all the attention it attracted, the US chief executive's "state visit plus" was more about pageantry, managing risks and deflecting potential problems. More indicative of Xi's plans was his speech at the Asia-Pacific Economic Cooperation summit in Vietnam, where he called for "profound change", and visits to Vietnam and Laos on which he sought to warm and deepen relations. Xi's predecessors governed a relatively weak and inward-focused China. That shaped a policy of hiding strength and biding time, deferring thorny issues for future generations. For Xi, the future will come within the years in which he hopes to continue wielding power in some form.

Today's China is an emerging great power, but it faces serious demographic, economic and environmental headwinds. That leaves a limited window of opportunity to realise Xi's "Chinese dream" of national rejuvenation at home and "new era" of regional primacy and global influence.

These grand visions are often dismissed as abstractions, but they are better understood as calls to China's massive bureaucracy to come up with concrete, incremental steps to realise them. When Xi speaks of a "community of shared future", he is calling for a paradigm shift away from a balance of power in the Asia-Pacific region in which most countries look to the United States for security, and to China as the economic dynamo. With his predilection for control and centralisation, Xi wants to move the region towards an increasingly Sinocentric order.

Driving this is a foreign policy based largely on chequebook diplomacy rather than security guarantees, and on bilateral arrangements and mutual interests rather than formal alliances. The party calls this approach "major-country diplomacy". It has three axes of power projection: economic, military and institutional, each of them interwoven with propaganda, public diplomacy and influence campaigns that can change to intimidation when necessary.

The economic framework is Xi's signature "Belt and Road Initiative". As a branding campaign that recasts China's "going out" policy as a set of New Silk Roads, it seeks to leverage China's comparative advantages in financing, construction and production to reshape international trade and investment patterns in ways that foster geopolitical and economic benefits for China. At its congress, the party embedded the belt and road in its constitution, signalling long-term, top-level political backing. That may increase completion rates for projects, but also makes correcting course trickier.

Bibliography

Alexander Wendt: *Social Theory of Internationl Politics*, Peking University Press, 2005.

Allen Carlson, *Unifying China, Integrating with the World: Securing Chinese Sovereignty in the Reform Era,* Stanford: Stanford University Press, 2005.

Arend, A.: *International Law and the Use of Military*, London, Routledge, 1993.

Atar Singh Jadoan: *Military Geography of South East Asia*, Anmol, Delhi, 2001.

Caplin, A. and Schotter, A.: *The Foundations of Positive and Normative Economics*, New York, Oxford University Press, 2008.

Chandra, R.: *Judicial System in Mechanical Warfare*, Lucknow, Print House (India), 1992.

Conway, G. 1992. *Sustainable Rural Livelihoods: Practical Concepts for 21st Century*. Sussex: Institute of Development Studies.

Deepak, B R : *India and China : 1904-2004 : A Century of Peace and Conflict*, Manak, Delhi, 2005.

Digumarti Bhaskara Rao: *Military Conversion : Impact on Science and Technology*, Discovery, Delhi, 2003.

Gao, Mobo: *The Battle for China's Past: Mao and the Cultural Revolution,* London, Pluto Press, 2008.

Gautam, P.K. : *Environmental Security : New Challenges and Role of Military*, Shipra, Delhi, 2010.

Gul, F. and Pesendorfer, W.: *The Foundations of Positive and Normative Economics*, New York, Oxford University Press 2008.

Hart, Oliver: *Firms, Contracts, and Financial Structure,* Clarendon Press, Oxford, 1995.

Heimanson, Rudolph: *Dictionary of Military*, N.Y.: Oceana Publications, 1967.

Huntington, S.P.: *The China Modernisation Military and the State*, N.Y., Vintage Books, 1964.

Ian Storey: *ASEAN and the South China Sea: Movement in Lieu of Progress*, Washington, D.C., Jamestown Foundation,2012.

Itoh, Mayumi: *Pioneers of Sino-Japanese Relations: Liao and Takasaki.* Palgrave-MacMillan. 2012.

Jack Kemp: *A Monetary Agenda for the World Economy*, Boston, Quantum, 1984.

Jones, W.H.: *Politics of Military*, London, Hutchinson, 1971.

Joon Ahn: *The Rise of China and the Future of East Asian Integration*, Asia-Pacific Review, London, Carfax Publishing Company, 2004.

Keane J.: *Democracy and Civil Liberty*, London, Verso, 1988.

Marie Lecomte : *Hindu Kingship, Ethnic Revival, and Maoist Rebellion in Nepal*, Oxford University Press, Delhi, 2009.

Mary, W.: *Military Space Force: the Cultural Dimensions of Authority*, Cambridge, Belknap Press, 1985.

Pesendorfer, W.: *The Foundations of Positive and Normative Economics*, New York, Oxford University Press 2008.

Radhakrishna: *Handbook of Military and Defence Services*, Sumit Enterprises, Delhi, 2009.

Raj Kumar: *Weapons and Military Technology*, Sumit Enterprises, Delhi, 2009.

Scott Rozelle: *Accelerating China's Rural Transformation.* Washington, DC: World Bank, 1999.

Smith, V. L.: *Papers in Experimental Economics*, Cambridge, Cambridge University Press, 1991.

Taylor, F. W.: *The Principles of Scientific Management*, New York, 1917.

Thapa, Deepak : *Understanding the Maoist Movement of Nepal*, Centre for Social Research and Development, Delhi, 2003.

Thubron, C.: *The Silk Road to China*, Hamlyn, 1989.

Ullman, D. G.: *Making Robust Decisions*, Trafford, 2006.

Vogel, Ezra: *One Step Ahead in China: Guangdong Under Reform.* Cambridge: Harvard University Press, 1989.

West, Thomas L.: and Jeffrey D. Jones: *Handbook of Business Valuation*, New York: Wiley, 1992.

Wood, A.: *The Corporate Economy*, London: Macmillan, 1971.

Woodward, J.: *The Oxford Handbook of Philosophy of Economics*, New York, Oxford University Press, 2009.

Index

❑❑❑